DEATH and DYING

IN WORLD RELIGIONS

Edited by
Lucy Bregman

Kendall Hunt
publishing company

Cover image © bonsai, 2009
Used under license from Shutterstock, Inc.

Kendall Hunt
publishing company

www.kendallhunt.com
Send all inquiries to:
4050 Westmark Drive
Dubuque, IA 52004-1840

Printed in the United States of America
10 9 8 7 6 5 4 3 2 1

CONTENTS

CONTRIBUTORS

William C. Allen received his Ph.D. degree from Temple University in 1997, where he is now Associate Professor of Religion. He teaches courses in the religions of India and Yoga and Tantric Mysticism, and has contributed articles on "Reincarnation" and "Deities of Life and Death" to the *Sage Encyclopedia of Death and the Human Experience*.

Rebecca Alpert is a rabbi and Associate Professor of Religion and Women's Studies at Temple University. She writes and teaches about Judaism and contemporary issues, and is the author of *Like Bread on the Seder Plate: Jewish Lesbians and the Transformation of Tradition*.

Lucy Bregman is Professor of Religion at Temple University. She is the author of *Beyond Silence and Denial: Death and Dying Reconsidered* and *Death and Dying, Spirituality and Religion*.

John W. M. Krummel received his Ph.D. in philosophy from the New School for Social Research in 1999, and has earned a second Ph.D. in the Religion Department at Temple University. He is Assistant Professor of Religious Studies, Hobart and William Smith College. His writings have been published in *Dao: Journal of Comparative Philosophy, International Philosophical Quarterly, Existentia, International Journal of Philosophy*, and other journals.

Theodore R. Lorah, Jr. held a Master of Divinity degree from Eastern Baptist Seminary, and a Masters in Church Music from Westminster Choir College. He studied as a graduate student in History and Religion at Temple University. He died early in 2009.

Joseph McGovern, an ordained Roman Catholic priest for 25 years, holds Master of Divinity from Saint Mary's Seminary in Baltimore, MD, as well as an M.A. in History from Fordham University and an M.L.A. in Ancient Near Eastern Religions from The Johns Hopkins University, Baltimore, MD.

Eve Mullen is Assistant Professor of Religion at Oxford College of Emory University. She holds a Ph.D. from Temple University and an M.T.S. from Harvard. She is the author of *The American Occupation of Tibetan Buddhism* (2001), a study of Tibetan Buddhist transnationals and their American hosts in New York City.

Terry Rey received his Ph.D. from Temple University's Religion Department. Formerly Professeur de Sociologie des Religions at l'Université Nationale d'Haïti, he is Associate Professor and Chair of Religion at Temple University. He is author of *Our Lady of Class Struggle* and *Bourdieu on Religion*, and co-editor of *Òrìsà Devotion as World Religion* and *Churches and Charity in the Immigrant City*.

Gisela Webb received her Ph.D. from Temple University in Religion. She is Professor of Religious Studies at Seton Hall University and has served as Director of the University Honors Program. She is the author of *Windows of Faith: Muslim Women Scholar-Activists in North America*.

Amy Weigand holds a law degree and a Ph.D. in religion. She is an adjunct professor in the Religion Department at Temple University, where she teaches courses in Asian religions and Death and Dying.

Pamela D. Winfield received her doctorate from Temple University's Religion Department in 2003, specializing in Japanese Buddhist art and doctrine. She is author of "Curing with Kaji: Healing and Esoteric Empowerment in Japan," in *Japanese Journal of Religious Studies*, and has received a grant from Asian Cultural Council of Tokyo. She is currently Assistant Professor in the Department of Religious Studies, Elon University in North Carolina.

ACKNOWLEDGMENTS

This anthology depends on the support and encouragement of many persons. I particularly want to thank my Chairs, Dr. Rebecca Alpert and Dr. Terry Rey, both of whom are contributors to the present edition. I also wish to thank the Dean of College of Liberal Arts, and others from her staff who worked to make publication possible in accordance with Temple's policies.

All of the other contributors were enthusiastic and supportive in working on this project. But I wish to single out the late Ted Lorah, whose learning and enthusiasm made him one of the biggest boosters of the anthology.

Finally, the many students in our "Death and Dying" classes also contributed, and I am grateful for their varied input over the years of teaching this course.

Lucy Bregman

INTRODUCTION

Death and Dying in World Religions

Lucy Bregman

What do the world's religious traditions tell us about death, dying, bereavement, and afterlife? How can we hear their messages, when these are often embedded in settings and cultures very different from our own? And, even if we can open ourselves to what these traditions say, why should we? What is the value of the study of religion for those interested in dying and death today?

This anthology was originally written for the students of Temple University's Religion Department course on "Death and Dying." We wished to introduce them to the wealth of traditions and perspectives in the world's religions, to make them aware of the many ways different religions have thought about what it means to die, to mourn, and possibly to continue in some after-death existence. We knew that our students did not always come with academic backgrounds in humanities, beyond the most basic level, let alone previous academic study of religion. Although most took the course for personal interest, many anticipated careers in the health care field, or in education, social work, or criminal justice. Moreover, as students at a large public university in a metropolitan area, they shared classes with others of extremely varied backgrounds. Some were the children of immigrants, some were immigrants themselves, and many brought cultural experiences of alternatives to the mainstream American way of death and mourning. We designed this anthology for them, and for similar readers who needed a non-specialist introduction written by scholar/teachers, and intended to be readable. This purpose is continued in this, the second edition, of the anthology.

We also aimed for a presentation of the varied religious traditions that was an introduction to the academic study of religion as a discipline. The academic study about religion grew out of theology and other branches of religious learning studied in seminaries, and also out of *Religionswissenschaft*, the "science of religions" begun in the 19th century European universities. The latter hoped to be "scientific" and objective, and was intimately tied to the study of exotic and ancient texts and languages. Today's religion study programs in American universities are a conjunction of these two origins, but the present volume is much, much closer to the second. However, it is not our aim to mimic an exact "scientific" model of knowledge appropriate to chemistry or physics. Nor do the essays in this book claim some absolutely "value-free" or "neutral" status. More modestly, we wished for presentations that attempt, insofar as this is possible, to be academically fair-minded. We want the emphases and visions of the many religions discussed here to be perceived, and we did not want the entire framework of the book controlled by particular agendas or understandings of our own era. For example, we did not want a survey of religions all ranked solely on how "psychologically healthy" their views on death and mourning seemed to us. While, when it comes to religion, there is no absolute "neutrality," there are ways to take seriously the concerns of religions other than one's own, and to instill a genuine sense of curiosity about the wide range of what religious traditions have taught. We do not ask that readers of this anthology abandon their own beliefs and commitments, but we do believe that knowledge of world religions will lead to better-informed judgments than have often dominated popular awareness and public debates. The latter have frequently been controlled by fears over what dangers religious "others" might represent, or by a secularist agenda that finds all religious commitments superstitious and a potential menace to rational thought.

What do the world's religious traditions say about death and dying, bereavement and afterlife? The common-sense answer is that religions have always concerned themselves with questions of death and afterlife. It defines what makes us human to be aware of our own future deaths, and to prepare for them and ritualize the deaths of our fellow humans. Religious traditions have held sway over these activities since the start of human prehistory. Yet this answer needs explanation, qualification, and an historical context. When the modern American "death and dying" or "death awareness" movement started in the late 1960s, it focused on the psychological experiences of the dying in large high-tech hospitals. The other topic of major concern was the sequence or "stages" of bereavement, or "the grief process." While religion occasionally was mentioned by those working with the dying and bereaved, it was not a primary concern. Indeed, it looks as if early research simply bypassed religious ideas and practices. The assumption may have been that religion had failed to offer realistic, non-denying perspectives on death, suitable for contemporary persons in a largely secular world. A new openness about death would have to leave traditional religious beliefs behind. Moreover, an emphasis on experiences such as anger or depression among the dying seemed to fly in the face of one of religion's major claims: that it could provide consolation, meaning, and peace in the hour of death. Was there a future for religion at all in American persons' dying and death? Reading materials from that era makes this sound like a reasonable question.

However, this picture has changed as religion itself is now more publicly visible, more explicitly in the news, than it was 40 years ago. Not only has there been a resurgence of religious movements worldwide which challenge secular assumptions about the world and modern life, but here in the United States there is greater awareness and appreciation of the roles religion continues to play in people's lives. "Appreciation" here does not always mean "positive regard for." To some persons, this resurgence of religion in public life is a disastrous intrusion of religion where it does not belong. For others, it shows the resilience and adaptability of religions, at least in the American context, to changed expectations and norms. For instance, many religious congregations have organized support groups and programs for the bereaved, activities that might have happened informally in years gone by but now are initiated self-consciously and intentionally to fill a perceived gap in compassionate service. Some of these changes are due to the influx of new immigrants whose arrival (after 1965 when the immigration laws changed) coincides with the emergence of the death awareness movement. These newer Americans who moved particularly into urban areas, brought their own religious and cultural practices into an American setting where religious pluralism was already an established norm. Not only is "religion" in the news more, but the diversity of "religions" is more evident and newsworthy than it was a generation ago.

Therefore, we could make the argument that it is important to study world religions in a course dealing with dying and death, because those planning careers in healthcare will no doubt encounter Buddhists, Muslims, and Hindus, as well as Christians and Jews. Knowing what all these people believe and practice at the time of life's end will help in caring for them and their families. Even if one finds their beliefs personally absurd or repugnant, learning about what they hold sacred is necessary in a world where major religions are no longer geographically separated from one another. Although contemporary discussions of death and dying still begin with the hospital setting, and the medical framework of doctors and patients, diagnosis and prognosis, we know now that this is not the exclusive set of categories used to cope with the human dimensions of the end of life.

But there are other deeper and more basic arguments for studying world religions in the context of learning to think about death. For many thousands of years, the majority of human beings did their deepest reflection within the frameworks of these religions. Questions about the meaning of human life, individual and communal, were set within frameworks of cosmic, universal meanings. Questions about the ultimate meaning of any one individual's life could be answered in terms of God's salvation history, or the ultimate nature of the world we know as *samsara*, the realm of ignorance, suffering, and death. To live as a thoughtful human being meant to live in relation to death, and the religious traditions placed death within the largest sphere of transcendent meanings. In this, the religious traditions can become resources, deposits of wisdom which can point us in directions our own limited minds and personal experiences would never have travelled on our own. The message of the death and dying movement today is that living in relation to death is still an intrinsic dimension of our human condition. It is not something we can escape, deny, or outgrow. At this level, then, we are set the same existential tasks as humans in the past and everywhere, and must struggle to find answers to them that will work for us.

The present anthology rests on this argument that world religions have something positive to contribute to understanding death and its meanings. Religions have not been made obsolete by science, since the medical-scientific knowledge about death is not the only kind that matters or has value. True, every American child knows more about disease and its causes than did any of the sages or leaders of the world's religions, yet the wisdom taught by the latter is still necessary to know what to do with the scientific knowledge our society has accumulated. Questions about doctors and their terminally ill patients subtly depend on assumptions about persons, their dignity and self-knowledge which originate in religious and philosophical teachings. Religions have a value in pointing persons beyond accumulated factual information about disease, toward an understanding of the human meanings of sickness, dying, and death. Indeed, awareness of this human dimension, and the need for wisdom in how to apply scientific knowledge, is probably greater now than it has ever been.

Does this mean that everything religions have had to say is equally positive and relevant to hear today? No, nothing of the sort is claimed by the authors of these chapters. To understand the contributions of religious traditions is to recognize how these continuously change in response to internal self-criticisms and external pressures. Religions are not static, and are indeed constantly negotiating with the life-experiences of their members. Some of these changes are dramatic and traumatic, such as the exile of the Tibetan religious leadership after the Communist invasion of Tibet. Others are more subtle but no less real, such as adaptation to different family roles among American Protestants. Some religions have ways to make changes "official," centrally mandated for all members. Others do not. No religion floats above the world, and even the most traditional will eventually respond to the impact of Western medical technologies and other shifts in the experience of dying.

However, in this anthology we have focused on stabilities more than change, and on the core mainstream sacred texts or major practices of each tradition. We want to show how these have continued to operate, to define the religious space given to death-related topics. The presentations of each religion are deliberately intended to be non-innovative and non-idiosyncratic. Cutting-edge theological interpretation, and experimental ritual practice is less likely to be included than the events surrounding the dying and death of "typical Catholic Maureen."

An explanation is needed about the distribution and ordering of chapters. In a scheme of mechanical equality, each religion should have an equal amount of space given to it. But the reality is that some religions, particularly Christianity and Buddhism, have made death a major topic in ways that others have not. We have therefore allocated two chapters for Christianity, while Buddhism receives a chapter of its own with a focus on the Tibetan branch of the tradition, plus massive presence in the chapters on China and Japan. However, the latter two chapters take the stance that it is impossible to untangle the mix of religions that inseparably work within both cultures to express people's religious responses to death; therefore, not "Buddhism" or "Daoism" but "China" and "Japan" are the really relevant divisions.

As for the order of chapters, it seemed most wise when writing for an audience of Western readers, to start chronologically in the West and then move into Asia and Africa. We have begun with two chapters that deal with traditions no longer "living," but of historical importance for the major religions that developed in both Western and Mid-Eastern civilizations. Ancient Mesopotamia also represents a particular type of religious system: a pantheon of gods and goddesses with shared roles in world-rule, a system no longer prominent but which once had great historical importance and durability. Ancient Greece, and especially the central philosophical teachings of Plato on the soul, death, and knowledge, continued to contribute to religious thought, even when the more specifically religious and ritual component of ancient Greece was no longer a living reality. These two ancient sources of Abrahamic traditions are followed by the unproblematic ordering of Judaism-Christianity-Islam. Putting the Protestant Christianity chapter before the Roman Catholic chapter, however, is not based on chronology or on a theological judgment about which is more "authentic." It is a decision made because the content of the Protestantism chapter covers the Christian tradition more broadly, while the Roman Catholic chapter picks up on what themes are of specific interest to that branch of Christianity. The Asian sequence of Hinduism, Buddhism with a focus on Tibet, China, and Japan is both geographical and to some extent based on religious indebtedness of the latter two cultures to Buddhism. African traditional religions are in some ways even more theological distant from what Western people find familiar, and here stand in for a range of religious possibilities that are often referred to as "primal" or "tribal" yet which have had developments and elaborations of their own.

There are omissions, we admit. The authors were selected to represent a range of religious traditions, but also for their familiarity with the course on "Death and Dying" taught at Temple. They were given the choice of which topics to cover, and how to proceed, so that in some cases there is extensive coverage of beliefs but little interest in practice, while other chapters focus almost exclusively on what people do. No attempt was made to impose a framework or religious agenda by directing each author to answer questions such as: "Is there a role for Purgatory in the religion you are writing about?" As already indicated, we did want presentations focused on the "core" of traditions, but left it up to individual authors to determine what that might be.

Each chapter includes a set of references or sources and a set of study questions. Some chapters have a glossary. We have kept endnotes to a minimum, and have aimed for accessibility without sacrifice of intellectual rigor and scholarly quality.

CHAPTER 1

Life Stinks, But Death Is Worse: The Ancient Mesopotamian View of Life and Death

Theodore R. Lorah, Jr.

Introduction

Three hundred years ago, there were some notions that civilization existed in Mesopotamia. There were accounts left over by the Greeks and Romans; it was known that statues and other artifacts were in what was then the Ottoman Empire, but very little was known about the ancient city states along the Tigris and Euphrates rivers. There was a rich post-Islamic heritage, but the ancient heritage was not well known. The same was true of Egypt, whose hieroglyphs were only unraveled following the discovery of the Rosetta Stone after Napoleon conquered Egypt in the 1790s. With the advent of modern archaeology in the 18th and 19th centuries, texts were discovered that brought to light whole new worlds of mathematics, business, astronomy, and religion. As the ancient Mesopotamian epics were discovered and deciphered, it was found that there were amazing parallels with the texts of the Bible.

When the Bible reported that Abraham came from Ur, it was now known just where Ur was located, in present-day Iraq, and certain similarities in religious content were noticed. When Marduk defeats Ti'âmat[1] the salt sea, and places half over a dome to be the heavens and half becomes the sea that supports the dry land, they noticed that God does the same in Genesis 1. The word translated "deep," *tehôm* in Hebrew, is etymologically related to the god Ti'âmat, the "deep" being the salt sea. Further, God divides the waters, placing half above a dome, the heavens, and half below, which supports the dry land. But in Genesis the violence of the earlier account is missing, and the focus is on creation by a God who makes all things "good." The flood stories were also clearly related, with the ancient Utnapishtim (or Atra-hasis) replaced by Noah. Even the sending of birds to determine where dry land existed and the offerings are parallel. However, in both cases the

1

theology is different, and that difference was significant. The Lord, Yahweh, created the flood to end evil, but in Mesopotamia it was gods angry at being deprived of sleep because of the noise. It was noticed that human beings are made of clay and the blood of a god in Mesopotamia, but Adam, generic for human in Hebrew, was made of Earth and breathed in to become a living being (*nepesh haya*). However, in Akkadian, the language in which this is found, there is no equivalent word for "spirit," and the word *napishtu*, like its Hebrew cognate, means "being" more than "soul." There is also a remembrance of this life coming from blood in Deuteronomy 12:23, "life is in the blood." These parallels gave added meaning to the biblical accounts, placing them in a new to us but older context of the ancient near east, sharpening their focus.

The reason all of this became available was because of the nature of the writing materials. If a city that used parchment or linen or reeds was burned, the writings were burned with them, as happened when the famous ancient library of Alexandria, Egypt was burned. But when writings are written in cuneiform on a clay tablet, it hardens, turning to a type of stone. So Ashurbanipal's library was found nearly intact. The only weak point was that tablets could be broken or chipped, such that lines were missing. These could often be amended either because of parallel lines later on or common sense, and those places are often enclosed within brackets.

One last question we need to ask is of what value was a religious tradition that lasted over 3,000 years? Does it have any relationship to modern ideas? Certainly as a parallel witness to the great Western religions based on the teachings of the Bible, they are helpful. But other relationships may also exist. Simo Purpola has written about the tree of life in Jewish mystical Kabbalah and demonstrated that it is parallel to the ancient Assyrian royal tree of life, with the ancient gods being replaced by attributes of the God of Abraham (Sippola, 1993). Thus, their influence has been used and changed and embroidered by Jews and Christians, keeping alive the hints of the old understandings about life. This is why modern people need to understand what was there, what was lost, and what the meaning of life and death was to people who lived with the forbears of modern Western religion.

The Geography and Origins of Mesopotamia

The ancient Mesopotamians were an inherently pessimistic people. They had no illusions about the nature of their life together, a life that was intended for servitude in a climate where temperatures reached 120°F during the summer, and where large stretches of desert surrounded their river-based city states. Reaching northwest along the twin rivers, the Tigris and the Euphrates, from the marshes along the mouths of the two rivers through the arid lands and into mountain climates, they experienced frequent droughts as well as frequent floods, especially near the Persian Gulf. It is no accident that the flood story originated in Mesopotamia. Michael Roaf notes that the climate of Mesopotamia today is similar to that of 10,000 years ago (Roaf, 1990).

However, animals were plentiful in less arid zones, with herds of gazelle, fallow deer, wild ass, and cattle found in all but the desert zones, where very little vegetation would grow. Agriculture was practiced by means of canals which irrigated the fields along the rivers. Buxton tells us that because of the similar levels of rainfall, it would have been impossible for all of Mesopotamia to be irrigated at once, so it was likely that the rights to irrigate were part of the ongoing warfare, in a way similar to today's conflict between Lebanon, Israel, and Palestine over water rights along the Jordan River and the Sea of Galilee. Despite the similarity of today's climate, the climate has indeed grown ever more arid from population pressure and overgrazing.

> It has been suggested with a considerable degree of probability that, owing to a phase of desiccation, the inhabitants of the regions of Arabia which were becoming increasingly arid pressed upon the more settled and rich agricultural populations of the lowlands . . . Brooks believes that the development of this drought is responsible for the rise of the great Mesopotamian empires. (Buxton, 62)

The first human beings to develop an advanced civilization there were the Sumerians, followed by Akkadians, Hittites, Babylonians, and others. But the city state civilization the Sumerians founded remained, though different city states became dominant in different periods of time. The Sumerians invented the cuneiform alphabet, which served as the alphabet for each successive language that came to be spoken there, much as ancient Latin and modern English share the same alphabet. "It was not a historical accident that the alphabet, supreme product of cultural borrowing and adaptation, should have arisen in the area of the absorption civilizations" (Brundage, 534). The Mesopotamians also became brilliant astronomers, who saw their gods in the stars, writing down their observations in cuneiform numbers on a base 60 system. It was they who shared astronomy with the rest of the ancient world.

Each successive dominant city state accepted the basic culture, and Sumerian itself became a "sacred" language, because it was the language of the earliest religious texts. One of the gifts of the Sumerian civilization was the religion of Mesopotamia, which appears to have been relatively stable throughout its nearly 3,000 year history. Although each city state had its own patron god, and while sometimes a god might have more than one name because of language differences, the basic gods and their relationships with each other and with humanity remained the same. The gods were often related to natural phenomena, e.g., rain or birth. Thus, we are looking at a culture that is vibrant yet stable. An example of that stability is found in the ancient texts themselves, although the epics have some variations depending on language and which city state revised them. For example, when Ninevah was excavated in the early 20th century, texts were found that named the Assyrian high god, Asshur, as the agent of creation rather than Marduk, the Babylonian high god. Even with those differences, the story itself remains nearly the same. E. A. Speiser summarizes this well.

Perhaps clearest of all is the fact that the underlying civilization enjoyed substantial uniformity throughout its long career. This is not to imply that it was a static civilization; its dynamic character is constantly in evidence. But the statement can be made and upheld that certain basic values present from the start retain their vitality to the very end. Dominant beliefs and practices which we notice under the Sargonids of Akkad, in the third millennium, are still in vogue in the first millennium under the Sargonids of Ninevah. The changes that the passing centuries bring do not affect the main framework (Speiser, 41).

Because of the constant influx of new people, based in ethnic groups largely differentiated by language, there are significant differences between central and northern Mesopotamia and the south in terms of climate and social life. "The vexing issue is to what degree these differences are ethnic ones" (Yoffee, 290). One of the differences between these groups was the issue of class. In the south, Sumeria, "there were no classes, only differences in wealth; and the private ownership of land was insignificant." While farther north, an oligarchy of noblemen ruled a rigidly stratified social system. Private and royal landlords, rather than temple-owned land, were the rule (Yoffee, 290).

However, in spite of these differences, all of the city-states belonged to a "Mesopotamian textual community" (Yoffee, 292). These shared texts provided Mesopotamia with "a moral and spiritual unity" (Cooper, quoted in Yoffee, 294). Despite ethnic and language differences, the religion of Mesopotamia, found in their texts, bound these diverse peoples together in a shared culture. One finds, then, that the temples were an important unifying aspect of these people's lives. But there was also an undercurrent of struggle between the temples and the rulers, each vying for dominance over the other, particularly in regard to the control of land. Yet, it did not matter which city state became hegemonic; the religious culture and customs brought a common belief structure that transcended economic and class differences, binding each successive empire to a common culture that varied in detail but shared the basic value structure offered in their religious texts.

Creation through Violence and the Battles of the Gods

A basic motif of the religion these people followed is violent struggle. The gods were a society that mirrored human society, because in their minds it was the basis of human society, which also resulted in violent struggle between peoples. Their story of creation is found in an epic called Enûma Elish. It tells the story of creation as a battle between Marduk, the high god, and Ti'âmat, the salt sea or the "deep." Ti'âmat was terrorizing the other gods, and Marduk was beseeched by them to end her tyranny. In a monumental battle that is vividly described, as Ti'âmat opened her mouth to roar, Marduk sent the raging winds to fill her, so that she could not close her mouth, her belly filling with wind.

He sent an arrow through her distended torso, splitting her heart and killing her. Then we read in Tablet IV:

> He split her open like a mussel (?) into two (parts);
> Half of her he set in place and formed the sky (therewith) as a roof.
> He fixed the crossbar (and) posted guards;
> He commanded them not to let her waters escape.
> He crossed the heavens and examined the regions.
> He placed himself opposite the Apsû, the dwelling of Nudimmud.
> The lord measured the dimensions of the Apsû,
> And a great structure, its counterpart, he established, (namely,) Esharra.
> The great structure Esharra which he made as a canopy
>
> (Heidel, *Genesis*, 42–3).

Then Marduk established the gods' residences in the sky, the Apsû becoming the sky, the heavens, while Esharra became the land where people live, both of which were constructed using the waters of Ti'âmat.

These ancient Mesopotamian gods were in a society similar to human society, with some gods having more power than others. Although they were immortal, they all still had to eat, and as one would find in any class society, the lesser gods were responsible for feeding the more powerful gods. The lesser gods found this onerous, however, so eventually they took up arms, surrounded the palace of Enlil (one of the high gods in the Babylo-nian version), and in words reminiscent of every labor disagreement complained: "[Excessive] toil has [killed us], / [Our] work was heavy, [the distress much]" (Lambert, 53). Since the inferior gods rebelled and would no longer work, it was decided to create humankind to bear the work of the gods. Humanity's purpose is simply to feed and care for the gods. This is not like Genesis, where humanity is to tend and care for a garden they also enjoy. This is a life of hard labor. No other task of importance is given to humanity. No wonder they were so pessimistic.

The task to create humanity was given to Belet-ili, the birth-goddess. If one reads the entire account, with purifying baths on certain days of the month, and a brick placed between the pieces of clay, it is easy to understand that this account is influenced by Mesopotamian birthing traditions. Furthermore, the understanding of what materials are used to constitute human beings is also clear from the text, and once again creation is tied to an act of violence, this time the killing of a god:

> Let one god be slaughtered
> So that all the gods may be cleansed in a dipping.
> From his flesh and blood
> Let Nintu mix clay,
> That god and man

May be thoroughly mixed in the clay. . . .
Wê-ila, who had personality,
They slaughtered in their assembly.
From his flesh and blood
Nintu mixed clay.

For the rest [of time they heard the drum],
From the flesh of the god [there was] a spirit.
It proclaimed living (man) as its sign,
and so that this was not forgotten [there was] a spirit.

Then Mami, the goddess, addressed the gods:

'I have removed your heavy work,
I have imposed your toil on man.
You raised a cry for mankind,
I have loosed the yoke, I have established freedom.'

After this she recited an incantation and snipped off fourteen pieces of the clay, placing seven on her right and seven on her left, symbolizing male and female. She placed a brick between them, and then in a broken fragment there is a reference to "the cutter of the umbilical cord" (Lambert, 59, 61). It has long been known from textual evidence that ancient Egyptian women gave birth squatting on two bricks, although one was not actually found until the summer of 2003. Could this indicate a similar custom?

What one learns is that humans are fashioned from blood and clay, the blood of a god and the clay that is the Earth, formed as male and female. We do not find here body and soul, as in the later Western tradition, but blood and clay, and one's personality is in the blood. Humankind's toil thus gives freedom to the lesser gods, who have been freed from the obligation to feed the other gods. This is not one of the happier pursuits fated for humankind. In *Enûma Elish* there is a variant version, in which the god slaughtered is Kingu, who convinced Ti'âmat to rebel; he is slaughtered and his blood used to create humanity offering a reason for humanity's evil ways, having been created with an evil god's blood (Heidel, *Genesis*, 47).

The word used in Akkadian indicates that the slain god's blood contained his "personality" (*temu*) (Lambert, 185). This is the root for the word translated "ghost," *etemmu* (Soder, Band I, 263), which does not mean "spirit." The two components of the dead are bone and ghost, whereas in life it had been blood and clay. The personality found in the blood becomes a different sort of creature after decay, a ghost that can be malevolent if the bones are not buried properly and the ghost is not properly given sustenance.

We also learn that while the gods are immortal, they can be killed in combat, as was Ti'âmat, or for a purpose, as with Wê-ila, whose blood was used to make humanity. However, human beings are completely denied immortality. The god of death, Uggae in Sumerian, was present before the creation of humanity. Therefore, death was not the result of some sin or fall. It was the way humanity was created: subject to the gods, in this case the god of death. Immortality belonged only to the gods, and humanity had no part of it. This is affirmed by the divine bar maid, Sidduri, when she tells Gilgamesh: "When the gods created mankind, they allotted death to mankind, (but) life they retained in their keeping" (Heidel, Gilgamesh, 138). This notion is also found in Tablet X of *The Gilgamesh Epic*, where Utnapishtim, the Babylonian Noah, tells Gilgamesh: "The Annunaki, the great gods, ga[ther together]; / Mammetum, the creatress of destiny, de[crees] with them the destinies. / Life and death they allot; / The days of death they do not reveal" (Heidel, Gilgamesh, 79).

Not content with the thought of dying, going to his fate, Gilgamesh sought a different fate, searching for a plant that guaranteed immortality, making one young when one ate it. It was at the bottom of the deep, so he tied rocks to his feet and descended to the sea floor. Upon acquiring the plant, he cut the stones off his feet and rose to the surface. However, as he was bathing in a pool of water: "A serpent perceived the fragrance of the plant; / It came up [from the water] and snatched the plant, / Sloughing (its) skin on its return. Then Gilgamesh sat down (and) wept" (Heidel, Gilgamesh, 92). As a result of this theft, snakes shed their skin and achieve youth, but humanity is still denied immortality and is doomed to age and die. (Even in the present day, the snake is the symbol of the healing profession because of its mythological ability to heal and regain its youth.) The will of the gods cannot be defeated. Humans serve and then "go to their fate." King Huwawa tells this to Enkidu, Gilgamesh's closest friend: "Who, my friend, is superior to death? / Only the gods live forever under the sun. / As for mankind, numbered are their days; / Whatever they achieve is but the wind!" (Wolff, 396).

The nature of humanity's service to the gods and obeisance to them is reaffirmed in Atra-hasis, an Akkadian version of the flood story. (In this version, Atra-hasis is the name for Utnapishtim in the Sumerian version.) In Tablet II we are told:

> Twelve hundred years had not passed
> When the land extended and the peoples multiplied.
> The land was bellowing like a bull,
> The god got disturbed with their uproar.
> Enlil heard their noise
> And he addressed the great gods,
> 'The noise of mankind has become too intense for me,
> With their uproar I am deprived of sleep' (Lambert, 73).

As a remedy for his disordered sleep, Enlil ordered a pestilence. Enki, Atra-hasis' patron god, interceded, telling Atra-hasis to offer a sacrifice to a particular god, and the pestilence ended. Again, humanity disturbed his sleep after twelve hundred years, and Enlil ordered

Adad not to allow rain to fall, that there might be a famine. Interceding again, Enki told Atra-hasis that the people should withhold their sacrifices from all the gods, except to offer one sesame meal loaf to the rain god, Adad. They did as instructed, and it rained and the drought ended. Again the gods were deprived of their sleep after 1,200 years. (After all, human beings breed like flies and never learn from their misdeeds!) The gods determined there would be a flood, but this time they forbade Enki to speak to Atra-hasis. Instead, Enki spoke to Atra-hasis' reed house, telling it to become a boat sealed with pitch, covered with a roof to make it watertight. An eavesdropping Atra-hasis took the hint. Animals were gathered, and the boat was roofed over, so for seven days while the flood raged, the survivors were safe in the reed boat. Survival for all of the Earth's creatures was dependent on a reed boat not sinking in the turbulent waters of the flood. Of course, while humanity was being drowned, no one was feeding the gods, so as the deluge raged:

> The Annunaki, the great gods,
> Were sitting in thirst and hunger (Lambert, 95).

After the flood abated, Atra-hasis offered a sacrifice, with the result that:

> The gods smelled the savor,
> The gods smelled the sweet savor,
> The gods crowded like flies about the sacrificer (Pritchard, I, 70).

Clearly, humankind is needed by the gods to fulfill its purpose of feeding and caring for the gods. But it is equally clear that the noise pollution of too many people is something the gods won't tolerate, either. Humanity must keep its place and reverence the gods without disturbing them. It is also interesting that the gods are described as being like a swarm of flies. This is not an image of deity that has been retained in the Western tradition. Summarizing the nature of these gods, E. A. Speiser comments about this religion: "Perhaps its two outstanding features are the human attributes of its gods and their identification with the powers of nature and the cosmos. It is on this last count that we have here a universalistic, and certainly a supranational, conception of religion" (Speiser, 43).

Going to One's Fate

Dying was known as "going to one's fate." And it was the only certainty in life (Cooper, 21). On two stelae found in Harran, we find the story of the death and mourning of the mother of Nabonidus, king of Babylon. She was 95 when Nabonidus ascended the throne, and she died in the ninth year of his reign at the age of 104, going to her fate much later than most people could even imagine.

Nabonidus, king of Babylon, the son whom she bore, laid her body to rest [wrapped in] fine [wool garments and] shining white linen. He deposited her body in a hidden tomb with splendid [ornaments] of gold [set with] beautiful stones, [. . .] stones, expensive stone beads, [containers with] scented oil, and [...]. He slaughtered fat rams and assembled into his presence [the inhabitants] of Babylon and Borsippa together with [people] from far off provinces, he [summoned even kings, princes] and governors from the [borders] of Egypt on the Upper Sea to the Lower Sea, for the mourning and [. . .] and they made a great lament, scattered [dust] on their heads. For seven days and seven nights they walked about, heads hung low, [dust strewn], stripped of their attire. On the seventh day [. . .] all the people of the country shaved and cleaned themselves, [threw away] their (mourning) attire [. . .] [I had] chests with (new) attire (brought) for them to their living quarters, [treated them] with food [and drink], provided them richly with fine oil, poured scented oil over their heads, made them glad (again) and looking presentable. I provided them well for their [long] journey and they returned to their homes (Pritchard, II, 107–8).

It can be seen from this text that mourning is intense for seven days, with people wearing dirty clothes, covering themselves with dust, offering sacrifices, wailing loudly, even the men showing extremes of emotion in the face of death, until the period of mourning is finished, at which time they shave, bathe, and put on new clothes. Here there is a parallel with the Jewish practice of "sitting shivah" for seven days in the house after a death. Professional mourners would also wail and lament along with the family and friends of the deceased. One lament of mourning is found in *The Gilgamesh Epic*, where Gilgamesh mourns his friend, Enkidu, who has died of a disease sent by the gods to punish Gilgamesh.

"Hearken unto me, O elders, [and give ear] unto me!
It is for Enk[idu], my [friend], that I weep,
Crying bitterly like unto a wailing woman . . .
An evil [foe(?)] arose and [robbed(?)] me.
[My friend], my [younger broth]er(?), who chased the wild ass of the open country (and) the panther of the steppe; . . .
Now what sleep is this that has taken hold of [thee]?
Thou hast become dark and canst not hear [me]" (Heidel, Gilgamesh, 62–3).

Burial took place in various places, but two were predominant. There were some cemeteries, especially for royalty, but most people were buried in vaults beneath their houses. And sometimes, in earlier eras, they were given simple graves dug directly under the floors. The living and dead shared the home, divided only by the floor. "The dead thus remained close to the survivors, who provided for them, while their graves were protected from desecration" (Heidel, Gilgamesh, 164).

The Underworld: The Realm of Erishkigal

The reason for this close proximity was that the grave was the entrance to the under-world, the realm of Erish-kigal and her consort Nergal, whose city lay under ground where the sun set. And it was the responsibility of the remaining family to guarantee that the grave was secure and to care for the dead in Erish-kigal's realm which one would enter, not to return unless the bones were disturbed.

> To the gloomy house, seat of the netherworld,
> To the house which none leaves who enters,
> To the road whose journey has no return,
> To the house whose entrants are bereft of light,
> Where dust is their sustenance and clay their food.
> They see no light but dwell in darkness,
> They are clothed like birds in wings for garments,
> And dust has gathered on the door and bolt (Nemet-Najat, 144).

Because the grave was the entrance to the realm of Erish-kigal, if a corpse was not buried, the ghost could not enter the realm of the dead and wandered the Earth, wreaking havoc on those responsible for its maintenance, its children and children's children. One act in warfare was to remove corpses from the grave and scatter the bones, which placed the local population at risk from malevolent ghosts even after the armies had left. Ashurbanipal, King of Assyria, described this when he captured Susa in 646 BCE: "I tore down, demolished and exposed the tombs of their ancient and recent kings who did not revere [the goddess] Ishtar, my queen. I took their bones to the city of Assur, inflicting unrest upon their ghosts and depriving them of memorial rites and libations" (Cooper, 28). "The worst curse that could be pronounced on anyone was: 'May his body fall down and not have anyone to bury it,' or 'May his body not be buried in the ground!'" (Heidel, Gilgamesh, 156).

> So soon as the body received the last dues, the *edimmu* [This is the same word as *etemmu*, ghost] descended into the "great earth" to the "house of darkness, abode of Nergal," "to the house whence whoso enters comes not out." According to the poem of Ishtar's Descent into Hades, it was a place fenced about with seven walls each pierced by one gate. A profound gloom reigned there at all times, and the dead, "clad like birds in garments of feathers," had dust for food and mud for drink! (Delaporte, 170)

Further, there were seven guards, one at each gate, who had to be entreated for entrance. The underworld bureaucracy was no better than that of the normal world of the living.

The dead were placed in the tomb in a shroud or a coffin, often buried in what is today called a "fetal position." Grave goods were provided with which entrance to the realm of Erish-kigal could be purchased, and it was the duty of the offspring, particularly the oldest son, to continue offering food offerings and ceremonies, called *kispu*, on a regular basis. This was important for the sustenance of those who were dead, as they could not work for themselves in the realm of Erish-kigal. Indeed, judgment in Mesopotamia was not based on ethical questions, as it was in ancient Egypt, where the heart was weighed against a feather to determine one's sinfulness. Judgment in Mesopotamia was based on questions of how well one's offspring cared for him. Questions of one's ethics were to be rewarded and punished in this world.

> Every fault, however, was punished in this world; just retribution required that virtue should be rewarded here. Man, created by his deity and for his service, had nothing to expect beyond this life, and sooner or later he must leave it to descend to the nether world from which there was no returning (Delaporte, 168).

The nature of Mesopotamia's understanding of judgment is found in the closing passage of *The Gilgamesh Epic*, where Gilgamesh has begged to have Enkidu return from the realm of the dead to tell him the nature of the underworld. At the behest of Ea, a high god, Nergal opens a hole to the underworld, "[That he may declare the ways of the underworld] to [his] brother" (Heidel, Gilgamesh, 99). Nergal opens the hole, and Enkidu's ghost rises to greet Gilgamesh. After embracing one another, they converse, and Gilgamesh requests:

> "Tell me the ways of the underworld, which thou hast seen."
> "I will not tell thee, my friend; I will not tell thee.
> (But) if I must tell thee the way(s) of the underworld, which I have seen
> Sit down and weep."
> "[My body (?) . . . .] which thou didst touch, while thy heart rejoiced,
> Vermin are devouring (it) as though it were an old [gar]ment.
> [My body (?) . . . . which thou didst] touch, while my heart rejoiced,
> [. . . .] is full of dust."

Gilgamesh then asks about the fates of different categories of the dead. "He who has no son, hast thou seen (him)?" While the dead man with only one son "Lies prostrate at [the foot] of the wall (and) weeps bitterly," the man with two sons "dwells in a brick structure (and) eats bread." The more sons to care for and feed the dead, the better the situation of the deceased in the underworld (Heidel, Gilgamesh, 99–100). The text breaks after the report about the man whose six sons still care for him. However, the questioning continues with those lost at sea, slain in battle, and finally ends with those who lie unburied and have none to care for them:

> "He whose body lies (unburied) on the steppe, hast thou seen (him)?"
> "I have seen (him).

His spirit does not rest in the underworld."
"He whose spirit has none to take care of him, hast thou seen (him)?"
"I have seen (him)."
"What was left over in the pot (and) pieces of the bread that were thrown into the street he eats" (Heidel, Gilgamesh, 101).

It is quite certain that the afterworld was a place where all went, but to which no one really wanted to go. It was also a place from which no one desired to return, because to return was to be a ghost wandering a world without food, without a home, without substance, and without hope.

Life in Mesopotamia was a life that was limited in scope. One was involved in the care and feeding of the gods, in caring for one's ancestors buried beneath the family home, and in obeying those in authority. It was not a life of great promise and hope. And after one died, one was entirely dependent on the good will of one's children for what little life existed in the city of Erish-kigal. It was a life that was difficult, and a death that was much worse. Therefore, the best advice was that given by Siduri, the divine bar-maid, who told Gilgamesh, who was mourning the death of his friend Enkidu (Tablet X):

Thou, Gilgamesh, let full be thy belly,
Make thou merry by day and by night.
Of each day make thou a feast of rejoicing
Day and night dance thou and play!
Let thy garments be sparkling fresh,
Thy head be washed; bathe thou in water.
Pay heed to the little one that holds on to thy hand,
Let thy spouse delight in thy bosom!
For this is the task of [mankind]! (Pritchard, II, 64)

Eat, drink, and be merry, for tomorrow we die.

Note

1. The transliterations are as close as possible without a particular transliteration font.

Selected Bibliography

Brundage, Burr C. 1949. The ancient near East as history. *The American Historical Review* 54, no. 3 (April): 530–547.

Buxton, L., H. Dudley, and D. Talbot Rice. 1931. Report on the human remains found at Kish. *The Journal of the Royal Anthropological Institute of Great Britain and Ireland* 61 (January–June) 57–119.

Cooper, Jerrold S. 1992. The fate of mankind: Death and afterlife in Ancient Mesopotamia. In *Death and Afterlife: Perspectives of World Religions*, ed. Hiroshi Obayashi. New York: Praeger.

Delaporte, Louis. 1925. *Mesopotamia: The Babylonian and Assyrian civilization*. New York: Barnes & Noble, Inc., 1970.

Heidel, Alexander. 1951. *The Babylonian Genesis*. 2nd ed. Chicago: The University of Chicago Press. First Phoenix Edition, 1963.

—————. 1949. *The Gilgamesh Epic and Old Testament Parallels*. Chicago: The University of Chicago Press. First Phoenix Edition, 1963.

Lambert, W. G., and A. R. Millard. 1969. *Atra-Hasis: The Babylonian story of the flood*. Oxford: Oxford University Press.

Nemet-Nejat, Karen Rhea. 1998. *Daily life in Ancient Mesopotamia*. Westport, Connecticut: Greenwood Press.

Pritchard, James B., ed. 1958. *The Ancient Near East, Volume 1: An Anthology of Texts and Pictures*. n.c.: Princeton University Press.

—————. 1975. *The Ancient Near East, Volume II: A New Anthology of Texts and Pictures*. n.c.: Princeton University Press.

Roaf, Michael. 1990. *Cultural atlas of Mesopotamia and the Ancient Near East*. New York: Facts of File Limited.

Sipola, Simo. 1993. The Assyrian tree of life: Tracing the origins of Jewish monotheism and Greek philosophy. *Journal of Near Eastern Studies* 52, no. 3 (July): 161–208.

Soder, Wolfram von, ed. 1965. *Akkadisches Handwörterbuch Unter Benutzung des lexikalischen Nachlasses von Bruno Meissner (1868–1947)*, bearbeitet von Wolfram von Soder, Band I. Wiesbaden: Otto Harrassowitz.

Speiser, E. A. 1995. Ancient Mesopotamia. In *The Idea of History in the Ancient Near East*, ed. Robert C. Dentan. New Haven: Yale University Press.

Wolff, Hope Nash. 1969. Gilgamesh, Enkidu, and the Heroic Life. *Journal of the American Oriental Society* 89, no. 2 (April–June): 392–98.

Yoffee, Norman. 1995. Political economy in early Mesopotamian states. *Annual Review of Anthropology* 24:281–311.

Study Questions

1. How does the violence of the Mesopotamian creation story compare with other creation stories, such as that of the Bible?
2. What does the story of Nabonidas' mother tell us about mourning?
3. Why were the dead buried under the floors of houses, rather than in cemeteries?
4. What is the responsibility of the living to their dead ancestors?
5. Why do you think the Mesopotamians were so pessimistic in both their purpose for living and in their conception of death?

CHAPTER 2

Death and the Afterlife in Plato and the Greeks

John W. M. Krummel

Where do we think our after-life beliefs come from? The Jewish tradition? The Christian faith? The Holy Bible? Try ancient Greece! In fact the ancient Greek tradition and especially Plato are a major contributing source for most of our ideas about death, the after-life, and the soul. Embedded in our western religions we find surviving major themes traceable to ancient Greek philosophy and religion. In this chapter we shall explore some of these ideas about death and the afterlife that we find in the ancient Greek world, mythical beliefs that the pre-eminent Greek philosopher Plato gathered and appropriated for the sake of propounding his own philosophical doctrine. We will then focus our attention upon the ideas expressed in the works of Plato. Finally, we will conclude the chapter by looking at how certain interpretations of Plato's ideas in regard to death and the afterlife came to impregnate the Abrahamic traditions. Generations after Plato, some of the more extravagant renderings of his ideas spurred the quasi-religious movement of Platonism, whose influences such as Gnosticism, we see within Judaism and Christianity in the early centuries of the common era. While the Platonist and Gnostic influence triggered many debates and controversies within Christian history, some views about the afterlife, more easily traceable to Platonism than to the Bible, are still accepted by many today who may think of these ideas to be purely Christian or Biblical. Thus, if we are to study death and dying in the religions of the west, a look at Plato and the Greek legacy ought not to be excluded.

Much of how we in the west view life and death and the structure of reality is as much a product of history as anything else. Ask the average American "Joe" who goes to church once in a while, about what he thinks will happen when he dies. He might tell you that his body will die but his spirit or soul will go to Heaven. But a belief such as this is really the result of the intertwining of numerous strands of perspectives, traditions, cultures, and religions that have come and gone, emerged within or penetrated into the western world, mixing with one another and then dissolving or evolving within the currents of history. Many of us take for granted that it is Judaism and Christianity, which we have inherited as our western legacy, that provides us with our vision of life, death, and afterlife. But in addition, some of our beliefs about death and the afterlife, even those that have been accepted within Judaism or Christianity, may be traceable to certain non-Semitic currents, such as Zoroastrianism, Gnosticism, and Platonism. The purpose of this chapter is to help ourselves become more aware of the historical and specifically Greek and Platonistic background of some of our normally taken-for-granted beliefs.

In Plato's works we come across ideas about the afterlife that may be comparable to those we find in the Indian religions as well as ideas that become inherited through various forms in the western traditions. The belief in reincarnation that we find expressed in Plato's works was not so unusual during the centuries surrounding the commencement of the common era and allows for possible comparisons with similar perspectives in the Indian religions. This belief, however, eventually lost its hold on the western mind due to the spread of Christianity. On the other hand, Plato's dualistic views about the separation of the mind/soul and the body, an idea foreign to the Biblical tradition, did eventually filter into the Abrahamic tradition in some form or another to exert a certain influence upon the minds of some intellectuals as well as the popular imagination.

The Idea of the Soul in the Classical Period

Both archaeology and literature (the epic poetry of Homer and of Hesiod, ca 700 BCE) express ideas about death and the afterlife, which later were presupposed and appropriated by some of the tragic poets such as Aeschylus (400s BCE) and philosophers like Plato. There is in Homer the idea of something like what we today call the "soul." The Greek word for it was *psyche*. As a "breath-soul" or "life-source," the *psyche* in Homer is a shadowy image of the body that gives the body life, enabling it to move with volition; it leaves at death to continue existing in the realm of Hades. While continuing to exist beyond corporeal extinction, it is now a mere shadow because it can no longer produce life and movement. Alongside this Homeric concept of the breath-soul, there also seems to have co-existed for some time as a popular belief the idea that the soul's substance was related to *aither* or to the stars. After Homer, there was also the idea of the *daimon* or "spirit," that becomes associated with the Pythagoreans. In Plato, both ideas are used. The general belief during Homer's time seems to have been that whatever it is that survives death continues existing—either in the tomb or beneath the Earth or in a far away place in the west. And, this after-life existence was supposed to be a "shadowy" reflection of one's earthly existence. Among conceptions of the place where the dead go, there is the House of Hades, called so for being ruled by Zeus' brother Hades, but which in the post-Classical period, becomes called simply Hades. There was also the idea of the Isles of the Blessed, ruled by Zeus' father Kronos or Zeus' son Rhadamanthys, where heroes go to live a pleasant life. Funeral rites were also generally regarded as a necessary prerequisite for the dead to enter the land of dead (North, 49–50).

In addition there may have been other ideas concerning death as well, associated with various cults, local rituals, mystery religions, etc. There was no official dogma to curtail the flourishing of a variety of beliefs.

The Idea of the Soul for the Presocratic Philosophers

During the 6th and 7th centuries BCE, the so-called "philosophers" were mostly "physicists"; that is, they were interested in the study of nature (*physis*). These thinkers regarded the soul as material (such as air, fire, water, etc.). For example, Democritus saw the soul was made up of spherical atoms spread through the body with the mind as a concentration of these soul-atoms. Anaximenes' conviction that the structure of the soul as breath was air was a popular belief. Heraclitus' view that the soul is made of fire is also a belief stemming from folk traditions. In many of the early philosophers prior to Socrates and Plato, we then find the belief that our soul is made of the same elements that constitute the cosmos and is structured and operates according to the same rules. That is, the human being is structured as the micro-cosm in correspondence to the cosmos as the macro-cosm. For Heraclitus, for example, the knowledge of the soul had some relevance to the knowledge of the structure of the cosmos. Understanding the soul in such material terms is in stark contrast to how Plato comes to conceive the soul as distinct in its essence from that which constitutes the material world. If the material world is a world of generation, change, and decay, then the nature of the soul in contrast to matter, for Plato, is something eternal and non-changing. But before we proceed to our discussion of Plato, let us first examine another important idea about death and the afterlife that makes its appearance prior to Plato.

The Idea of Reincarnation Amongst the Pythagoreans, the Orphics, and Empedocles

In some of the western fringes of the Greek world such as in south Italy and Sicily, the belief in reincarnation became popular amongst some religious groups as well as philosophers and entered popular thought by the end of the 6th century BCE (see North, 57). Reincarnation is also known as metempsychosis or the transmigration of the souls. It is the idea that the soul, surviving through many cycles of birth and death, lives on through several lives. In some versions of this belief, the soul, after a long time, manages to escape from this tediously repeated incarnation to return to what is supposed to be its original happy state. Around this same period, we find a similar idea of the cycle of rebirths and redeaths and the goal of escaping it in Indian religions, namely *samsara* and *moksha*. One might surmise that the idea was widespread from the Mediterranean to western Asia and India during that time. Implicit in this doctrine of reincarnation was the idea that after death the soul is judged and accordingly rewarded or punished, whether in the afterlife or the next life (North, 58).

In the western part of the Greek world, this idea of reincarnation, which may be traceable to the Orphic sect, became associated especially with Pythagoras. Pythagoras, known today as the mathematician who discovered the Pythagorean theorem, was also a religious thinker of sorts and he founded a community in Crotan in southern Italy in the mid-6th century BCE. Pythagoras' doctrine of reincarnation is closely related to his view of the *psyche*, which he regarded as the essential self or personhood as well as the life-giving principle of the individual human. Pythagoras regarded this soul as morally significant. That is to say, it is morally responsible for the choices it makes. However, he also recognized that it is limited by the body. Aristotle's and Pindar's comments seem to suggest that after its death the soul according to Pythagoras' belief must face a divine judgment, followed by reward for the good or punishment in the underworld for the wicked—but with the hope that the wicked may eventually be released from punishment. After appropriate punishment or reward, the soul may then be reincarnated. The suggestion is also made that the best souls after repeated incarnations may eventually be able to reach the isles of the blessed after death. Much of these ideas are comparable to what become later described in Plato's *Gorgias* (523a–b). However, aside from such writings (Aristotle's commentary and Pindar's poem possibly written for a Pythagorean patron), there appears to be no firm evidence that the Pythagoreans held the purpose of life to be the escape from the wheel of rebirth. The goal of existence rather was to exist *within* the cosmos "in a state of emotional repose and intellectual acuteness" (Fideler, 36). For this sake the adept was to undergo various forms of training, including abstinence from meat and obedience to certain rules and ethical conduct, to overcome sensuous desires and self-ishness. Such purification of the soul was meant to improve one's rebirth. On the other hand, impurity could pull one down in the hierarchy of living beings, from a human body to an animal body in one's next incarnation. The soul itself was viewed to reflect the entire universe as a micro-cosm linked together with the macro-cosm of nature, other living beings, and the gods. Thus the aim of the Pythagorean religion was *not* to leave this harmonious cosmos but rather "to become aware of, and enhance the function of, transcendent harmony *in* the natural, psychological and social orders" (Fideler, 36).

By the 5th century there were other religious individuals and groups who were known to adhere to the doctrine of reincarnation, but the most famous would be the religious society of the Orphics and the Bacchants. Some trace the Orphics all the way back to the 8th century BCE and consider it to be the precursor that influenced the Pythagoreans. Those called the Orphics, of which not much is known, were supposedly people who engaged in various initiation rituals into mysteries. Some of these were said to depict the terrors of Hades. They believed in the divine origin of the soul and that the body is a kind of prison which entraps the soul until it has paid the penalty for pre-birth sin. The soul is bound by the wheel of rebirth to a series of reincarnations. The observation of certain rites and ceremonies, abstinence from meat (vegetarianism), ethical conduct including non-violence and abstinence from animal-sacrifice, etc., for the Orphics were the means to purify the soul from its sins and to eventually thus free it from its bodily prison. Once thus saved from rebirth and bodily existence, the soul can return to its original divine status. Thus it is the Orphics, rather than the Pythagoreans, who explicitly sought to escape the wheel of rebirth. Their view of the soul has been inherited not only by the Pythagoreans but also in a certain sense by Empedocles, and also Plato as we shall see in the next section.

Later in the mid-5th century BCE, Empedocles (490/495–ca435 BCE), another western philosopher, claimed to have lived the lives of a boy, a girl, a bush, and a fish, and hints at the doctrine of reincarnation in his idea that existence extends before "birth" and after "death." This may be his incorporation of the Orphic-Pythagorean doctrine of reincarnation. Empedocles called the soul *daimon*, and suggested it to be a fallen god of sorts, a divine spirit that fell from its original state of bliss to become incarnate in the body. He also seems to suggest that the "god" (*daimon*) in each of us is a fragment of the cosmic or celestial Sphere from which it fell, and that eventually it is to be re-united with the other fragments and with all other things into one cosmic divine "Holy Mind" that makes up the Sphere. The *daimon*, thus imprisoned in this prison of flesh, longs to escape it. However, it is tossed from one incarnate existence to another, transforming from plant to animal to human. He, like the Pythagoreans and the Orphics, also believed that meat-eating further binds the soul with sin. Thus, to escape from this repeated incarnation, purification from sinfulness, involving abstinence from meat, was necessary.

The Dualism of Plato

Plato (428/27–347 BCE) appropriated in his works much of the after-life myths covered above. We find references in his works to metempsychosis (reincarnation), the soul as imprisoned in flesh, purification, after-life judgment, etc. These were ideas coming from popular religion, mystery cults, and mythologies, already familiar to his readers of that time. Plato's major concern seems to have been the promotion of the philosophical way of life, of which Socrates was the exemplar, and it is most likely for this sake that he appropriates the various after-life beliefs already known to his readers of that time. This particular concern of Plato's is manifest, for example, in the noticeable shift in the notion of the soul (*psyche*) from Homer's breath-soul and the tragic poets' soul as the vehicle of passions to Plato's soul as the center of intellectual and moral activity, which needs to be cared for through philosophy. Whether Plato himself meant them literally or not, one nevertheless cannot deny the influence these after-life myths—employed within the Platonic scheme—had upon subsequent thinkers and religionists, who comprised the so-called Platonist or Neo-Platonist movements. It is the Platonists and Neo-Platonists who then inculcated some of these Platonized after-life beliefs into the Abrahamic traditions. Thus, in order to understand some of the popular and philosophical after-life notions within the broad cultural sphere of European Judeo-Christianity (as well as Islam), a familiarity with these after-life myths incorporated into Plato's thinking is one starting point. Let us now look at the ideas about death and afterlife that we find expressed in Plato's works.

The main character in Plato's dialogues is Socrates (469/470–399 BCE), who in real life was Plato's teacher. Socrates was a man who enjoyed questioning and conversing with people, and he went around the public squares of Athens, questioning the so-called "wise."

In doing so he won a gathering of young followers who liked to witness Socrates' conversations with other famous, powerful, and/or wise men. Unlike the Sophists who charged money for their teachings, Socrates did not claim to be a teacher and neither did he charge money to those who listened to him speak. In Plato's dialogues, we find that Socrates understood true knowledge as starting with the knowledge that one does not know—that is, the acceptance of ignorance. Only with this recognition of one's ignorance can one start upon the path of inquiry that would lead to knowledge. Socrates, however, had proved irksome to many of the powerful and supposedly wise men of the city, whom he had publicly humiliated through his open-air conversations with them. Socrates eventually was charged by certain powerful men of the city with the corruption of youth and impiety (in rejecting the traditional Greek gods) and sentenced to death. It was Socrates' execution that inspired Plato, one of his students, to start writing, and his early works appear to have been written in defense of Socrates, as if to explain to his fellow Athenians that they had misunderstood Socrates. A related purpose also was to promote the life of inquiry that Socrates had lived. Eventually Plato himself gained a following, and he started what has been regarded as the first "university," the Academy (*Akademia*) in 387 BCE. Death is an important theme that appears throughout Plato's works and the fact that it was the death of his teacher that inspired him to start writing and teaching may have something to do with this. We will now look at several of Plato's writings which discuss death and wherein views about the afterlife make their appearance.

The *Apology* and *Gorgias* are two works from the early period of Plato's career, in which discussions of death and the afterlife make their appearance. The *Apology* was Plato's own rendition of the trial of Socrates of 399 BCE at the age of 70, under the accusation of Meletos. In this dialogue, Plato has Socrates express some ideas about death in his speeches. In his first speech, Socrates is agnostic in regards to what happens to the soul after death. But because of our very lack of knowledge about what the afterdeath will be like, Socrates affirms that the fear of death amounts to a foolish claim to know what one does not know (*Apology*, 29a–b). In his final speech, Socrates expresses the conviction that because his mysterious inner voice, his *daimon* (spirit), which always prevents him from doing what he ought not to do, did *not* prevent him from coming to court, the outcome of his sentencing will be good. He speculates that death either will be a nothingness like dreamless sleep or the soul's translocation to the realm of the dead (Hades). In either case the outcome will not be bad. The latter case, however, would be good in particular because then he would be able to converse with men like Homer and Hesiod, Orpheus and Musaeus (*Apology*, 40c–41a). Although there is reference to after-life judgment, there is no mention of the doctrine of reincarnation in this text as there is in later dialogues.

The various after-life myths discussed above, including the ideas of reincarnation, punishment, and judgment, do however get incorporated into some of Plato's other dialogues after the *Apology*. Many scholars today consider these appropriations of myth to be rhetorical devices used to enforce his point—namely, the imperative to live the philosophical life, a life in the pursuit of wisdom and virtue. For example, in the dialogue *Gorgias*, life is seen as a sort of death with the body as the tomb. On the other hand, death is seen as the separation of the soul from the body (*Gorgias*, 524b) which served as the soul's prison during its life on Earth. The soul's after-life fate is taken to depend on a judgment of its earthly deeds and general character. After the body dies, the soul, marked by its actions in life (which may remind one of the Indian view of *karma*), goes to a meadow where it will be judged naked by Rhadamanthus, Aeacus, and Minos, three sons of Zeus (*Gorgias*, 524a). The judge views the soul, with its markings of deeds no longer veiled by the body, and pronounces his judgment, sending the soul upon either of two roads (*Gorgias*, 524d–525a). Aside from the road leading from the world of the living to this meadow, two other roads lead off from the meadow, one to the Isles of the Blessed, where the good (the "philosophic" souls who have lived "just and pious lives") are sent to be forever happy; and one to Tartarus, "the prison of payment and retribution/punishment," where the wicked who have lived in an "unjust and godless way" are sent (*Gorgias*, 523a–b, 526b–c). If curable, the wicked endure "therapy" in Tartarus and are eradicated of their wrongful desires but only through pain and suffering (*Gorgias*, 525b). But if not curable for the reason of committing the worst and ultimate crimes, the wicked endure eternal punishment, for the benefit not of themselves but rather for others. That is, while they themselves do not derive profit from their punishment, they are made into spectacles so that others seeing them under the most horrendous tortures, profit by taking their examples as warnings (*Gorgias*, 525b–c). According to R. E. Allen, the elements in this picture have several sources: the meadow is from Homer, the Isles of the Blessed is from Hesiod, the after-life judgment is in Aeschylus and Pindar, and the notion that the soul is judged naked, morally uncovered, may be of Orphic or Pythagorean origin (Allen, 227–29). However there is yet no mention here of reincarnation as in *Phaedo* and the *Republic*. In any case we see Plato here incorporating various popular after-life mythologies for the sake of ethics, driving the point that the virtuous soul is (or will be) a happy soul.

From the middle period of Plato's career, both *Phaedo* and the *Republic* provide us with views of death and the afterlife. *Phaedo* takes place as a conversation amongst Socrates and his friends who are visiting with him in prison on the day of his execution (399 BCE) to bid him farewell. During this conversation Socrates explains to his friends his view of the human soul. He shows neither fear nor resentment for he has good hope that he will join the company of "gods and good men" (*Phaedo*, 63b–c). His reason is that one who has spent a good life is likely to attain a blessing in death (*Phaedo*, 63e). The good life is the life of philosophy and philosophy as such is the practice that prepares one for death and dying (*Phaedo*, 64a). To say that philosophy is the preparation for dying does sound strange to our present-day ears. Socrates explains that life's most sacred concern is to "philosophize." The Greek word for "philosophy," *philosophia*, means the "love of wisdom." For mortals faced with death, philosophy in its pursuit of wisdom also can provide the meaning of life and existence. Taking over the view of death as the separation of the soul from the body, Socrates expresses his view that philosophy frees the soul from bodily or material concerns to instead orient it toward eternal truths of the non-material. This serves to prepare the soul for its separation from the body in death. Thus "dying before death," as the acceptance of one's coming separation from the body in death, is the profession of the true philosopher. A soul able to know eternal truths then has the good possibility of attaining eternal peace in death.

The picture of the "underworld" (Hades) in *Phaedo* is somewhat similar to the one in Gorgias, but also includes the doctrine of reincarnation, and is as follows. With the body's death, a guardian spirit escorts one's soul to a place where other souls are gathered to face trial. Then in accordance with one's judgment, one is led by an appointed guide to the "House of Hades" through a path with many forks and crossroads. But those who are still attached to the body hover around the visible world until they are led by force. The worst criminals are shunned by others and must wander alone. Each one reaches the place most suitable to it (*Phaedo*, 107d–108c). The more pure the soul, the higher the region it reaches to be released from the clutches of the Earth and to dwell in freedom without the body (*Phaedo*, 114b–c). Those who have been purified by philosophy then attain the vision of true reality above the hollow spheres of the Earth (*Phaedo*, 109b–110a). Those who have led good lives but without philosophy are sent back down to Earth to be reborn. Those who are to be punished in Tartarus, as in *Gorgias*, are of two kinds, the curable and the incurable. The former are those who can win the pardon of who they have offended in life. After spending a year in Tartarus, they may then be sent back to Earth to be reborn. The incurable, on the other hand, never emerge out of Tartarus (*Phaedo*, 111–114). The *Republic* also describes a comparable scenery of an after-life meadow where souls are judged and sent through either an opening for the unjust to below the Earth or an opening for the just into the heavens in the sky, with judges sitting in-between the two passageways. There are also souls coming back to the meadow from either of those two realms of bliss or torture, after having spent a long time there, headed for their reincarnation on Earth (*Republic*, 614c–615b). Similar views about the afterlife as consisting of judgment, punishment, and reward, followed by reincarnation, are expressed in *Phaedrus* (*Phaedrus*, 248c–249c) from Plato's later period. Plato's utilization of these reincarnation and afterlife myths may or may not be meant to be taken literally. What is clear, however, is his belief that philosophy is what provides value and meaning to life. It is for this sake that intellectual activity, in Plato, takes the place of the purification rituals and ceremonies of the Pythagoreans and Orphics.

Related to this emphasis upon caring for the soul's intellectual and moral health is Plato's understanding of the mind-body relationship. This aspect of Plato's philosophy becomes very influential subsequently. I am referring to the so-called mind-body dualism, which becomes explicitly formulated in *Phaedo*, as a part of Plato's influential metaphysical theory of how the cosmos is structured. On the one hand, human beings possess reason through which they enjoy insight of eternal truths. But, on the other hand, we are also immersed in the physical world of sensible things that exercise influence upon our desires and impulses, serving to fetter our rational soul. This is a development of the Pythagorean idea of the body as a prison of the soul and the Orphic view that the soul ought to be purified from the influences of the body. Plato, however, constructed an elaborate metaphysics of how reality is composed of two realms, the material and the intelligible, and incorporated the soul/mind-body relationship into this cosmological scheme. The views expressed in *Phaedo* about the soul, life and death, and the afterlife, are thus intricately linked to Plato's metaphysics (i.e., his conceptions about how reality in general is structured) and consequently epistemology (i.e., his theory about knowledge) as well. Socrates in prison tells his friends that the good philosopher is not concerned with the pleasures of the body such as food or sex. The good person instead turns away from the body and toward the *psyche* (soul, mind) and to the realities that the *psyche* grasps (*Phaedo*, 64d–e). In terms of knowledge, what the body's sensations grasp is unclear, imprecise, and deceptive (*Phaedo*, 65a–b). Genuine knowledge then cannot be sensible knowledge and must rather involve the pure reasoning capacity of the mind without the body's senses (*Phaedo*, 65b–c). The objects of such genuine knowledge, comprehended by the *psyche*, are universal concepts—timeless truths and eternal ideals—such as justice, goodness, beauty, etc. *in general* (*Phaedo*, 65d). These abstract truths, the "Ideas" (or "Forms"—depending on how one translates the Greek word *idea* or *eidos*), are contrasted with what the bodily senses grasp, which are particular sensible objects. The particulars that the body grasps through its senses are changing realities existing inside time and space in this physical world, for example, the wilting flower that was once beautiful or the good act of mowing the lawn, efficacious at least for a while. The universal concepts, on the other hand, are never changing and eternal in meaning, existing outside of time and space. The capacity to know these timeless realities is an indicator of the soul's immortality. But the truths of the physical world are contingent and provisional, liable to change and to that extent, illusory. It is only because our *psyche* is temporarily fused with the body that it is the victim of illusions and desires that result in discord and wars. To attain peace one must then focus one's attention upon what the *psyche* grasps without help from the body's sense; one must escape the body to attain "pure knowledge" and see "things in themselves" with the *psyche* alone (*Phaedo*, 66b–e). Plato thus regards philosophy as a "purification" of the soul that cleanses the *psyche* from the contaminating influences of the body to prepare it for its release in the body's death. He sees it as a practice that trains one for death so that one will be ready to find pure knowledge in Hades, the realm of the dead (*Phaedo*, 67a–68b).

Reference in *Phaedo* is also made to Plato's theory that learning is actually the recollection of the insight the *psyche* had prior to birth—the timeless universal truths ("Forms"). The sense-perception of particulars, as the imitations or examples of these universals, only serve to remind the soul of them (*Phaedo*, 72e–73e). Learning, triggered by sensation, is the recollection of these universal truths that we forgot at birth. To an extent then the senses of the body are useful for this end, helping us to recover that lost knowledge. For example, seeing two chairs equal in size or color may help us to understand what "equality" means. However, equality itself ought not to be confused with the equal chairs (see *Phaedo*, 74b–d). Just as the *psyche* existed apart from the body and prior to the body's birth, so do these "Forms," like equality, greatness, smallness, goodness, etc., exist in a separate realm of the non-physical (*Phaedo*, 74e–76a, 76d–77a).

What our foregoing discussion shows is that there is a correspondence in Plato's mind between his anthropology (theory of human beings), epistemology (theory of knowledge), and metaphysics (theory of reality). The human being is constituted of two elements, the mind/soul (*psyche*) and the body; the universe involves two realms, the realm of the universals ("Forms") and the physical sensible realm of particulars; and while the *psyche* can attain pure knowledge of the Forms, the body through its senses deal with the physical sensible objects of the world. Thus, like the Forms that are eternal and non-changing, independent of material or physical contingencies, the *psyche* or soul is likewise immortal and has the capacity to ignore, at least to a certain extent, the bodily needs. While the body with its senses is a useful tool, the soul is the user and hence ought to be the body's master just as the physical world of particulars is shaped and ordered according to the Forms ruling from above (*Phaedo*, 79c). As the universal exemplars (Forms) are more god-like than their particular examples (physical things), so is the *psyche*, the soul, more god-like than the body. As these Forms rule the world of particulars that "share" (or "participate") in them, so does the *psyche* rule the body. Plato's dualism thus entails a hierarchy in the order of beings: there are two sorts of things but one is superior to the other; likewise there are two elements that make up the human being, but one element, the soul, is superior to the other, the body. When the soul ignores bodily cravings to pursue truth alone, it orients itself toward the realm of "the pure" (Forms) and therein experiences "wisdom" (*Sophia*) (*Phaedo*, 79d). The philosopher ("lover of wisdom") thus aims to purify the soul by freeing it from bodily interference as much as possible to attain knowledge of true reality, the Forms. This activity prepares one for final separation from the body at death. It is this hierarchical dualism with an ethics of ascendance from the lower to the higher that becomes inherited later, via the Platonists, and mixed with Abrahamic views.

What happens then to such a purified philosophical soul according to *Phaedo*? Like *Gorgias*, Plato in *Phaedo* also makes use of the older after-life myths. In death, freed from worldly stains, the pure soul goes to Hades to be with the gods (*Phaedo*, 80d). On the other hand, the impure soul contaminated with desires, is dragged back down by its desires and attachment to pleasures to Earth where it is forced to wander as a ghost around graves, longing for the physical, until it is reincarnated to be bound by the characteristics of its previous life and to fulfill those desires (*Phaedo*, 80e–81e). For example, one who practiced gluttony may become reborn as a donkey, one who practiced tyranny may become reborn as a hawk, and one who practiced social virtue but out of habit and without philosophy, may become reborn as a human being, etc. (*Phaedo*, 81e–82b). But the lover of learning, the practitioner of philosophy, whose soul has been purified by having kept away from bodily pleasures, goes to the realm of the gods (*Phaedo*, 82b–c, 82e–83c). Using the myth of reincarnation, Plato thus bids his readers to ignore and withdraw from bodily pleasures and the deceitful senses and to focus upon the intellect alone as much as possible. This intellectual faculty, the mind, as the *psyche*, is the substantial core of the self that sustains its own health through the process of reasoning or intellectual activity as exemplified in Socrates' life. As the life-giver of the body, it can never admit the opposite of life, death, and thus, Socrates asserts, must be immortal (*Phaedo*, 105c–106d). Salvation of this immortal element of the self from the clutches of the body and of repeated rebirth requires both learning and ethical conduct. Socrates stresses that it is only its upbringing and education, the non-material goods, that the *psyche* takes to its afterlife, and that these can be beneficial or harmful. Virtue as such requires life-long vigilance and discipline and resistance against the bodily influences (*Phaedo*, 107c–d). It is thus Plato's conviction that the care of the *psyche*, as the intellectual and moral core of one's humanity, ought to be the primary duty while alive. Let us now see how this Platonist dualism left its mark upon later Western conceptions of death, including Jewish and Christian views (and in Islam as well).

Platonism in the West

With the acceptance of Plato as a major thinker, much of the above-mentioned ideas concerning death and the afterlife became widely circulated throughout the Western (Mediterranean and Greco-Roman) world. It is interesting to note how during the few centuries before and after the beginning of the common era, the encounter between this Platonistic view of the self as an immortal but disincarnate substance and the very different set of views about the self as forming an integral whole involving body and soul, belonging to the Biblical and post-Biblical apocalyptic traditions of Judaism and Christianity, led to both creativity and tension as these two cultural spheres encountered one another throughout the Mediterranean world. Unlike the Greeks, for example, the Pharisees who dominated Judaism for a while refused to separate the soul and the body. This was connected to their belief in resurrection as an embodied life—although this came to be seen as a kind of transfiguration of the old body into the new. Paul propounds the same sort of belief in his letters, warning against dualistic conceptions. In the Hellenistic world (of Greeks and Romans), the Christians came in contact with radically different (non-Hebrew) perspectives on death, including the Platonistic idea of the duality of the cosmological structure and the immortality of the soul. Thus as Christianity, which initially began as a Jewish apocalyptic sect spread throughout the Gentile world, Hellenistic-inspired beliefs, perhaps traceable to Plato, became prevalent even within Christianity. With the spread of Greek philosophy and in particular the popularity of Platonist influenced ideas, even Jewish and Christian thinkers came to express views traceable to Plato. Alexandria in Egypt was especially a hotspot for Jewish and Christian philosophers under the influence of such Hellenistic ideas and Greek philosophy. The problem with the Platonistic idea of the immortal disembodied soul that separates from the body immediately at death, for early Christians like Paul however was that it makes the course of history irrelevant and the Messianism of Christ—his suffering, death, and resurrection—meaningless (see Goldenberg, 103–4).

From around the 4th century BCE, Greek Platonist dualism became combined with Near Eastern mythology and astrology to form the movement of Gnosticism. Gnosticism developed alongside Christianity and flourished during the 1st and 2nd centuries of the common era to influence Christianity. The Gnostics, inheriting Plato's dualism, divided the world into matter and spirit and viewed the body (*soma*) as the tomb (*sema*) of the soul. The body makes the soul forget the divine knowledge it possessed prior to birth. Its only salvation is through reception of knowledge (*gnosis*) revealed by a heavenly redeemer—identified by some Gnostics with Christ. The happy consequence of this *gnosis* would be the return, with the body's death, to the heavenly home outside of the evil and imperfect cosmos created by the Demiurge, a lesser power than the one true God. Salvation as such would be an escape of one's inner divine spark possessing immortality from the world of death and decay. However, the Gnostics stirred controversy for a while amongst the Christians with their dualistic cosmology according to which God is *not* the creator of this material world and according to which Christ as divine Logos could *not* have participated in the evils of human life: birth, suffering, death. For the orthodox Christians, this renders Christ's life meaningless, and hence the Gnostic influence had to be eradicated—and yet Plato's influence survived within Christianity.

Among Christians of the 1st century, there were thinkers like Clement of Alexandria (c.150–250) who under the influence of Platonist hierarchical dualism, denigrated earthly and historical life in favor of the realm of immortality. Clement's student Origen (c.185–251/4) was another important Christian thinker who participated in the intellectual discussions of Alexandria. Also under the influence of Greek Platonist philosophy, Origen divided the world into spiritual and material realms, with the implication that spirit is good and matter is evil. Salvation then for Origen, akin to what we saw in Plato's *Phaedo*, is one's restoration into the realm of pure spirit. In speculating about the eternity of the human soul, he even suggested its pre-existence, another idea that we already saw in Plato. However, this idea was later condemned by a church council of the 6th century. Although the ideas of reincarnation or the pre-existence of the soul have been expunged from Christian beliefs, popular ideas of the afterlife as being spiritual rather than embodied that survive today may then perhaps be traceable to such Platonist influences upon the Western mind.

Within Judaism as well there was some tension between historic and Messianic eschatology with its view to eventual bodily resurrection and the philosopher's and mystic's preoccupation with the soul's immortality in distinction from the body. But eventually eschatological and apocalyptic ideas became combined and discussed in terms of Platonist and/or Gnostic ideas. The Jewish philosopher Philo Judaeus (20 BCE–50 CE) of Alexandria in Egypt during the 1st century CE blended Platonistic ideas into the Jewish tradition to claim that we are composites of mind and body but in our "rebirth" after the body's death we shall be unbodied, free from composition. Claiming that there is a similarity between Plato and Moses and arguing that the same God spoke through Greek philosophy and Jewish religion, Philo interpreted rebirth or resurrection in Platonistic terms as an escape from the bodily jailhouse. Another example of a major Platonistic thinker of the Jewish tradition, but over a millennium later, would be Moses ben Maimon or Maimonides (1135/38–1204) of medieval Spain. At this time belief in resurrection was made by the rabbis a required principle of Jewish belief and the rabbinical tradition taught that the denial of resurrection is heresy. Accordingly, Maimonides affirmed the doctrines of final judgment, the coming of the Messiah, and the resurrection of the dead. However, he also interpreted this "world-to-come" as a world of disembodied spiritual bliss where the soul lives on for eternity without the body. How this idea of disembodied spiritual existence squared with the idea of resurrection was never made clear by him. The belief of some Reform Jews of today in the immortality of the purified soul may perhaps be traceable to this Platonistic strand of influence.

We ought to at least give due credit to the ancients, with an awareness of their living influence upon our ways of thinking. And Plato ought to be recognized as one of those ancients who has shaped our minds, including our worldviews and religions.

Selected Bibliography

Brumbaugh, Robert S. 1966. *The philosophers of Greece*. London: George Allen & Unwin.

Dresser, Horatio W. 1926. *A history of ancient and medieval philosophy*. New York: Thomas Y. Crowell Co.

Fideler, David. 1988. Introduction. In *The Pythagorean Sourcebook and Library*, trans. Kenneth Sylvan Guthrie. Grand Rapids, Michigan: Phanes Press, 1987.

Goldenberg, Robert. 1992. Bound up in the bond of life: Death and afterlife in the Jewish tradition. In *Death and Afterlife: Perspectives of World Religions*, ed. Hiroshi Obayashi. Westport, CT: Praeger.

Hutchison, John A. 1969. *Paths of faith*. New York: McGraw-Hill.

Keck, Leander E. 1957. Death and afterlife in the new testament. In *The Presocratic Philosophers*, eds. H. Obayashi, G. S. Kirk, J. E. Raven, and M. Schofield. Cambridge: Cambridge University Press, 1983.

North, Helen F. 1997. Death and afterlife in Greek tragedy and Plato. In *Plato: Complete Works*, H. Obayashi. Plato. ed. John M. Cooper. Indianapolis, IN: Hackett Pub., 1997.

Plato (ed. & commentary, R. E. Allen). 1984. *The dialogues of Plato*, vol. I. New Haven, Yale University Press.

Plato. (trans. G. M. A. Grube). 1977. *Plato's Phaedo*. Indianapolis, IN: Hackett Pub.

R. J. Zwi Werblowsky. 1997. Judaism, or the religion of Israel. In *Encyclopedia of the World's Religions*, ed. R. C. Zaehner. New York: Barnes and Noble Books.

Study Questions

1. What concepts of the afterlife were present in Ancient Greece?
2. What is Plato's dualism, and how does it affect his view of humans, knowledge, and the structure of reality in general?
3. How does the hierarchy of Plato's dualism relate to life lived in preparation for death?
4. What does Plato mean by "purity" and "purification"? How does Plato/Socrates understand the purification of the soul?
5. How has Plato's view influenced later religions?

CHAPTER 3

Death and Dying: A Jewish Approach

Rebecca Alpert

Jews date their origins back to the Ancient Near East, approximately 1,000 years before the time of Jesus. The early history of the Jews is chronicled in the Hebrew Bible (known to Christians as the Old Testament). The Hebrew Bible is the root of later Jewish legal and cultural traditions, but Judaism as we know it today is based fundamentally on the writings of the rabbis (200 BCE–500 CE) and the books known collectively as the Talmud. Although these teachings were codified in the medieval era, and adapted and modified during modern times, they remain the central traditions of Jewish practice and thought until today.

Jewish traditions emphasize the values of learning, prayer, living properly, and doing good deeds. Jews view study as a holy endeavor. They focus on the Hebrew Bible and Talmud, which are the sacred texts, but have always been interested in the knowledge to be gained from philosophical, literary, and scientific sources as well. Jews pray, traditionally, three times daily and also have special holy days. The Sabbath, which is observed each week from sundown Friday to sundown Saturday is the most important Jewish holiday. It is a time for refraining from worldly activities to concentrate on sacred study and spend companionable time with family and friends, eating and singing. Other significant holy days are Passover in the spring and the Days of Awe in the fall. On Passover, Jews celebrate the liberation from Egypt and their beginnings as a people in the land of Israel in ancient times. The ten "Days of Awe" begin with the Jewish New Year, Rosh Hashanah, and end with Yom Kippur, a day of fasting and self reflection. Jews also emphasize the importance of daily behavior and living properly. Jews are required to "keep kosher" which means to observe certain dietary rules including not eating pork or shellfish and not mixing foods that contain milk with those that contain meat. Jews are also expected to promote the values of peace, caring, and justice in their communities and toward all human beings.

The Jewish approach to death and dying is based on three basic concepts.[1] First, in Judaism, death is seen as a natural part of life. Second, Jews understand the body to belong to God and as something to be treated with honor and respect even after death. Jews don't agree about what happens to the soul, but this is also not so important in Jewish teaching. Last, the human community is obligated to mourn for the dead and to carry their memory. The key factor in understanding the Jewish approach to death and dying is to understand that Judaism is focused more on practice than belief. As such, this chapter will examine what Jews do when someone dies, and how they mourn, rather than what Jews believe about what happens to a person after death.

Death and Life

When the first Jews came to America in the 17th century, the first thing they would do was purchase land for a cemetery. While this may be surprising, Jewish law and custom require that Jews be buried in a Jewish cemetery, and ensuring that the dead have a proper resting place is as important as caring for those members of the community who are living. Jewish customs require that you prepare for your death and the death of your relatives in a variety of ways. In addition to being sure that your financial and personal obligations are in order (the stuff of making wills and purchasing burial plots), it has been a Jewish custom to write what has come to be known as an ethical will. In addition to leaving your loved ones material objects, Jews are supposed to reflect on the values that they would like to be sure their children, grandchildren, and others to whom they want to leave a legacy, follow.

Another way that Jews make preparation for death during their lives is in the celebration of the holiest day of the Jewish calendar, Yom Kippur (The Day of Atonement). On Yom Kippur the individual takes account of his or her life, and makes restitution with God and with humans for their misdeeds of the prior year. Many of the rituals associated with this practice are meant to remind Jews of the ultimate point of atonement, the one we face when we die. In one sense, Yom Kippur can be viewed as a rehearsal for death. On Yom Kippur you have the opportunity to be both the *met* (the dead person) and the *avel* (the mourner) simultaneously, and then to re-emerge into life renewed when the Day ends, reminded both of the fragility of life and of the possibility life offers of beginning again.

Most people are aware that Jews fast on Yom Kippur. Jews also refrain from having sex and wearing leather or jewelry (signs of affluence and beautification). These acts of self-abnegation symbolize one's own death as a retreat from life. They are also the customs one observes in mourning. Wearing white and dressing in a *kittel* are other examples of how Yom Kippur functions as a symbolic death. You literally dress in the clothes you will wear to the grave. White is the color of the shroud one is dressed in after death, and the *kittel* is the gown that is placed over the shroud. Finally, and most important, one of the prayers that is recited on Yom Kippur as part of the atonement ritual is called the *Viddui*, or confession. In this prayer, a Jew catalogues the wrongs that he or she has done during the year, and asks for forgiveness. This is the prayer that the Jew is obligated to recite on our deathbed, and which the most ritually observant Jews also recite daily.

We are also mourners on Yom Kippur, as we light candles for all of our family and friends who have passed away. The Yom Kippur ritual also includes a special memorial service (one of four during the year) to honor and remember those who have died. There is also a service on Yom Kippur called the Martyrology, when we remember not only our friends and relatives, but all Jews who lost their lives in the past *al kiddush ha shem*, to honor God's name, as martyrs. At this point in Jewish history, we particularly remember those, Jews and others, who died in the Holocaust, and the Israelis and Palestinians who have lost their lives in the violent clashes in the Middle East. But we also remember those who were martyred during the Crusades and the Inquisition and in earlier eras.

K'vod Ha Met: **Honoring the Dead**

While other traditions ponder the significance of the soul, Jewish teaching about death focuses mostly on the body. Jews do not doubt the existence of the soul, but most Jewish thought sees body and spirit and inextricably connected during life, and Jewish texts do not provide a clear picture of what happens to the soul after death. With the exception of the medieval Jewish philosophical tradition, which does ponder the fate of the soul, the focus of Jewish law and custom around death is primarily about how to treat the body of the deceased. Jews see the body as a holy vessel, a gift from God. Jews are instructed to take good care of the body to preserve its health in life and its honor after death. When rituals and customs around death are focused on the body, it is understood that while the soul or spirit (or breath or life force) may have departed, the body still retains the individual's holiness, and must be treated with honor and respect.

A story from the Talmud will illustrate this point. Rabbi Meir had a son whom he loved very much. His son died on a Friday, and his wife, Beruriah, concealed this fact from him for a day so that he would enjoy his Sabbath rest unperturbed, since Jews do not bury or mourn on the Sabbath. At the end of the Sabbath, she asked him what he would do if a King entrusted his most precious jewel to them, and then asked for it to be returned. He responded that he would care for it and return it, and he rent his clothes at that moment, knowing that his son had passed away. The story illustrates the idea that our lives are a gift from God, and our bodies are merely on loan to us, to go back to God when the time comes.

Jewish tradition prescribes a variety of customs to help people deal with the reality of death as part of life, and to make sure that we respect the body of the dead person as a vessel of holiness. The customs and beliefs described below are based on Jewish legal tradition. While many Jews do not follow these customs, or even know about them, many of the customs are undergoing a renaissance in contemporary Jewish life. As people in society have become more interested in ancient rituals and customs in recent years, observance of traditional Jewish practices around death and mourning has become more common. It is also true that even Jews who define themselves as secular (who are Jews because they see Jewishness as an ethnic and not a religious heritage) find themselves wanting to learn about and observe customs related to death. This may be because death is something they fear, or because it reminds them of their connection to their history and ancestry, or because they want to honor the wishes and customs of prior generations. Jewish funeral directors, for example, will be sure to inform the families of the deceased about traditional practices, and funeral directors are more willing to cooperate with communal organizations that want to help Jews observe these customs. Yet it also remains the case that for many Jews who are not Orthodox, many of these customs are unknown and unobserved, and Jews are buried according to American custom which derives primarily from Protestant tradition. The differences will be clear as these customs are described below.

When a Jew dies, the first act that takes place is to place the body on the floor. This symbolizes the return to the Earth that is a hallmark of Jewish practice surrounding death. "From dust you come, and to dust you return" (*Genesis*, 3:19) is a key to understanding the goal of Jewish practice. Of course, this ritual cannot take place if death occurs in a hospital setting. But those present at the time of death are required to do two things. First, they should tear their clothing, an act that is part of the ancient mourning practices in the Hebrew Bible. Second, those present recite a blessing, *Baruch ata Adonai, dayan ha emet* (Blessed are you, Adonai, Righteous Judge). They do this out of respect for being in the presence of a dead body. Of course, it may seem strange to the modern sensibility to praise God's righteousness at the moment of someone's death, but this too is in keeping with the idea discussed above that death is a natural part of life, and that even at this terrifying moment when a loved one is no longer alive, Jews are to remain mindful of the gift of life, and of the idea that death is not to be feared but is part of a natural process.

Jews also honor the dead through a series of acts in preparation for the funeral and burial. From the moment of death until the body is placed in the ground, it is never to be left alone. A person called a *shomer* (guard) remains with the body during that entire period. The person may recite *Psalms*, although the contemporary custom suggests that the *shomer* may also read other poetry or literature that the deceased person might have enjoyed.

A group of volunteers from a local synagogue, called a *hevra kedisha* (holy society), then prepares the body for burial. The body undergoes a ritual washing (*taharah*) and is then dressed in simple linen shrouds (*tachrichin*). Men (and today women) are also dressed in their own *tallit* (prayer shawl) and then dressed in the *kittel* (gown) worn on Yom Kippur. In Israel, the body is wrapped only in these garments. In the United States and other European Jewish cultures, the body is placed in a coffin as well. The coffin should be made only of wood, preferably plain pine, and not include any metal. As soon as possible thereafter, preferably not more than 24 hours after death, the funeral takes place. These customs insure that the body will decay quickly, and return to dust.

Immediately preceding the funeral, official mourners repeat the ritual that takes place at the time of death, known as *keriah* (tearing the garment). They tear their clothes (for a parent, over the heart, and for spouses, siblings, and children, over the right breast) and recite the blessing, "Blessed are You, Adonai, Righteous Judge." The rending of clothes (more often a small black ribbon that is affixed to the clothing) expresses their grief; the blessing formula reminds them that even at this moment of grief, they still praise God who created a world that includes death as a part of life. Judaism does have categories of official mourners. You are an official mourner if the person who died is your parent, child, spouse, or sibling. These individuals are the ones who participate in the *keriah* ceremony and who sit in the front row at the funeral service. In recent times, the partners of gay and lesbian people, and other members of extended family and friendship networks (especially grandchildren as people live longer and grandchildren are themselves adults) have been included as official mourners, although this is not the universal custom.

Although those attending the funeral often greet mourners beforehand in an effort to offer comfort, according to Jewish tradition the actual mourning process does not begin until after the burial so that the focus of the funeral continues to be honoring the deceased and not comforting the mourners. Until the time of the burial, the mourners are not technically in a state of mourning, but are in a category called *aninut*. During *aninut*, those close to the deceased have only one obligation and that is making sure the arrangements are made to prepare the body for burial.

The funeral is usually quite simple. There is no liturgy dictated for the funeral, but certain rituals have become customary. The funeral continues to focus on honoring the dead. The ceremony is most often conducted by a rabbi, but need not be according to Jewish law. It is simple and usually takes no more than 20 minutes. In keeping with that simplicity, Jews generally do not have flowers at the funeral. The ceremony consists of reading a few psalms and perhaps some music or poetry that the deceased might have liked. The main focus is on the *hesped* (eulogy). The goal is to present the deceased in a positive but also realistic light. The eulogizer is expected to describe the good that the deceased did, but not to exaggerate it. The funeral ends with a recitation of *El Mohle Rachamim*, the memorial prayer, which asks that God, who is full of compassion, grant a perfect rest to the spirit of the person who died.

Often the funeral takes place in a chapel at the funeral parlor, but for a respected member of a synagogue community, the funeral can also take place in the synagogue. Still others hold the funeral ceremony at the cemetery, either at the site of the grave or in a chapel on the premises.

The body is carried to the burial site by pallbearers, although their role is mostly symbolic. They accompany the coffin to the hearse, and carry the coffin at the cemetery to the grave. This custom is also in keeping with honoring the dead. The shomer who has been reading psalms from the moment of death also continues his or her accompaniment of the body to the grave.

The ceremony at the grave is also very brief. It consists of reading a few psalms and recitation of the *Kaddish*, the Jewish memorial prayer that mourners will continue to recite throughout the period of mourning that will be described in greater detail below. The most important custom that takes place at the grave is the actual burial. It is Jewish custom for the mourners to fill the grave after the coffin is lowered. Many do this symbolically by placing several shovels full of dirt on the coffin. But it is becoming more common to observe the traditional practice of filling the grave completely. This is the final act of honoring the dead person. From here, Jewish custom begins to focus on the mourner. To symbolize that transition, those attending the funeral form two lines, through which the mourners pass upon leaving the grave. As the mourners pass, those on line greet them with the words, "May the One who has comforted mourners comfort you in the midst of the gates of Zion."

Jewish tradition considers attending the funeral and burial of people with whom you are acquainted, whether you know them from synagogue or other communal organization, from work or your neighborhood, to be very important. The Talmud teaches that accompanying someone to the grave is the greatest of all *mitzvoth* (good deeds) because that person cannot repay the kindness. It is also appropriate to give a donation to a cause that the deceased cared about in order to honor their memory.

After the acts for honoring the dead are completed, the attention then turns to comforting the bereaved. Before we look at mourning customs, however, it is important to mention several practices that are popular in American culture that raise issues for Jews given the focus on honoring the dead, remembering also humans are dust and return to dust: cremation, embalming, or viewing the body before the funeral.

Embalming and Viewing

Jews believe that to respect the body involves a process that recognizes that the body should not be preserved in any way. Therefore, embalming is not a common Jewish practice. The body should be buried quickly[2] and placed directly into the ground so that it can, as suggested in *Genesis*, return to dust. The process of embalming (like the idea of creating hermetically sealed coffins made of things like metal that do not quickly decay and will preserve the body) is not in keeping with Jewish custom. Yet embalming is also understood as a necessity in some circumstances. For example, if a body needs to be transported to its burial place, the law requires embalming for health and safety reasons. Also, if the funeral cannot take place within the appropriate 24 hours because it is necessary to wait for family members to travel back for the funeral, their needs take precedence. Today, often refrigeration is available, and that would be preferred. But there are circumstances that require embalming, and it is an acceptable alternative. The custom of viewing the (embalmed and cosmetically prepared) body the night before the funeral is also discouraged by Jewish tradition for similar reasons. The body when prepared in keeping with Jewish tradition is dressed in a shroud, with the face covered, and is not meant to be viewed. The viewing of a cosmetically restored body is not considered respectful of the dead, and leads people away from a realistic sense that death is a process of decay.

Cremation

Cremation is another act discouraged by Jewish traditional practice. The body should be allowed to decay in a natural process, and burial is understood to provide that process. The generations after the Holocaust also saw burning bodies as too close to the experience of the Jews who were sent to crematoria. But as evidence of Jews being buried in mass graves by the Nazis as well comes to light, and as younger generations are more removed from this experience, this explanation becomes less important. Many Jews are moved by the ecological advantages of cremation over burial, and Jewish cemeteries and religious leaders have become more willing to perform funerals and memorial services for those who choose cremation, and also to allow their burial in Jewish cemeteries. Yet it is still the case that burial is much more common than cremation among Jews today.

Other contemporary practices based on medical technologies that don't seem to be in keeping with the Jewish ideals of honoring the body and seeing the body as belonging to God and therefore not to be tampered with by human endeavor need to be examined. The Jewish approaches to such phenomena as euthanasia, organ donation, autopsy, and suicide have also undergone much rethinking over time.

Euthanasia

Jewish tradition has always taken a positive attitude toward medicine and Jews have been in the forefront of medical research. Ancient Jewish texts support the idea that humans are partners with God in creation, and human beings are obligated to seek health and healing. The body belongs to God, so the individual has a strong obligation to take care of the body and to promote health. One consequence of that idea is that Jewish texts oppose any act by a human being that would hasten death. Therefore, Jewish law does not promote euthanasia under any circumstances. In recent times, however, many Jewish scholars have rethought this position. New technologies can keep the body alive in some circumstances way past any time when the person would be considered alive by the traditional Jewish criterion of breathing; Jewish scholars have argued that it is in some cases appropriate to remove those technologies, or as it is expressed in the vernacular, to "pull the plug." It is also appropriate in many cases not to begin to use those technologies in the first place, but to allow the process of death to take place in a natural way. Scholars often refer to the ancient story of the death of Rabbi Judah, the author of the Mishnah, a 2nd century legal text of great importance. As Rabbi Judah lay dying in an upstairs bedroom, his students downstairs kept praying for him, and their prayers kept him alive. Knowing that Rabbi Judah was ready to die, the servant who worked in the house dropped a pitcher. The loud noise disrupted the prayers, and Rabbi Judah's soul was allowed to depart. Although this is only a story and not a legal text, it has provided a warrant for contemporary scholars to argue that in certain circumstances humans may intervene to end life.

Suicide

If Jews are not generally permitted to assist in the death of another person, then it follows that taking one's own life would also be viewed in a negative light. The same principle applies: the body belongs to God, and humans are only caretakers. It is obligatory for the human being, then, to care for his or her body, and it is not permissible according to this logic, to end one's own life. Traditional Jewish law therefore does not permit a suicide to receive any rites that honor the dead. However, this rather harsh approach is almost never adopted. First, Jewish law recognized that these rules are very difficult on mourners, and are counter to the important rule that mourners should be comforted. There was also an understanding that most people who commit suicide are not acting out of free will or with full mental capacity. The law therefore requires that for someone's death to be defined as a suicide, the person would have had to committed the act in the presence of witnesses to whom they proclaimed the act as a suicide. The definition is so stringent that almost no one falls into the category. Nonetheless, the law remains to discourage people from committing suicide, given the Jewish tradition's preference for preserving life.

Organ Donation and Autopsy

Jewish tradition also opposes organ donation and autopsy. These are both considered acts that do not honor the dead, because the dead must be honored by the proper burial of all parts of the body. (This principle is so far reaching that it includes burying body parts that were surgically removed during the person's life prior to their death if at all possible.) However, Jewish law has become less stringent about these practices in more recent times. While honoring the dead is indeed an important part of Jewish tradition, saving a life (*pikuah nefesh*) is always understood to take precedence over this and other commandments. Advances in medical science make autopsy an opportunity for research into inheritable diseases, and it is permitted under these circumstances. (And, of course, autopsy is permitted if there are legal requirements in the cases of suspected suicide or homicide.) Organ donation is also now widely practiced among Jews. While not all organs directly save lives, most Jewish teachers follow the principle that quality of life is an important concept as well, and many people will live better lives as a result of organ donation.

Jewish Mourning Practices

Jewish mourning begins when the family and friends of the deceased return from the burial site. Often, a pitcher of water is left outside the house where the mourning observances are taking place (house of mourning, or *shiva* house) for people to wash their hands symbolically on return from the cemetery. This custom probably has its roots in magic and superstition (to wash off the experience of being in a cemetery among the dead), but also takes on the symbolic meaning of a transition toward the next important phase: comforting the mourners (*nihum avelim*).

Traditional Jewish teaching places a high value on making sure that those who are experiencing grief receive adequate support from the community. Just as it is important to attend a funeral, community members are expected to participate in observances around mourning. Some members of the community in fact don't attend the funeral so that they can make sure preparations are made in the house when the mourners return. The first thing the mourners do is sit together and eat a meal, called, appropriately, the meal of consolation, *seudat havra'ah*. It is customary to eat round foods, like eggs and lentils, as a reminder of the cycle of life and the continuity between birth and death. The mourners also light a candle which burns for the seven days of mourning.

The name of the first phase of the mourning process is *shiva*. *Shiva* means seven in Hebrew, and indicates the number of days that this first phase of mourning is observed. Often this is referred to as "sitting shiva," because one of the customs is for the mourners to sit on low benches for the duration of this period of time. Mourners are also expected not to leave the house, except for the one day during the seven when shiva is not observed, the Jewish Sabbath. From sundown Friday until sundown Saturday the seven day process is interrupted, and mourners are expected to go to synagogue. Otherwise, they remain in the house. So the observance is actually not a full seven days. Any part of any day also counts in the seven, so the day of the funeral is always counted as day one, and Friday daytime and Saturday evening are also included. And the seventh day ends after the morning prayers take place.

It is preferable to observe shiva in the house where the deceased lived so that the mourners can be surrounded by things that remind them of the person who died. Where this is impractical, shiva can be observed in the home of one of the mourners, and if necessary mourners can observe shiva in their own homes individually. When not in the home of the deceased, mourners often bring photographs and other keepsakes to display to remind them of the life of the person who has died.

Mourners observe various other customs in addition to sitting on low benches as a symbol of their grief. They cover the mirrors in the house to help them keep their attention focused away from themselves (and probably as a result of old superstitions that the spirit of the dead might appear in the mirror). The mourners also refrain from sex, do not wear leather, bathe for pleasure, cut their hair, or wear cosmetics or perfume as we observed was the case during Yom Kippur. They are also not permitted to study, as study is considered a great pleasure in Jewish tradition. These customs help the mourner to focus on the grieving process. Staying home for the seven days also promotes concentration on the mourning process. If, however, it is a hardship not to go to work, mourners may observe only three days of this process, and more liberal and secular Jews in general follow the custom of a three day observance.

During shiva, mourners do two things. They have prayer services in their homes, and they receive visitors who come to comfort them. In keeping with the requirement to comfort the bereaved, members of the community are expected to make a visit to the house of mourning. It is traditional for the mourners to set the tone of the conversation, and not to offer greetings to their visitors, to indicate their status as outside the world of regular social intercourse. This gives the mourner the opportunity to experience his or her grief as he or she is experiencing it at the moment. This helps the visitor remember that the mourner is not expected to take care of the visitor's needs. The visitor can play a vital role in sharing stories about the deceased that will help the mourner in their grieving process. If a visit isn't possible, a note (or even an email) is considered most appropriate.

Visitors are also expected to participate in prayer services at the house of mourning. Jews pray three times daily, although the afternoon and evening services are often collapsed into one prayer time. For a prayer service to take place, Jews require the presence of a minyan (10 Jewish men for Orthodox Jews, 10 Jewish men or women for all others). Community members come to the shiva house for morning and evening prayers. During the prayer service, mourners often take the opportunity to reminisce about the deceased. They also recite the Mourner's Kaddish, or the memorial prayer for the dead. Kaddish means holy, and the Kaddish prayer is used in a variety of ways during most Jewish prayer services. It is recited in Aramaic, the ancient language Jews spoke during the time of Jesus. The Kaddish is actually a doxology, or prayer of praise of God. Surprisingly, it makes no mention of death whatsoever. Yet it is the central prayer that is used during the period of mourning and throughout the Jewish year to memorialize the dead. The text follows:

Mourner:
Let God's name be made great and holy in the world that was created as God willed. May God complete the holy realm in your own lifetime, in your days, and in the days of all the house of Israel, quickly and soon. And say: Amen.

Community:
May God's great name be blessed, forever and as long as worlds endure.

Mourner:
May it be blessed, and praised, and glorified, and held in honor, viewed with awe, embellished, and revered; and may the blessed name of holiness be hailed, though it be higher than all the blessings, songs, praises, and consolations that we utter in this world. And say: Amen.

May Heaven grant universal peace, and life for us, and for all Israel. And say: Amen.

May the one who creates harmony above, make peace for us and for all Israel, and for all who dwell on earth. And say: Amen. (Reimer's translation)

From this we once again learn the lesson that for Jewish tradition, death is a part of life to be accepted and for which we praise God and God's creation. At the same time that Jewish tradition emphasizes the importance of recognizing that life goes on, it also affirms that people need a process and customs to help them grieve. Shiva makes provisions for both aspects.

Shiva ends on the morning of the seventh day after the morning prayers. The mourners and those present walk around the block, symbolizing the end of shiva and their return to the everyday world. After this intense mourning period, Jewish tradition defines another period of time, *sheloshim*, or Thirty. During the month following a death, mourners do not attend celebrations such as parties or weddings, but otherwise, they return to their daily work in the world. After the loss of a parent, mourners extend the restrictions of sheloshim for one year. During this time, they also observe a daily recitation of the kaddish. For many, this returns them to an involvement in synagogue life as they must be present for daily services to recite the Kaddish with a minyan. In traditional Judaism and in Orthodox Judaism to this day, this daily recitation is incumbent upon sons but not daughters. It was this particular imbalance that led many Jewish women to rethink their roles in Jewish life and to demand equal rights. This custom of daily Kaddish recitation and reflection on the death of a parent has led several contemporary Jewish thinkers, like Leon Wieselthier, Esther Broner, and Ari Goldman, to publish memoirs about the power of this experience. Other Jews who don't feel bound by the restrictions of traditional Jewish customs recite Kaddish publicly when they can, but also recite it privately each day for the year long period.

Between two and eleven months after death it's customary for Jews to hold an unveiling of the tombstone at the cemetery. The service for this is also quite brief and mostly involves removing a covering from the stone, reading the words written there, and reciting the memorial prayer and the Kaddish. When leaving the gravesite, it's also customary to place a pebble or small rock on the grave. The rock is your personal marker that indicates you've come to visit.

After the mourning period ends, it is still incumbent upon Jews to perform rituals to remember their loved ones. Four times a year, on Yom Kippur, and the three pilgrimage festivals (Sukkot, Passover, and Shavuot) there are communal memorial services as part of the prayer service, and these are also times when Jews are reminded to visit the graves of their relatives and friends. Jews light candles that burn for 24 hours in memory of their dead at these points, and also on the Yahrzeit, or anniversary, of someone's death. For a parent's yahrzeit, you are also expected to go to synagogue to recite Kaddish.

These regularly established mourning rituals indicate the most important dimension of the way Jews conceptualize the role of death. Death is not a tragedy, but something that is incorporated in to daily life. Having a child to say kaddish for you and being part of a community that will perpetuate your memory is as close as Jews get to an understanding of immortal life. There is little Jewish concern about the afterlife, although Jewish philosophy posits a resurrection (for some of souls, for others of body) at the end of days. Jewish texts also describe the *olam haba*, or world to come. These texts provide descriptions of what the world to come will be like (there will be peace in the world; every day will be like the Sabbath; the righteous will have a reward). But these depict hopes and aspirations for a possible future world, not a definitive conceptualization of life after death. For Jews, individuals live on primarily in the memory of those whose lives they influenced and changed.

Notes

1.   While different Jewish groups today approach rituals and beliefs differently, and Orthodox, Conservative, Reform, Reconstructionist, Israel, and secular Jews will differ in the emphasis they place on each of these rituals and beliefs, this essay will present a general introduction to traditional practice.
2.   Certain Jewish holy days, and the weekly observance of the Sabbath, take precedence over this rule, and funerals are postponed if the death falls in too close approximation of these times.

Selected Bibliography

Alpert, Rebecca T. 1997. *Confronting mortality and facing grief: Jewish perspectives on death and mourning: An advanced guide for adult study.* Wyncote, PA: Reconstructionist Rabbinical College.

Diamant, Anita. 1998. *Saying Kaddish: How to comfort the dying, bury the dead, and mourn as a Jew.* New York: Schocken Books.

Gillman, Neil. 1997. *The death of death: Resurrection and immortality in Jewish thought.* Woodstock, VT: Jewish Lights.

Goldman, Ari. 2003. *Living a year of Kaddish.* New York: Schocken Books.

Lamm, Maurice. 1969. *The Jewish way in death and mourning.* New York: Jonathan David.

Levy, Yamin. 2003. *Journey through grief: A Sephardic manual for the bereaved and their community.* Jersey City, NJ: KTAV.

Riemer, Seth, ed. 1997. *Reconstructionist Rabbinical Association Rabbi's Manual.* Wyncote, PA: Reconstructionist Rabbinical Association.

Solomon, Lewis D. 2001. *The Jewish tradition and choices at the end of life: New Judaic approach to illness and dying.* Lanham, MD: University Press of America.

Wieseltier, Leon. 2000. *Kaddish.* London: Picador.

Study Questions

1. What three concepts guide the Jewish response to death?
2. What is the role of the *hevra kedisha* in the Jewish community?
3. Why has Jewish tradition prohibited both embalming and cremation? What positive values are demonstrated in burial practices?
4. What are the principle mourning commandments and prohibitions?
5. While the Kaddish prayer does not seem to mention death directly, what Jewish views does its recital teach?

CHAPTER 4

Protestant Christian Views of Death, Dying, and Afterlife

Lucy Bregman

Death, Salvation, and "Eternal Life"

The Protestant branch of Christianity includes a wide range of religious groups and denominations, from Assemblies of God, Baptists, Episcopalians, United Methodists, and many who are unaffiliated with any major denominational body. There are now Protestant Christians found worldwide, and indeed the fastest-growth areas for this branch of Christianity lie in Africa, Asia, and Latin America. However, this chapter will focus principally on English-language and North American Protestantism. We will treat Protestant Christianity not as a separate religion, but as one branch of the wider Christian faith. Therefore, some introduction to major themes of Christianity is in order.

Christianity from its origin has been a religion of salvation. Theological ideas such as atonement, reconciliation, justification, and redemption all are ways to express how, due to the death and resurrection of Jesus of Nazareth, the basic relation between God and humanity has changed. Human beings had all become estranged from God, but God's answer was the sacrificial death of his Son, making possible eternal life for those who believed and trusted in the person and work of Jesus. The God known to Christians is the same God of the Hebrew Scriptures. What God began in ancient times through a covenant with Israel (recorded in what Christians began to call the Old Testament after their own collection of writings became the witness to the "New Covenant" or "Testament") now is fulfilled and completed in Jesus Christ. Christians argued about how much of Jewish law and ritual one needed to observe, but by the 2nd century of the common era at the latest, there were clearly two separate religious groups. What Christians never repudiated included Judaism's belief in God as Creator and ruler, and the hope for a complete redemption of a creation now flawed and disordered. Intrinsic to this hope was a vision of a world re-created so that death and violence would be no more. Death, sin, estrangement from God, and injustice were all part of the old era, while the "world to come" would be a reign of peace and eternal life. Among Jews at the time of Jesus not all of these ideas were universally held, but Jesus' parables clearly assume that some condition beyond death awaits all. Even if he did not use the stories to inform his hearers about the afterlife, he taught that a universal resurrection from death would arrive, brought in by God at the end of time. A part of this resurrection, a very important part, was the judgment by God of both the righteous and the wicked, followed by their reward and punishment. In the meantime, would the dead have any conscious experience, or would they all be "on hold" in their graves? Jesus' parable of the beggar Lazarus and the rich man (*Luke* 16:19–31) assumes the former: the dead feel, hope, speak—but are separated by a gulf from each other and the living.

Perhaps more important for the early development of Christianity was the Gospel of John's message of "eternal life" through Jesus, a life that begins now in the world but stretches into the transcendent era of God. "Whoever hears my word and believes him who sent me has eternal life and will not be condemned; he has crossed over from death to life" (*John*, 6:24). As this passage indicates, a transition from death to life is both a statement about physical death and a metaphor for a transformed relation with God. Christianity, then, uses the language found worldwide in initiation-oriented groups: one's old ordinary existence is "death," and one's new and eternal life begins when one participates in the group's rite (for Christians, baptism). The Apostle Paul uses this language extraordinarily effectively in encouraging new Christians to turn away from their past identities and embrace new life: "Count yourselves dead to sin but alive to God in Christ Jesus" (*Romans*, 6:11).

These themes are the shared legacy of all Christians. They reveal that death was never taken as merely a natural event, nor was it fundamentally *neutral*. It was always a minus, a negative, something from which to be saved. One crosses over from death to life, even when what we ordinarily think of as "life" can be viewed as estrangement from God and therefore a kind of "death." The positive vision behind this is of a life in and with God, eternal and available to humans today, a life that helps those who live it frame their experiences and relations from an ultimate and eternal perspective. The risk is that ordinary everyday life, identified as "death," will seem merely a way-station to an afterlife, and therefore a miserable burden to endure. Christians have occasionally slipped into this second stance; to exalt the world to come they have felt they must trash the world we now inhabit. The Bible does not exactly validate this stance, but it is possible to find individual passages to support such views.

We should repeat that the above religious motifs are the shared inheritance for all Christians. Protestant Christians build upon them, but with the exception of eternal punishment for the wicked—the reality of Hell—very rarely question them. The Bible so clearly teaches a resurrection and judgment of the dead that it seemed outside the scope of Christianity to develop alternatives to this, or to claim that death as a "natural event" is the complete ending of one's existence as a person. However, this doesn't mean that the branch of Christian theology known as "eschatology," teachings on last things, has been free from conflicts. The conflicts have been over specific issues and elaborations within the above framework.

Protestant Themes: The Reformation Legacy

Within the totality of Christianity as a world religion, the Protestant movement has two beginnings: an historical beginning, as a 16th-century protest against perceived abuses and deviations in the Roman Catholic Church, and a theological origin in the Bible as the final norm for faith. The Reformation, begun in 1517 by Martin Luther in Germany, intended to reform the Catholic Church, not create a new religious body side by side with the existing one. But that was what actually happened. However, the new movement did not intend to replace *everything* already done by Christians. Many of the beliefs held by Protestants, even the most vehemently anti-Catholic Protestants, were and remain direct legacies of late-medieval western Christianity. For instance, pious self-help books on how to die in a state of faith (the *Ars Moriendi* literature) had been popular among European Christians before the Reformation (ever since the 14th-century Black Plague epidemics, when the threat of sudden and horrible death hung over everyone) and continued to be read and re-printed after it, by Protestants as well as Catholics. This kind of writing depended upon literacy, a certain level of individualism, and awareness of dying as a special spiritual situation. These were all features of early modern Protestants' faith.

However, as the name "Protestantism" implies, the Reformation was a protest movement, carried out by reformers who believed that the Bible contained all the knowledge of God and salvation necessary for Christians. "Tradition"—i.e., the teachings of the Catholic leadership or *magisterium*—was not considered a second valid source of authoritative doctrine. Some Protestants, such as Mennonites, tried to bring the church back so that it looked like the New Testament Church of *Acts of the Apostles*, while others, including both Martin Luther and John Calvin, kept the model of a church which as a visible institution encompassed the entire society. This was even more true for the Reformers in England, where a national church (Church of England) kept many more Catholic features than other Reformation movements. But all accepted the principle of *sola Scriptura*, Scripture alone, as the standard for faith. What they argued about was how to interpret the Bible, especially when the questions they ask were simply not those the Biblical authors ever considered or would have found important.

What did Protestants of the 16th century believe the Bible taught about life, death, and afterlife? Their overriding concern was to establish a sure and certain basis for a right relation with God, based on God's own decision to save (the doctrine of "election") and personal faith of believers. The overall picture was focused on individual faith in Jesus Christ as savior, with "faith" understood as personal trust rather than knowledge of facts about Jesus and salvation. Most of the emphasis on "faith" was to contrast it with "works," using the arguments of Paul found in *Romans* and *Galatians* in the Bible. The implication of this for the Reformers and their followers was that a sacramental/ritual relation to Christ was not enough, and indeed provided a false security in the face of one's utter need of divine grace. Thus, a sacramental rite for the dying vanished from Protestantism, while facing death in the presence of Christ became an intensely inner experiential matter.

But perhaps the most dramatic change at the time of the Reformation was in Christian beliefs and practices related to the destinies of the dead prior to the Last Judgment. Latin medieval Christianity had developed the idea of Purgatory, a place where the unperfected dead could be "purged" or purified from their sinful habits and dispositions. Meanwhile, the living could assist them by paying for a priest to say masses on behalf of the recently dead; this was believed to shorten the period of purgation. Such a doctrine, the Reformers believed, could not be found in the Bible. Therefore, it could not be made a central article of Christian teaching. Consequently, the practice of saying masses on behalf of the dead souls in Purgatory was abolished among Protestants. No masses for the dead meant lessened income for priests, but popular suspicions about those who made money off the dead fueled this change. (These suspicions sound today a lot like criticism of the American funeral industry!) In place of Purgatory, the Reformation left salvation and damnation entirely in the hands of God, whose "election" of believers for salvation was an absolute, unconditional decree. Were some who died still imperfect "unready" for Heaven? Didn't they need purgation, cleansing? From a Protestant point of view, this is an entirely wrong question. God saves, God alone saves; all are unworthy, all depend ultimately upon God's mercy. Gradiations of more or less purity or worthiness miss the point entirely. And, once in the hands of God, the dead dropped out of the picture.

Did this mean that Protestants were more likely to be anxious about their own impending deaths, since they could no longer count on either sacramental absolution or a place in Purgatory? Or, were they more energetically confident that since God had saved them, and God alone was fully trustworthy, they could depend upon God all the way? Both attitudes appear. A very famous Protestant book from the late 17th century, John Bunyan's *The Pilgrim's Progress from This Life to the Next*, captures both. This is an allegory of Christian life, laid out as a journey from "The City of Destruction" to the "Celestial City." The road is filled with trials and dangers, but the glorious destination awaits those who seek it rightly. At the end, the hero, Pilgrim, and his friends, come to a swift and deep river and must cross it. In this metaphorical picture of dying and death, the faithful Christian must not be overwhelmed by fear—and yet, false confidence in one's own goodness is an even worse trap. There is no guarantee that a Christian will not fear death, or that death will be an easy experience. Yet one of the pilgrims declares as he is about to enter this ordeal:

> This river has been a terror to many; yea the thoughts of it also have frightened me. But now . . . I stand easy . . . The waters indeed are to the palate bitter and to the stomach cold. Yet the thoughts of what I am going to, and of the conduct that waits for me on the other side, doth lie as a glowing coal at my heart . . . I have formerly lived by hearsay and faith, but now I go to where I shall live by sight and shall be with him in whose company I delight myself. (Bunyan, 282)

Therefore, although death itself remains a negative, Christian hope diminishes its power, and a confident and courageous stance transforms what is bitter and cold into "a glowing coal." Note, however, that it is the sure expectation of a destination and a meeting with one's own beloved risen Lord that inspires this vision.

Bunyan's book was a favorite for hundreds of years; it was, next to the Bible, *the* most popular book in the American colonies and through the 19th century. Roughly speaking, it is the same vision that inspires many classic Protestant hymns, including "Amazing Grace," still Americans' most popular religious song. First comes salvation through faith, then life's "many dangers, toils and snares," then a place "beyond the veil, a life of joy and peace." Grace, God's guiding and abiding presence, continues on through dying and crossing over from this world to the next, where

When we've been there 10,000 years,
bright shining as the sun,
We've no less days to sing God's praise
Than when we first begun.
     (words by John Newton)

Evangelical Protestantism: Triumphant Dying and Familial Heaven

The second era of Protestantism began in the mid-18th century, with the Methodist movement founded by John Wesley in Britain. This style we will call "Evangelical Protestantism," and it has influenced Protestants everywhere (except Iceland). This movement was started as a "revival" to win the hearts and souls of those who had lost connection with the more institutional, traditional, and routinized forms of the Church of England. It emphasized "a personal relation with Jesus as Lord and Savior" and the centrality of the Bible. I have put the first phrase in quotes, because the words have become a kind of code or shorthand for a particular religious stance. Very briefly, Wesley and the early Evangelical movement believed that "second-hand religion" was no religion, and that personal experience of salvation was necessary for everyone. Not that Luther hadn't believed this, but he had not, seemingly, re-shaped the entire practice of the religion to insist on it. Wesley and the Evangelical movement stressed the real and visible experience of conversion and a "converted life" that followed from it. Could anyone actually achieve "sinless perfection" in this life? Yes, with God's help, and social support from other believers, Welsey believed that this was possible.

Evangelical Christians did not change any of the already-existing Protestant doctrines about death and afterlife. There were no arguments about resurrection, Heaven, judgment, and barely a murmur about the punishments of Hell. But due to the very optimistic stance of Evangelicals about the possibility of a transformed life, the hope for a "triumphant dying" became the norm. Wesley's case-history of the "perfected" Christian, a

Jane Cooper, was actually the history of a dying woman, who dies not just without fear, but in a state of exaltation. "Her face were full of smiles of triumph and she clapped her hands for joy" (Wesley, 345). This norm of triumphant or ecstatic dying makes the passage quoted from Bunyan appear mild and cautious, just as it makes psychological ideals of "acceptance" seem wimpy. It also led to a renewed fascination with deathbed scenes and last-minute conversions. An Evangelical would hope that his or her own dying could be a witness to others of the power of the Holy Spirit and faith in Christ to override all fear of death. Undoubtedly this actually worked in many cases. But one wonders now how oppressive some of the consequences of this ideal can be; not everyone, even with strong faith, can go out singing. Moreover, the added fear of being "a poor witness" haunts heirs of this expectation.

Another shift in attitudes and expectations seems to have followed in the footsteps of Evangelical piety. This one does involve a different emphasis than had been officially marked off in the past. In the case of Wesley's movement, the Methodists stayed within the structure of the institutional Church of England only until his death; then, they reconstituted themselves as a separate religious body. In the British American colonies, almost all religious groups were voluntary associations of like-minded persons, drawn together for worship and continuously needing to define themselves as different from other voluntary groups. This pattern, in place by the late 18th century, meant that the ideal of a whole society sharing *one* religious life, was already doomed. Religion became a private decision, a matter of one's personal choice and conscience. Individual faith, and individual "converted life," rather than public communal spiritual life, became the standard brand of American Protestantism. Although almost all who live within this model assume this is "that old time religion," in fact it is far more individually-based than what Luther, Calvin, and the other early Reformers had in mind. The controversies this created for church organization—the technical term is "polity"—flourished during the 18th and early 19th centuries. But its implications for a vision of "last things," a Biblical vision of "A New Heaven and a New Earth," also were felt. How?

If Christian faith is a matter of my personal relationship with Jesus Christ, and not a matter of a large-scale institutionalized social order, does that mean *no* human relationships mean anything? No, not at all. For the Evangelicals and those influenced by them (actually, practically all Protestants to some degree), the family was the one sphere beyond the individual where Christian faith could be visibly expressed. A Christian home was the one institution where Christ could reign. The religious exaltation of such a home came at a time when families themselves were changing. Farm families were large, multigenerational, and economic producers; the newer, urban, and middle-class families were much smaller, "nuclear," and consumed goods and services. Paid work took place outside the home, and the family was more and more seen as a refuge from the harsh, unChristian wider world of public life. While we may assume that people have always cared about their families, the new style of family life meant that they cared very deeply about far fewer persons, and the family unit became a life unto itself, isolated from other, larger-scale groupings as it had not been before.

And so, it is from this development that the hope to look upon one's Savior in the Celestial City starts to include the hope to reunite with one's own dead family members. If that hope had played a role for persons at the time of the Reformation, let alone before, it was a shadowy private and wistful hope. It was not a central motif of what people expected in the afterlife. But by the 1850s that is what it became. A collection of *Death-Bed Scenes* gathered by a Protestant pastor reveals this. Paradoxically his best example of an "ecstatic die-er" expects to meet her mother in Heaven, and also is certain that her young and healthy husband will soon join her there. "But what would Heaven be without Jesus!" she exclaims (Clark, 130). Somehow, Jesus now finds a niche among one's personal loved ones, although neither the dying woman nor the pastor who recorded her experience saw it this way.

More popular presentations of Christian afterlife hopes did make this shift. "Heaven Our Home" became populated with one's beloved dead, especially dead children. A nuclear family will, in this life, come to an end as its members grow up and form families of their own. In Heaven such a family can be preserved eternally, although what this would actually mean is hard to imagine. What can be termed "Modern Heaven" is thoroughly human-centered, and even cluttered with all the specific, particular good things of this life (see McDannell and Lang, 1988). It is a place of leisure and personal growth, a kind of celestial retirement village. Is this what Protestantism officially teaches? No, or at least, not with this emphasis. Nor is this humanized, familial Heaven unknown to Roman Catholics. But it is a development whose results are everywhere in popular culture. It reinstates one lost aspect of Catholic Purgatory—namely, a connection between the living and the dead (who, traditionally, needed the help of the living to shorten their purgation). Now, dead grandparents watch over their grandchildren, dead South Philadelphians celebrate their 30th wedding anniversaries in Heaven, and familial relationships dominate people's hopes for what the afterlife will be like. "Being met on the other side" is how some hospice team members speak of this, "being met" not by Jesus or saints, but by one's own beloved dead.

Because of this, it became unfashionable to mention the possibility of eternal separation from God, the traditional painful fate of the wicked. But there were also good theological and ethical objections raised against the traditional doctrine of Hell. Could a loving God truly condemn people forever for sins which, however evil, were finite in scope and effects? If the purpose of earthly punishment is rehabilitation (a view which emerged in the 18th century) then Hell is truly pointless; no possibility of rehabilitation could come from an everlasting punishment. These objections have not stopped a large number of Christians from continuing to accept some version of Hell but its importance diminished as "Heaven Our Home" dominated popular afterlife hopes.

20th Century Focus: Healing

Protestantism did not stop with the Evangelical movement, however widespread and adaptable its style has proved. Twentieth century Protestantism proved to have new vigor and new influences, especially as it spread into every continent and among a very wide assortment of peoples. Perhaps the most impressive development is the Pentecostal movement within Protestantism, for this has come into places such as Latin America where more traditional forms of Protestantism were barely known. Pentecostalism is the name for the religious movement that focuses on "gifts of the Spirit" given at the festival of Pentecost (*Acts*, 2) as the visible sign of the believer's faith and God's presence in his or her life. These gifts feature glossallalia ("speaking in tongues") and prophecy. But along with this comes a sense of reviving the fullness of New Testament Christian experience (remember, for Protestants the true origin of their faith is to be found in the Bible). And this experience clearly included healing through the power of the Holy Spirit.

Here we have a really good example of Protestantism's continued adaptability. Pentecostal Christians universally accept the traditional beliefs about resurrection, Heaven, Hell, and judgment. They fit well within the Evangelical framework as described above. But an emphasis on spiritual healing has been a feature of Pentecostal practice which resonated with other Protestants, so much so that groups traditionally very far removed in style and doctrine, such as Presbyterians and Episcopalians, will now be willing to hold services especially devoted to healing. Some groups, influenced by Pentecostalism but outside its by-now traditional structures, are especially devoted to healing as a ministry and a metaphor for the whole process of salvation through Christ. Songs such as "I am the Lord Your Healer" rely on this image, without repudiating more traditional ones such as justification.

What does "spiritual healing" mean here? And why should it have made a come-back, at a time when contemporary scientific medicine has seemed so powerful? Do Protestant pastors who pray for healing from the Spirit compete with doctors? No, very very seldom is the relationship seen as one of either/or. Instead, the focus on healing may be part of a movement to reclaim the sphere of health and illness from the domination of medical experts, and return it to ordinary persons. Although some versions of "spiritual healing" focus on celebrity "healers" and their special powers, the vast majority of those who accept some version of spiritual healing do so more democratically, as the gift given to all believers rather than to just a few. While only a trained doctor can diagnose and treat a disease using Western scientific medical methods, every Christian may pray for healing, lay hands on the sick, and feel assured that God wants to heal. Sometimes the real competition is not between scientific medicine and spiritual healing, but between Protestant Christian versions of the latter, and indigenous practices such as *Espiritismo*, systems of folk healing which have long been part of traditional cultures.

Does a fascination with spiritual healing have implications for Christians' views on death and dying? I believe it does. On the positive side, healing cuts through the body/soul dualism of much traditional Christianity. If God wants to heal, God takes bodies seriously and positively, God does not deal exclusively with disembodied souls. Not too many Christians have ever actually denied this, but a focus on healing reemphasizes that the body is a part of creation and a good gift from God. It is not first and foremost an obstacle, a nuisance, or an embarrassment. Even if the ultimate hope for an eternal life does not include the body as we know it now, revering the body as the site of God's healing action means taking embodiment seriously and positively. But there is a shadow side to this as well. Healing and health are pluses, not minuses. Death, then, becomes even more of a minus than it was anyway in Christianity. If health is God's plan, always and everywhere, then death is God's enemy, always and everywhere. Pentecostals have not been the only ones to speak this way (in fact, they have usually not been the loudest in making this claim), but a focus on healing has helped create a climate in which military imagery (God's defeat of death) is as prominent as it is in scientific medicine. We will examine this issue later in this chapter.

Funerals, Mourning, and Graves

Protestants have always been suspicious of "ritual," a leftover from Reformation polemics against the Roman Catholic sacramental system. Does that mean there are no rituals at all among Protestant Christians? Of course not. Baptism and the Lord's Supper (Holy Communion, Eucharist) are practiced by all Christians. So are funerals. But remember how the Bible, particularly the New Testament, has been viewed as the authentic norm for faith, and we can understand how funerals, post-funeral death rites, and mourning are not Protestant concerns. In the New Testament, what follows death is resurrection, not a funeral or mourning. This means that "bereavement" in the contemporary psychological sense is not a religious topic for Protestants, or indeed, any Christians. The repudiation of Jewish law (*Torah*) early in the ancient church meant that no practices such as Jewish *shiva* were ever religiously binding on Christians. Nor is there any mandate in the New Testament that believers in Jesus be funeralized, although this surely happened. The minimal reference to grief following a death in Paul's *I Thessalonians* 4:13 is hardly encouraging of attention to either funerals or bereavement: "Brothers, we do not want you to be ignorant about those who fall asleep, or to grieve like the rest of men, who have no hope." What follows is an elaboration of early Christian hope for the return of Christ and the universal resurrection of the dead. Even if this does not equate to "Do not mourn at all" it certainly shows how what follows death in Christianity is resurrection, not attention to the immediate situation of those left behind.

Given this emphasis, it is not surprising that the traditional Protestant funeral was marked with a solemn, somber reminder that "To dust we shall return," that death is the universal destiny of all. Eternal life is available to those who believe in Jesus as savior, but a traditional funeral functioned to proclaim the Gospel of salvation from death in the midst of death. Burial in the Earth was accompanied by hope that, at the end of time, God would raise all the dead. Those whose bodies were destroyed by fire, or dismembered, or lost at sea would not be at a disadvantage, but the ideal was clearly to keep the body as God's good creation intact. The purpose of the funeral was to proclaim that a Christian life of pilgrimage through this world had ended, and an eternal life received already here in the world was now coming to fulfillment. If one were to ask, "Does the funeral happen for the dead person or for the living?" the traditional Protestant answer would be: The funeral is for the glory of God, to announce the Lordship of Christ as savior from death. The deceased is not saved or lost by anything done at the funeral. What *can* happen is that others present will be reminded that they too will die, and that all of them should repent and turn to Jesus Christ as their savior. Thus, their role is not as mourners, but as the future dead. Some Protestant churches emphasize this by having an "altar call," an explicit plea for personal commitment to Christ, as part of the funeral service. Many others would find this unnecessary; if the funeral is a genuine Christian funeral, this is what people are going to be thinking about anyway.

But beyond the funeral, there is no set religiously-required duty, nor anything explicitly Christian about whatever mourning practices people observe. Local custom may be as stern and specific as any religious teachings, but it is local customs that are left in charge. One very, very widespread custom was the ban on the re-married of widows until after a year of mourning had elapsed. This seems to have been a way to ensure that any children born would be known to be offspring of the dead husband. It was not a question of making space for emotional grief. Assigning proper paternity mattered; a widower, on the other hand, could remarry very quickly and often did. Wearing mourning clothes (assuming people could afford special clothing) was a reflection of this social role of "mourner," but once again, no direct religious mandate for this practice could be derived from the Bible or any Protestant church confessional statement. Even today, when such public roles for mourners are almost entirely gone, the role of custom still structures behavior at death for many Protestants. "We knew that someone had died when we saw the minister's wife bringing Jell-o salad," said one Protestant from rural Pennsylvania, commenting on how "ritualized" even a non-ritual tradition can become.

An effect of the Protestant Reformation's opposition to Purgatory was to avoid any hint of contact between the living and the dead. Once the dead were dead, they were in God's hands, and there was nothing the living could do for or with them. One should not pray for them, as in Roman Catholicism. This suspicion of all contact between the living and the dead harks back as well to the Old Testament's prohibition of mediums and necromancy (deliberate attempts to contact the dead for fortune-telling). Protestants alert to this will be especially hostile to cultural practices involving regular communication with ancestors, such as are found in Africa and Japan. When one joins a Protestant church, one renounces any attempt to contact the dead, or to maintain an "ancestor altar" in one's home. By and large, this is not a North American concern, and few persons would confuse a teenager's consoling awareness of his dead grandmother's presence with necromancy. Indeed, there is probably more leeway now on this issue among North American Protestants—at the popular level at least—than ever since the Reformation.

For pre-industrial North Americans, the typical Protestant funeral was followed by the simple burial in the cemetery either right by a church (such as at Old Pine Street Presbyterian Church and St. Peter's in the Society Hill district of Philadelphia) or in a family burial ground. Individual headstones were the rule, and yet the early ones from the 17th and 18th centuries were not very "individualized." Bible verses, a stark design of a death's head, and the name and dates of the person were about the limit. These burial grounds could not accommodate urban populations, and in the 1830s new and less church-identified cemeteries were established (Laurel Hill in Philadelphia was an early one). These removed the dead further from the living, but also permitted a space for them apart from the church grounds, literally and symbolically. This was the era of elaborate tombs, ornate graves, and visits to the dead marked by deep emotional mourning on the part of families. Although such burial places were religiously-segregated (no Catholics, no Jews; both groups had their own cemeteries) they were not religiously-based or religiously-sanctioned; the sense of the church as a community that included both the living and the dead faded even more than it had at the time of the Reformation.

Today, most Protestants are willing to accept cremation as an appropriate form of body disposal, even if for many conservatives it is less good than the traditional burial. The real diversity here is not by religion, but by area of the country. The South, heavily Protestant and also heavily traditional, prefers burial, while the far West leads the rest of the country in cremations. Protestant countries in northern Europe have been even more willing to substitute cremation for burial. In America, some pastoral debate arises not over cremation but over whether to provide a funeral for someone who was not a church member, not a Christian, or whose death was under dubious or controversial circumstances. Suicides, drug overdose deaths, those whose lifestyles went against church moral codes, and persons who clearly rejected Christ: should these be given a Christian funeral? Because few Protestant churches have any centralized authority to provide directives, almost all such decisions are left up to the pastoral wisdom of the local minister who will perform the funeral service. Once again, holding a funeral for someone is not believed to enact or ensure that person's salvation, and denying someone a funeral risks appearing uncharitable and uncompassionate.

We have described what might be called the "mainstream" American Protestant pattern in this discussion. Variants certainly existed: an African-American New Orleans funeral included a street procession, joyful and vigorous music, and a sense of community celebration. Yes, this cost more, but going out in style seemed to many a statement of one's happiness at having been alive, and a measure of how many people would miss you when you were gone.

But it costs more! Today, Protestants are caught in the dilemma of how much or little to acquiesce to the "American way of death," especially a preference for ostentatious funeral gear marketed to consumers by the funeral industry. Should there be a return to the simplicity of starkness of small-town funerals and burials? Or is the New Orleans pattern—a big party where people actually have a good time—more what contemporary Americans want? This is not addressed as a religious issue, and to the best of my knowledge few Protestant groups have taken stands on it, let alone attempted to enforce these.

When Protestants have tried to revise funeral services, they have tried to use theological ideals such as "emphasize Jesus' resurrection, not death" with very mixed results. Complaints from mourners that the funeral should be a time when they have permission to cry and feel sad led to further revisions. Today, the motif of "celebrating a life" is a widening practice, one that is both celebration and personalized for the individual who died. But its religious meanings have not been explicitly explained, or linked to the more traditional ideas we have described.

The "Holism" vs. "Dualism" Question

In recent Christianity, the use of such language as "Death is God's enemy" and "the defeat" of death flourish, far more so than in the past. Most of those who use it claim it is Biblical. Is this fascination with military imagery for death a sign of Protestants' recovery of the Biblical worldview, or is it a capitulation to the fantasy of scientific medicine, which hopes to defeat death through human control? Perhaps it is both, simultaneously. Because scientific medicine often sees death as personified enemy, it became prevalent in some Protestant circles to claim that the Bible, or at least the New Testament, supports such a view. Because science and medicine both accept that the person is an embodied whole, so Christian theological writers began to find "holism" rather than a traditional body/soul dualism in the Bible. Some of these ideas appear in official church documents more than in the everyday hopes of ordinary believers.

Is death "the enemy of God"? The most vigorous advocate of this position was a German Biblical theologian, Oscar Cullman. Does the Bible teach "immortality of the soul" or "resurrection of the dead"? For Cullman, these were two absolutely opposite hopes, and the former was clearly un-Christian, Platonic, and false (Cullman, 15ff.). No matter that Luther, Calvin, Wesley, and many other Protestant spokespersons had never noticed such an opposition, or that the Bible itself does not clearly teach it. Nowhere in the New Testament, including Paul's own writings, is "Death" personified in this fashion, as a malignant enemy of God. The real enemies of God are Satan and his legions of demons, in the Gospels, not "Death." There is no Biblical warrant for a figure of an old man such as the Grim Reaper. Even calling Death "a defeated enemy" treats it as a He, a personal attacker. A great deal of Biblical scholarship responding to Cullman shows how mid-20th century, not 1st-century, concerns about "defeating death" dominate this discussion (see Cooper, *Body, Soul and the Life Everlasting*).

But Cullman and his followers had an important point to make. The body/soul split seems too remote from the way science and medicine view humans, and it seems escapist in the face of devastating history too. Imagine a total nuclear war; only a few sickly people left alive on a poisoned Earth, but a crowd of souls in Heaven. Who could desire this as a goal to hope for? Whether or not the Bible is as anti-dualist as Cullman claimed, there is a widespread Christian recovery of the sense of this created material world as good. The human being, an embodied dweller in this world, is who God saves—not an ethereal, disconnected soul. This theological development is shared by conservative and liberal Protestants (and by many Roman Catholic Christians). But it *has* made death seem more "un-natural," more an evil intrusion into God's creation rather than a fact that affects the body but leaves the soul unblemished and unharmed. Even for those who accept the traditional idea that "death is the separation of the soul from the body," this renewed emphasis on holism and the goodness of life makes death seem more of a wrench, a sad departure, a difficult passage. A bereaved father expresses this:

> In our day we have come to see again some dimensions of the Bible overlooked for centuries. We have come to see its affirmation of the goodness of creation. God made us embodied historical creatures and affirmed the goodness of that . . . But this makes death all the more difficult to live with . . . Death is seen rather as the slicing off of what God declared to be, and what all of us feel to be, of great worth. (Wolterstorff, 31–32)

Death is the slicing off of God's good creation, and indeed an "enemy" of what God originally intended. We may, even as people of faith, lament the deaths of those we love, for God did not want death in the world. The title of the book from which this quote comes is *Lament for a Son.* For the bereaved father, such a cry of pain is not a sign of faithlessness, but of real appreciation of what God has made.

But this view emerges as another very traditional Protestant reading of the Biblical texts has been abandoned or deemphasized. A traditional reading of Paul's *Letter to the Romans* (particularly Ch. 5) links death to sin as the consequence of disobedience. God inflicts death on humanity as punishment for sin. Therefore, a sense of sorrow and contrition belongs among the Christian responses to death, even for those whose faith in Christ allows for a different and hopeful stance. Note that it is not "Hell" or a negative judgment linked to death in this way; death itself is a penalty, a mark of how all share in Adam's sinful nature. While some theological thinkers would now remove the "judicial" imagery, they would also want to retain the sense of primordial guilt, fault, and negative that clings to human death, even if resurrection is also part of the picture. The title of a contemporary Protestant religious thinker's book, *God, Guilt and Death,* by Merold Westphal, about sums this up.

However, it is precisely this sense of death as intrinsically punitive which has faded or been rejected both by other Protestant thinkers and by pastors. Not only does this theological theme not console either the dying or mourners, it is hard to correlate this idea with medicine or biology without massive reinterpretation. We cannot really imagine a death-free human being, and whatever the original meanings of the story of Adam and Eve and their Fall (*Genesis,* 3) the idea that humans could have endless physical life (had we not sinned) just seems impossible to correlate with any recognition of ourselves as biological organisms. No matter how symbolically we interpret the *Genesis* story, or the theme of "death as punishment for sin," this problem remains. Few American Protestants want to dwell on this dilemma.

Universal Eschatology

Early in the 20th century, a leading Protestant thinker scoffed at the beliefs of those who saw in contemporary history the Biblical "end-times" such as depicted in the book of *Revelation*. How could any modern person take such ideas seriously? But those who did certainly had the last laugh, even though as of this writing the trumpets have not sounded and Christ has not returned in glory. Throughout the same historical period that saw wars of unprecedented destructiveness, many Christians have found these developments to be ultimately meaningful, in a larger plan of God laid forth in Scripture. While ideas about "end times," the rapture of believers (being caught up in the clouds to meet Jesus, in *1 Thessalonians*, 4:17) and the final judgment are rarely applied to issues of individual death and dying, these are indeed part of the totality of Protestant perspectives on death. Visions of the death of everyone, a universal cataclysm brought on by God according to his plan, are found in the Bible, and have never been officially repudiated by any Christian church. They have been de-emphasized, and fixation with them condemned. Certainly, the Bible itself gives no encouragement to those who want to set exact times and dates. But against a solid tradition of Protestant individualized focus on personal salvation, universal eschatology, teachings of "last things," allows some room for a collective, worldwide vision of what God wants to accomplish in history. As warfare eventually included the complete obliteration of cities, and the possible complete obliteration of all life, Biblical images of total destruction seemed compelling, however horrendous.

Yet of all death-related theological topics, this has possibly been the most divisive in recent years. How much credence to give "end-time" concerns? Whether or not to leave room for a vision of "Armageddon"? Is the Biblical picture of the end of the Earth as we know it suitable for a disaster movie, filled with special effects? Should any practical changes in one's life be made, if one accepts the nearness of the end of life as we know it? When a secular group of activists mobilized around the slogan "We must prevent Armageddon!" even a Christian hostile and suspicious toward "end-time" beliefs noted that "Armageddon is something God brings about, it is not for us to prevent it." Unlike many of those who simply dismiss such beliefs altogether, this person recognized that they are part of the Christian legacy. Once again, these eschatological beliefs play no role in how individual Christians meet their dying or how other Christians mourn the dead. They are, however, part of the larger stage of history within which individuals die. They are elements in the Protestant Christian response to mass death and modern destructive power.

Conclusion

The story of Protestant Christianity's perspectives on death and dying should end on the note of contemporary worldwide diversity. While some of the original Reformation churches have remained very clearly northern European and North American, others now find most of their members in Asia, Africa, or Latin America. It is possible to talk of

"Protestant legacies" and perspectives, but the whole picture would look different if we had begun by depicting the faith and death-related issues facing an impoverished AIDS sufferer in Uganda. Or, from the perspective of a person from Japan where Christianity spread in opposition to both Buddhist tradition and local practices dealing with ancestors. Moreover, ideas about death have a different meaning in an environment where infant death is common, and malnutrition is more prevalent than obesity. What all share as Protestants is the Bible, and the emphases on personal faith in Jesus Christ; what all share as human beings is the sad inevitability of death, one's own and that of others. While some issues of top priority for North Americans may involve negotiating a high-tech medical system, and making decisions for "end of life care," these may not be possible concerns elsewhere. North Americans face "the funeral industry" and must become smart consumers to determine which of many services provided by the funeral home they really want or need, while elsewhere Protestant Christians rely on extended families and neighbors to provide what really matters to them.

What Protestants do share is the awareness that, through Jesus Christ, those who believe have crossed over from death to life. In this life, and in a life that transcends it, faith in Jesus' eternal life is the most central and universal Protestant stance toward death.

Selected Bibliography

All Bible quotations from *The New International Version*. (1984 International Bible Society).

Bregman, Lucy. 1999. *Beyond silence and denial: Death and dying reconsidered.* Louisville: Westminster John Knox.

Bunyan, John. 1964. *The Pilgrim's Progress.* New York: Signet.

Clark, Davis W. 1855. *Death-bed scenes.* New York: Carlton and Phillips.

Cooper, John. 1989. *Body, soul and the life everlasting.* Grand Rapids, MI: Wm. B. Eerdmans.

Cullman, Oscar. 1965. Immortality of the soul or resurrection of the dead. In *Resurrection and Immortality*, ed. Stendahl, Krister. New York: Macmillan.

McDannell, Colleen, and Lang, Bernhard. 1988. *Heaven: A history.* New Haven: Yale University Press.

Wesley, John. 1981. A plain account of Christian perfection. In *Selected Writings and Hymns*, eds. John and Charles Wesley. New York: Paulist Press.

Wolterstorff, Nicholas. 1987. *Lament for a son.* Grand Rapids, MI: Wm. B. Eerdmans.

Study Questions

1. What does the concept of "salvation from sin and death" mean in Christianity? Why is death in itself "negative" rather than "neutral"?
2. What was the impact of the Protestant Christian principle of "Scripture alone" on beliefs about death and afterlife?
3. What changes have occurred in Christian expectations about dying? Heaven? Hell?
4. Why are funerals and mourning not important Christian theological topics?
5. Is Christianity "dualist" or "holist" regarding persons, bodies, and souls? Explain the debate over this issue.

CHAPTER 5

The Roman Catholic Views of Sickness, Death, and Dying

Joseph A. McGovern

Four Central Roman Catholic Beliefs

Roman Catholicism is the largest branch of Western Christianity. It was separated from Protestant Christianity during the Reformation of the 16th century. Its specific teachings, articulated against the background of the Reformation were codified at the Council of Trent (1545–1563) and underwent a major upgrade during the Second Vatican Council (1963–1965). Several beliefs distinguish Roman Catholics from many of their reformed brethren, namely: the role of Tradition in addition to Scripture; the belief in seven sacraments, the existence of Purgatory and the Communion of Saints. These will affect the Catholic views of sickness, death, and dying.

Tradition: In Roman Catholicism, Scripture does not stand alone but must be interpreted. Unlike many of the reformed traditions which allow for individual applications of the Scripture, under the inspiration of the Holy Spirit, the Catholic Church feels that if an interpretation is to be normative and binding on all its members, the interpretation must be done through the Church. In many cases, such as anointing the sick, we shall see that the official teaching of the Catholic Church would be different from the holdings of many Protestants who may accept an anointing of the sick, but deny a sacramental nature to the anointing. We should also note that the texts, upon a reasonable reading, can legitimately be interpreted either way. In Catholicism, however, the use of Tradition would make the Sacrament of Anointing the Sick the most important interpretation.

Sacraments: The Catholic Church believes that sacraments, as defined at the Council of Trent, are outward signs or symbols, instituted by Jesus (and this institution is often clarified through the Church's use of Tradition) to provide grace the believers need at many critical stages of their lives: birth (Baptism), coming into childhood (Eucharist and Reconciliation), coming of age (Confirmation), entering into a mature vocation in life (Marriage or Holy Orders), and the end of life (Anointing the Sick, with a sub-ritual "Commendation of the Dying"). Sacraments have also been defined, in the more contemporary era, as ritualized meetings or encounters between God and humans. For the

Roman Catholic (and many other denominations as well), sacraments are not merely pious customs, rather they are powerful symbols which, when celebrated in Faith, actually bring about the spiritual reality which they symbolize.

Catholics also believe in **Purgatory.** The concept of Purgatory certainly dates back at least to St. Augustine (fl. 400 CE) and probably earlier, since unlike many things when Augustine refers to it he does not bother to explain it. He seems to take it as a given that people will understand what he means by it. Purgatory is a non-physical place or state between the end of this life and Heaven in which a person is purified of sins and imperfection. Following *I John* 5:10–18 in the New Testament, Catholics believe in *levels* of sin. One may commit a venial sin (which weakens but does not destroy one's relationship to Jesus, for example, using foul language) or a mortal sin (which does break one's relationship to God, for example, deliberately murdering one's neighbor). Mortal sins are forgiven through the Sacrament of Reconciliation (which is preferred) or through perfect sorrow and repentance for the sin ("perfect" meaning one repents because one has done wrong, not because one fears Hell). Venial sins are forgiven through the same two means and also by imperfect sorrow (meaning one is repenting because of the fear of Hell). In each case, however, there would be a lingering issue of justice, meaning that the sin has thrown one's life out of balance and it must be made right again. Purgatory is a state (beyond physical place or time) in which one eliminates this imbalance in one's life so that one may say a perfect "Yes" as a response to God's gift of love for eternity. It might be easiest to understand Purgatory by thinking of what happens when a person wants to give up smoking: he knows he wants to say "yes" to freedom, but the effects of years of smoking make that difficult and painful. At the end, however, he will be happily smoke free. Purgatory plays a major, if often unspoken, role in the Catholic approach to sickness, dying, and death. The beauty of Purgatory is it provides a place for the ordinary person who may not have the faith of a great saint, but who certainly does not deserve Hell. Once one attains the state of Purgatory, one will eventually attain Heaven and the vision of God. This is the basis for many Catholic prayers for the dead, to help the deceased through Purgatory and into Heaven as easily as is possible.

The prayers for the dead lead us into the final idea from Roman Catholicism, namely the **Communion of Saints.** This means that all members of the Church are related to one another or in communion with each other. It comes from the simple observation that on Earth people may help each other with worldly tasks, and the Communion of Saints extends this ability beyond this world. The *Church Triumphant* is saints in Heaven, the *Church Suffering* is the souls in Purgatory, and the *Church Militant* is the Church here on Earth. There are some interesting facts about the various members of the Communion of Saints. Saints in Heaven do not need prayers; they are already with God, but they can pray and intercede for those here on Earth and probably for those in Purgatory. The souls in Purgatory can pray for those on Earth, but can do nothing except suffer to help themselves. Those on Earth can benefit from the prayers of the fellow communicants in both

Heaven and Purgatory, and they can use intercessory prayer to ask for help from those in Heaven and can offer prayers and good works (in a spirit of manifesting faith) for those in Purgatory. What this means is that we do not have neatly compartmentalized groups of believers, rather death is only a temporary separation which affects what people can do, but they are always capable of helping others to get to Heaven.

We should note that over the centuries the above four indicators, especially sacraments and Purgatory, have often been described in very concrete and legal fashion, arguably *too* concretely or *too* legalistically. Symbols always suffer when they are made too concrete and forced within the boundaries of space, time, and the limitations of the human mind. We should keep in mind that whenever the Catholic Church has spoken in an apparently concrete or legal fashion, it always does so poetically in order to maintain the flexibility and openness of the symbols. If we forget this, and insist only on concrete and legal readings of Church teaching, the beauty of the Catholic Church's teaching suffers a great deal of diminution.

The Earliest Traditions

We should recognize that the great majority of the early traditions are shared, in a greater (e.g., Episcopal Church) or lesser (e.g., Evangelical Churches) degree with other Christian denominations.

Most scholars today feel that the earliest parts of the Gospels to be completed were the passion narratives. These would later be redacted with other documents, both written and oral, to form what are now the four canonical Gospels (in order of their completion) of *Mark*, *Matthew*, *Luke*, and *John*. The passion narratives all stress the reality and redemptive value of the suffering and death of Jesus. This would become especially important in later years as the Church had to struggle with the issues of Gnosticism (from Greek *gnosis* a secret knowledge—this stressed the value of knowledge over faith or good works) and Docetism (from Greek: *doceo* to seem—this claimed that Jesus only *seemed* to be human and *seemed* to suffer and die but in reality did not). Roughly contemporary with the formation of the passion narratives we see Paul state very bluntly that if Jesus did not suffer and die, then Christians are the most foolish people ever to have lived. What we are seeing is the emergence of a theology that suffering and death have a value in the Christian view of the world. In addition, through the passion narratives and the Pauline material, the Church began to articulate the view that death had been overcome through the suffering, death, and resurrection of Jesus. Paul in Romans contrasts the "old Adam" (i.e., the Adam of the book of *Genesis*) with the "new Adam," namely Jesus. Just as the old Adam brought death as a punishment to all humanity, so the new Adam, Jesus, brings the possibility of life for all.

In order to appropriate the gift of life, Christians were required to join themselves to the suffering, death, and resurrection of Jesus. This was done in a practical manner through living a simple life of relative self-denial in imitation of Jesus' suffering, and in a ritual manner through Baptism. The Early Church preferred that a new believer be baptized by going down three steps (in mimesis of Jesus' three days in the tomb) into a pool of blessed water (symbolizing chaos, death, and the need for a new creation), being immersed three times and then ascending three steps (both in honor of the not-yet-defined Trinity of Father, Son, and Holy Spirit). The person to be baptized wore regular clothing to the baptistry, removed it for entry and upon coming forth was re-clothed in white garments as a sign of new life. We should note that in places where climate or persecution made immersion either life threatening or extraordinarily impractical, one could baptize by simply pouring water on the person's forehead. We should also note that the very early book called the *Didache* (c. 75 CE) refers to this Trinitarian baptism as being "Baptized in the name of the Lord Jesus."

There are explicit references to joining one's own death to that of Jesus (and hopefully joining in his resurrection as well) found throughout the early Church Fathers. Two references will be sufficient. Ignatius of Antioch (c. 106 CE) in his *Letter to the Romans* (#4) states regarding his coming martyrdom by animals: "I am the wheat of God, and am ground by the teeth of the wild beasts that I may be found the pure bread (i.e., Eucharist) of God." The slightly later (c. 144 CE) *Martyrdom of Polycarp* notes that when Polycarp was burned alive for faith, the arena did not smell of roasting flesh but had the "aroma of baking bread" with the bread again standing for the Eucharist. Both of these indicate that the early Christians wished to join their death to that of Jesus, echoing the earlier Paul who says, ". . . if we die with Christ we shall surely live with Him [Christ]." We also see that the Eucharist is a focal point of both life and death for the Christian.

Regarding suffering, the Church looked to *Jas* 5:14–15 in which the writer states: "Is there anyone sick among you? If so, let them call for the priest (or elders, literally *presbyters*, a word which lacks some clarity in translation) who will anoint the sick person with (holy) oil, praying for him." It is then indicated that the prayers will help the person spiritually and bodily. We should note that this belief is a good example of the role of Tradition. Roman Catholics, following Tradition, have always read this letter as being the underlying Biblical command for the Sacrament of Anointing the Sick formerly called Extreme Unction. In this sacrament, the priest anoints the sick person in order to help the individual join his suffering to that of Jesus. The reformers, especially Martin Luther, while accepting that *Jas* is in the New Testament, expressed doubts about how normative it should be and most of the reformers explicitly reject the connection between the text and the later sacrament.

We see a veneration for the holy dead emerge very early as well. In the cases of both Ignatius and Polycarp cited above, Christians venerated their remains and celebrated their victory over ordinary death by praying in their memory on the anniversary of their deaths. This should not be confused with worship of the dead, it is simply a veneration of someone who has gone before and who can help (through prayer) those who are still struggling on Earth.

We should also note that Christian veneration of the saints marks a major change from both the Jewish and Pagan traditions. These other groups tended to keep away from dead bodies and tombs. The Christians were very comfortable with them.

Dark and Middle Ages

In the Dark Ages (c. 430 CE–950 CE) and Middle Ages (950–1350 CE) death was an omnipresent fact of existence. It would be the great equalizer during times of plague, with paintings of a dancing grim reaper taking all, from lord and lady of the manor through the lowliest peasants in his dance of death. There was a great deal of emphasis on the fear one should have at the Last Judgment. This is illustrated by the Medieval hymn *Dies Irae* (Day of Wrath) which stresses the need as well as the practical impossibility of being as prepared as possible for the judgment.

There was also a certain amount of comfort with death as well. It was common for various local congregations to venerate relics, which were items associated with saints, holy people who were assumed to be in Heaven praying for the people on Earth. Relics were most commonly bones, prayer books, or clothing of the saint. It is a well documented fact that many of these "relics" have been proven to be frauds, but that does not diminish the world view that they expressed, namely: that the Church Triumphant could and would intercede for the Church Militant and the Church Suffering. The veneration of relics certainly shows a high level of comfort with the presence and care of the deceased.

For a person who is sick or dying, there has been a sacrament presently known as the Sacrament of Anointing the Sick. This has its roots in *Jas* and at diverse times in Church history went under various names: holy oil, unction [sacred anointing] of the sick, blessing of consecrated oil, unction of God, office [in the sacrament] of the unction. The emphasis, as revealed in the various names, may stress the importance of different aspects of the sacrament: the oil, the anointing, the sick person, God, and arguably the sacramentality of the act. Irregardless of which aspect may be emphasized at a given time, however, the underlying purpose of the sacrament is to help the dying person join their death to that of Jesus. The Sacrament of Anointing the Sick seems to have been renamed "Extreme Unction" during the late 1100s. Whether this was done because it would be the extreme or final anointing of a person's earthly life or (somewhat less likely) because it was the last in a series of anointings for the person, including Baptism, Confirmation, Holy Orders, etc., is now unknown. Another name, "sacramentum exeundum," the "sacrament for a person about to depart [this life]," also appears at the same time, perhaps anticipating the distinction that 20th-century Catholics would make between rituals for the sick and the dying. We should note that this was not officially defined as a sacrament until the 1439 Council of Florence. This does not reflect a lack of consensus about its sacramentality as such but rather the Catholic Church's reluctance to officially define or teach anything unless there is a compelling reason to do so. For much of Christian history this was accepted by almost everyone as a sacrament or quasi-sacrament, but in the

1300s and 1400s many felt that certain heretics of the time had denied its place as a sacrament, thus providing the need to define it as such. It was defined again at the Council of Trent and its basis in the teaching of Jesus was set forth for the first time. Again, there was a practical reason for this, as many of the Reformers had denied its place as a sacrament.

The use of the Anointing of the Sick as a sacrament, not just for the sick but especially for the dying, shows a relatively high level of comfort with the possible redemptive values of sickness and death when joined with the suffering of Jesus. It is important to see the continuity with the early church in that again we have the sick or dying person being helped to join her own suffering and death with that of Jesus in order to triumph over death.

During the Dark and Middle Ages, there were at least 10 saints who were venerated as a patron saint of death and dying. These would include Mary, the Mother of Jesus, who suffered the death of her son; Saint Anne, who was the grandmother of Jesus; Stephen, the first martyr; Joseph, who is absent from the public life of Jesus, and thus is thought to have died with Jesus and Mary at his side somewhat earlier; Martha, the sister of Lazarus whom Jesus restored to life; the archangel Michael, presumably for his power over Satan and his minions; the Magi from Matthew's Gospel who were patrons not so much of the dying but of everyone who is on the road to not just death but a good death by seeing Jesus as the Magi did at the end of their long journey. There were also more particularized saints whose intercession at death would be sought by discrete groups such as crusaders, those in danger of sudden (but non-military) death, those in danger of death on the open roads, mothers who had lost their sons (either in childhood or adulthood), etc.

The reader will note that no matter what station in life a person occupies, there is always a consciousness not only of death but of a saint to help. This is a clear indicator of the "Communion of Saints." This stress should not obscure the fact that there was also a great deal of fear about the Last Judgment, but from our perspective in history, across a wide chasm of time and culture, it is hard to determine if this was a raw fear of the Judgment in and of itself or a cautionary fear, meaning one should keep the ultimate consequences of all one's actions in mind at all times. This writer prefers the latter view, but there are others who prefer the former.

The Church published a series of booklets, at least since the beginning of printing, to help parish priests prepare their flocks for the inevitable death and last judgment. This involved a series of guided meditations on the Passion and Death of Jesus as well as prayers for intercession from various saints. The saints seem to have been included because they were often saved in a miraculous (e.g., Mary Magdalene) or last minute (Dismas, the "good thief" of the Gospels) manner. Despite the notations of the perils of the Last Judgment, the stress seems to be on the possibility of salvation if one is open to Jesus. We should note that there were a large number of female saints whose intercession was sought at the hour of death. Again one cannot help but get the impression that the stress is preparation for the Last Judgment in the hope of a happy verdict rather than on death and judgment simply as machines of terror.

After death, one would have Mass celebrated for them and then would be buried in sacred ground, a consecrated cemetery. From the 300s through the late 1400s, burial grounds were commonly found in cities for most Europeans. If one were to die in open and flagrant sin, one could be denied burial through the Church and denied access to consecrated ground as well. We should understand this concern for the body in contrast to various Gnostic heresies which seemed to have abounded during the Middle Ages (and other times as well). Gnostics, who have been around at least since the dawn of Christianity (see above), denied the reality of Christ's body, his suffering, death, and resurrection. In addition, they taught that the best way to die was to separate oneself (self, here, meaning soul only) from the body. The Church eagerly anticipated the reunion of body and soul at the resurrection. Thomas Aquinas (fl. 1270 CE) openly speculated that the soul would in some manner be incomplete until it was joined by the body at the resurrection. So, as part of a member of the Communion of Saints, the body would be treated with dignity and respect until it could rejoin its partner at the resurrection.

At the end of the Middle Ages and during the early Renaissance, we do see some "worldly" individuals who express a great deal of disdain for this life and hopelessness in the face of death. These people, however, seem to be the minority and would be in opposition to mainstream beliefs.

Reformation

In the 1500s, Western Christendom was fractured into many denominations. We shall be concerned with the Roman Catholic branch of Christianity.

While the actual foundation for the Reformation was laid by subtler forces such as the printing press, the rise of literacy, and nationalism, the actual spark for the Reformation was the "sale" of indulgences. As noted above, those on Earth, the Church Militant could pray and do good works for the Church Suffering in Purgatory. Prayers and other good works (done with Faith) were often described as indulgences. The theory of indulgences was not really a problem at the time; prayers and good works, done as part of the Communion of Saints, could help the deceased. The problem was that by the late 1400s, the good works in question were too often gifts of cash, often to expand the art collections of various less than ideal Popes. This stress on cash would properly enrage Martin Luther and many other scholars and reformers.

It appears that at first Martin Luther merely wanted to reform the doctrine of Purgatory, that is, make it more reliant on a change of heart and less reliant on monetary gifts. There are surviving Reformation tracts (e.g., Andreas Bodenstein von Karlstadt in 1523, going through at least seven editions) which followed Luther's lead and tried to re-establish the spiritual nature of Purgatory. In many cases, however, they retained the idea of a state of cleansing, but rejected one of the essential Catholic ideas of Purgatory, namely ability of the living to pray for and assist the deceased. By 1530 (the probable date of Luther's *Repeal of Purgatory*) the idea of Purgatory was practically eliminated in the

Reformed traditions. This has importance beyond Purgatory itself, however, because the Reformers would deny the Communion of the Saints insofar as they would deny the ability of the living to help those in Purgatory as well as the ability of those suffering to pray for those on Earth. In some instances, Luther in effect branded the idea of helping those in Purgatory as a form of necromancy. Obviously necromancy would be forbidden by both Scripture and Tradition. This will be a major difference between the Roman Catholic and reformed theologies of the dead.

During and after the Reformation, Roman Catholicism would retain the concept of Purgatory, but it would spiritualize the idea. During the Reformation, the issue of money had dropped from important discussions of Purgatory and the stress would be on prayer and faith manifested in good works. The question must arise: Then why did the Roman Catholic Church retain and adapt Purgatory while the reformers ultimately had to reject it? The answer lies in Tradition. It is highly questionable whether or not one can find a direct scriptural justification for Purgatory. The reformers, who rejected 1 and 2 Maccabees from the canon of the Old Testament, felt there was no scriptural basis and thus rejected Purgatory. Roman Catholics, in accepting the canonicity of these books, have a scriptural warrant for Purgatory, although it is minimal. Since Roman Catholics have always stressed Tradition as well as Scripture, they were able to rely on a very long tradition which explicitly favored belief in Purgatory. In addition, the traditional concept of the Communion of Saints endorsed Purgatory as a practical matter as well. Thus, even without a clear scriptural mandate, Roman Catholics would be able, perhaps even compelled, to retain the doctrine of Purgatory while the reformers would face an equally strong compulsion to eliminate it.

A side effect of the rejection of Purgatory was that the Reformers tended to marginalize the dead, practically as well as theologically whereas the dead continued to be a major factor in Catholic practice and theology. In the 50 years previous to the Reformation, there had been some burials of the dead outside city walls, usually for medical reasons, such as fear of contagion from one of the various plagues that commonly ravaged Europe. After Luther's rejection of any contact between the living and the dead, we see that reformed cities tended to bury everyone outside their walls, often using medical necessity to justify it as a "temporary" measure and then never returning to the earlier practice of burial within the city. Catholic cities often tried to retain the custom, but with varying degrees of success. Complicating the issue is that there was an emerging medical consensus that burial within a city *was* (for Catholics and Protestants) unhealthy, there were issues of overcrowding in the cities and there were many cases of people, especially leading citizens, who were officially Catholic but supported or at least sympathized with many of the reformers' ideas.

At the end of the Reformation, during the Council of Trent, the Catholic Church restated the sacramentality of the Anointing of the Sick, articulating its foundation in the words and actions of Jesus and the early Church. The fact that it was a sacrament formalized and ritualized the manner in which it would be celebrated. We should note that while the intent was that this would be Extreme Unction and the dying would be the primary persons to benefit from this sacrament, the Catholic Church did not restrict it to the dying, it was clearly left available for the sick as well. This can be seen in the 1614 edition of the *Roman Ritual*, which clearly indicates the sacrament may be celebrated for the sick as well as the dying. From an official theoretical and theological perspective, the Council of Trent is critical for Roman Catholicism until the 1960s. There will be occasional modifications to the *Roman Ritual* which will affect how sacraments would be celebrated, but there would not be any official new theology until the Second Vatican Council. The First Vatican Council, 1870, ended very prematurely and did not teach anything of substance regarding the sick and dying.

In practice, Catholicism would be somewhat different from the theories of the Council of Trent. From Trent until several years after Vatican II, the "ordinary" Catholic would perceive Extreme Unction as being only for the dying rather than the sick. One of the ways in which a reticent family could inform a loved one of an unfavorable prognosis from their doctor was by having the priest arrive and anoint the person. The message "you are dying" was unmistakable. The present writer, along with many of his contemporaries, can remember, as late as 1982, encountering a great deal of resistance to anointing "healthy" (i.e., people who were not expected to die immediately) people.

It is most likely that the various bishops and other leaders gathered at Trent did not anticipate that it would be 400 years until the next ecumenical council within the Roman Catholic Church. That would be the situation, however, and it would result in making the decrees and customs of the Council of Trent very concrete, arguably too concrete.

Vatican II and the Present Time

In the 1960s, Pope John XXIII convened the Second Vatican Council or Vatican II in order to "update" (*aggiornamento* in the Pope's words) the Catholic Church. Extreme Unction would be greatly adapted to the modern world. Extreme Unction would become the Sacrament of Anointing the Sick or the Rite of Anointing the Sick with a separate subritual titled the Commendation of the Dying. This in effect would separate the sacrament into two distinct rites. The language of each ritual section would clearly indicate whether the prayer was hoping for a speedy recovery or a happy death. We should note that such prayers are never made to manipulate God, rather to intercede for a hoped for outcome but always with the proviso that the prayer is subject to the will of God.

The changes made for care of the sick and dying may be summarized as follows:

1. Having, in practice but not in theory, two separate rituals, one for the sick and one for the dying. This would make sick people more open to receiving the sacrament since it no longer expressed a belief that the person would die soon.

2. A stress on community. Both aspects of the sacrament could be celebrated privately, i.e., with the priest and parishioner being the only ones present, or it may be communal in which case many people come to church or (more commonly) a health care

facility chapel, and most prayers are celebrated as a group. The group would include not just the sick and dying but also any friends or family they may wish to invite as well as any members of their health care team (doctors, nurses, nurses' aides, etc.). This helps to alleviate the sense of isolation felt by many sick and dying people. We should note that celebrations of the sacrament are not limited to Roman Catholics; anyone who wishes to attend and join in praying is welcome.

3. A newly emerging sense that (quoting Cicero) "old age itself is a sickness"; the Catholic Church now celebrates the sacrament communally for residents of nursing home and assisted living facilities. Moreover, in previous centuries, the sacrament generally could only be received one time "for each condition"; as medicine advanced this was relaxed to once a year for chronic conditions, and now the custom would be monthly for chronic conditions. None of these sickness-oriented anointings would interfere with the ability to celebrate the Commendation of the Dying for the same person at times of need.

4. There is also a debate about whether or not ordained deacons can serve as primary ministers of the sacrament. Many, perhaps most, theologians today feel they can in theory, but the problem is that someone who is receiving the Commendation of the Dying would also want to receive the Sacrament of Reconciliation also known as Confession, at the same time, and only a priest may celebrate the latter sacrament. Deacons can, however, be employed in the communal celebrations of anointing for anointing, praying, etc.

5. Independent of sacraments, the Catholic Church, in most dioceses, will now allow the spouse of a Roman Catholic to be buried in a Catholic cemetery. This is a sign of respect for the dignity of the individual, the dignity of other religious traditions, and the dignity of the marriage bond.

6. In addition, today suicides and "public" or "notorious" sinners may be banned from burial in consecrated ground. This has a long history, but we should note that today the burden of denying such a burial would rest on the one seeking a ban, rather than on the family of the deceased.

A Typical Roman Catholic Death and Burial

I would now like to walk the reader through a "typical" death within the Roman Catholic tradition. Be aware that the Catholic Church in the United States is divided into "dioceses," and there are slight variations among diocese. Each diocese is headed by a bishop or archbishop who sets policy (after consulting with members of the diocese and perhaps other bishops as well). But generally, they will be similar.

We start with Maureen Smith, a composite Catholic. She is 50 years old, she attends Mass every Sunday at her local parish, and her doctor has told her she needs to go to the hospital for a series of tests. She consults with her local priest and asks if he could celebrate the Anointing of the Sick for her and her family. They all want the celebration to be in the family home (they could also request it at church or the hospital). Father agrees.

In attendance would probably be: Maureen Smith, her husband, her three children, one grandchild, several friends and neighbors, the priest, and perhaps a leader of song.

The priest arrives carrying the holy oil in an oil stock made of brass and often gold plated. There is usually a ring affixed to the base so it does not fall after becoming slippery from the holy oils. In addition, the priest will bring the Eucharist or Holy Communion in a sacred vessel called a pyx usually made of gold plated brass. The priest will also bring a stole, a piece of cloth which drapes over both shoulders and around his neck. This is a symbol of his office as priest and a sign that whatever he is doing while wearing it is being done in his official capacity as a priest. Commonly the stole will be purple or white in color. If a deacon is present, he would also wear a stole, but it would drape over only one shoulder. In the Catholic Church priests are all men, and at the present time deacons are also exclusively men.

Father will usually meet Maureen privately, hear her Confessions, and grant absolution before beginning the Anointing of the Sick. Confessions would be heard in privacy, and the priest is bound by the Seal of the Confessional not to directly reveal anything he has heard. After Confession, Father would enter a large public room, often the dining room. The table will have been transformed into a temporary altar, with a white cloth upon it with a crucifix (Catholics prefer a crucifix with the image of Jesus' body on the cross, many Protestants prefer the plain cross), lighted (preferably) beeswax candles, the holy oils, a Bible, and the Ritual Book for the Anointing of the Sick. Father will try to involve as many people as possible in actually celebrating the sacrament; this helps foster a greater sense of community.

There will be prayers and Bible readings, selected in advance from a standard list, which all stress the hope that God will bless the sick woman, give her the strength to join her own suffering with that of Jesus, and that if it God's will she will be quickly restored to health. The priest will then bless the oils and will anoint Maureen on the forehead (which is where all prayer and actions begin) and on the palms of her hands (since most human activity until recently has been in some form of manual work).[1] It is then common for all present to share in a sign of peace and good wishes for each other, which can be very emotional. Father will then give Maureen (perhaps other Catholics as well) the Eucharist.

Maureen enters the hospital the next day. Her prognosis is bad, and she is sent home. While she is home, Father will generally bring her the Eucharist once a month, and will provide an opportunity for Confession and spiritual direction if she wishes. Prior to Vatican II, Father would always visit on the First Friday of the month, since Catholics have been encouraged to receive the Eucharist on First Fridays. There is a long standing (but unofficial) belief that if one receives communion on nine First Fridays in a row, one will have the opportunity to go to Confession right before one dies. The present writer must add here that his own experience, while anecdotal, has certainly borne out the truth of this belief. Post-Vatican II, Maureen will be able to receive more often than First Friday. Her neighbors may be installed by the parish as extraordinary ministers of holy communion which will allow them to bring communion from church (it must previously be consecrated or transsubstantiated by a priest) to her at home or in the hospital. It is still customary, however, for the priest to visit at least once a month so that Maureen will have the opportunity to go to Confession if she so wishes. She may also receive the Anointing of the Sick regularly from the priest as well.

Maureen continues to receive help from the Church in this manner for as long as she needs it. Then one night she gets really sick. Her husband knows she is dying. He calls the ambulance and Maureen enters the emergency room at the local hospital. Her husband knew enough to call ahead to the hospital and tell them Maureen is Catholic. The chaplain will be waiting when she arrives. This time there will not be a formal celebration of the Anointing of the Sick as there had been before she entered the hospital for her tests. The chaplain will celebrate (assuming she appears to be dying) the sub-ritual called the Commendation of the Dying. The holy oils will have been blessed some time ago, so no time will be spent on blessing them. Instead of a personal and private Confession, the chaplain may ask Maureen, "Do you want absolution for your sins?" and upon receiving an affirmative answer, he may ask if she is sorry for them and then give her absolution without the need for private Confession. Given the chaos of most hospital emergency rooms, private Confession is not possible. We should note that if Maureen is unconscious (and perhaps dead), this would be one of the very few times the Church will celebrate a *conditional* sacrament. Normally at the end of Confession the priest will say, "I absolve you of all your sins in the name of the Father and of the Son and of the Holy Spirit. Amen." If she is unconscious and perhaps dead, the priest will say: "*If you are still alive*, I absolve you . . . etc." The sacraments are only for the living; that is why it is conditional in cases where a person may be dead or alive.

After receiving absolution for any sins, Maureen will then be anointed, again on the forehead and palms of the hands, assuming these are accessible. If not, a person may be anointed anywhere. If Maureen is not clearly alive, the anointing will be done with the same "if you are still alive" precondition. If Maureen is conscious, she will receive communion, only this time it will have a special name, Holy Viaticum, from a Latin term meaning something which helps a person on a long trip. After Maureen has been absolved, anointed, and given communion, these will all be recorded in a special book, the *Sacramental Registry*, in the hospital chaplain's office.

If Maureen dies that night, Father (either the local priest from the parish or the hospital chaplain) may visit with and console the family. The next step is to make arrangements for her funeral. Maureen's family goes to the funeral director of their choice, who then calls the parish and arranges for the time of the next blessings. To be buried from a Catholic Church, Maureen must have been a "practical Catholic" during her life. This term is generally defined by the local pastor or bishop, and varies greatly. Generally the person must have some formal affiliation with a parish, but technically according to the *Code of Canon Law* which is written in Rome and binds everyone, a person should be considered a practical Catholic if they were baptized and have never renounced the faith. Many local churches impose more stringent rules, but in theory these could be appealed, to Rome if necessary. But Maureen went to Church every Sunday when she was well, so there is no doubt at all that she is a practical Catholic.

There is often a Vigil or Wake Service celebrated in the funeral home the evening before Maureen will be buried. In earlier days, the priest celebrated this. Today, because of a shortage of priests, it may be celebrated by a priest, deacon, or even a seminarian. In rural areas, the leader may be a lay person who is not in any official ministry at all. There is a great deal of variation at Wake Services. While there is an "official" text, the Wake is a sacramental (an informal ritual, which is close to being a sacrament but is not a sacrament), so the priest celebrating it has a great deal of flexibility. Someone with very little training would be more likely to exactly follow the guidelines in the ritual book (since they are written by experts and have been used successfully for many years). There is usually a call to prayer, followed by Bible readings (which a family member may read if they are able and wish to do so), often there is a sermon-like (but very brief) reflection on the Christian meaning of death, then antiphonal prayers between the celebrant and congregation, and a conclusion. We should note that everyone at the funeral home is welcome to join the Wake Service, one need not be Catholic. The casket may be open or closed during the service. The only requirement is there should not be the appearance that people are praying to the deceased, rather they are praying for the deceased (cf. Communion of Saints, above).

The next morning, family and friends may visit the funeral home. After last farewells, the body is to be reverently transported to the church for a Funeral Mass. Prior to Vatican II, one would have a Requiem Mass in which the emphasis would be on preparing for the Last Judgment and the sorrow experienced by all at the loss which takes place in death. The vestments, or ritual garments, worn by the priest at Requiem Mass were commonly black as a sign of mourning. The Requiem Mass would ultimately stress the joy of the resurrection, but it would be a very muted joy. In contrast, today's Funeral Mass is marked by a sense of celebration that the deceased is with God. The Church does not deny that the family may have some suffering because of the separation caused by death (and a wise priest will preach on this subject as well the resurrection), but the Church wishes to stress that the loss is only temporary. In contrast to the black vestments of the Requiem Mass, a Funeral Mass commonly uses white vestments (the same color used on Easter) as a sign of rejoicing in new life.

The casket is greeted at the door of the church by the priest (who may be joined by a deacon, or in a large parish another priest) who sprinkles holy water on the casket to recall Maureen's baptism. Then they will place a white cloth on the casket (removing the American flag at this time in the case of a Veteran). As this is done the priest will say (referring to both the holy water and the white cloth), "On the day of her baptism, Maureen was clothed with Christ. At the time of the resurrection, may she join Him in eternal life." This clearly recalls what we saw earlier, that the Catholic believer joins their sickness and death to that of Christ, especially in baptism, so that she may join in His resurrection. The casket is then brought into the church, behind the priest. The casket is normally closed in church during Mass. The exception to this would be for a priest who is generally buried in his vestments. The casket is often kept open for his last Mass on Earth.

The casket may be incensed at various times during Mass. This has a very long tradition and there are two reasons. The first reason is the incense involves another sense (smell), and the more senses involved the better. It ascends up as a form of fragrant smoke, a sign of the prayers of the congregation for the deceased. In addition, in earlier times, before embalming, it would also mask any odors.

The Bible readings for the Mass and the sermon generally reflect the theme of Christian death and resurrection. While it is common for the preacher to adapt the message to the life of the deceased (pointing out good deeds she did while alive) it should not be a eulogy. The rest of the Mass proceeds very much like an ordinary Mass until the end. At the end, the priest goes to the casket, and says special prayers for the deceased. For a few years, it had been common to allow family members to deliver a reflection (or even a eulogy) at this time. The most recent (promulgated in 2004) edition of the general instruction section of the *Roman Missal* states that there should "never" be a eulogy of any kind. The problems with family-led reflections was they stressed the individual as individual rather than as a member of the Church and its Communion of Saints. They often highlighted loss over resurrection and in far too many cases the reflections were attempted by people who had absolutely no skills in public speaking.

The casket is then led back to the hearse for transport to the cemetery. At the rear of the church, there may be people from certain societies with which Maureen was affiliated. There commonly are members of the Rosary and Altar Society, a group of women parishioners which dates back at least to the Irish immigrations of the 1840s. This is a burial society in which the members help and pray for one another in their time of need, as well as helping to maintain the physical upkeep of the church sanctuary. Prior to Vatican II members of this society were the only women allowed in the sanctuary of the church. There can also be members of certain occupations, such as police, fire department, or armed forces. The Catholic Church does its best to work with these groups in having a dignified funeral which reflects the public service job of the deceased.

The body is then brought to the cemetery. Ideally, Maureen's parish priest (the same one who anointed her when she entered the hospital for tests) would accompany the family to the grave. There would then be a consecration of the grave (if that had not been done before, for example, if Maureen is being buried in a military cemetery), or a simple blessing of the grave, asking God's grace of eternal rest. There would be a call to prayer for those gathered at the graveside, then a Bible reading, a few more prayers for Maureen, and then a commendation of the body as it enters the grave.

After burial, everyone returns home, or sometimes may have lunch together. Among Irish Americans, there is still a strong preference for the "Irish Wake" after the funeral. Everyone returns to the home of a designated family member, the priest (or in today's Church the deacon may have to go in the priest's place, because of manpower shortages) also attends. The priest then moderates a discussion of the deceased, putting to rest any unfinished business people may have with her. Unfinished business may range from anger ("Why did she eat so much salt and have a heart attack?") to loving farewells (people wishing they could have been at her side when she passed away). The priest represents the parish in general as well as the universal Church. He is also there as a semi-professional facilitator, to make sure that people do not end up with overpowering and unresolvable grief. If he sees that, the priest makes certain that he and others follow up with the person.

It is very common to have a Mass celebrated for the deceased (remember, with the Communion of Saints the living can help the dead through prayer) on the first month's anniversary. Many devout families will try to have a Mass said every month for the deceased, and will make a donation, e.g., of a Ritual Book, chalice, etc., to a parish in memory of a deceased loved one. This is usually something which will be used during Mass for the foreseeable future, and may be engraved with the name of the deceased. It is universal in the Catholic Church to have Mass celebrated for all the deceased members of a given parish on November 2. This is All Souls' Day and a time when Catholics pause to meditate on life, death, eternal salvation, and do so by praying for those most in need of their prayers. While a Catholic will especially pray for family members, she will also pray for all the recently deceased from her parish on this day. While there is no obligation to attend Mass on November 2, many churches find themselves filled.

Maureen will have an immediate personal judgment after her death. Catholics generally feel there is a need for a combination of faith and good works. There is no set formula. Most Catholics prefer the teaching of St. Thomas Aquinas (fl. 1270 CE) "for a reckoning of my good things, I trust God's justice, for a reckoning of my bad things, I rely on God's mercy." The exact details of the judgment are debated; some feel God judges the dead, others feel God simply shows the deceased their life (good and bad, acts of commission and acts of omission), and the deceased respond in trust, despair, or a trust which needs some help. Realizing that no one has been through the judgment and come back to describe it, most Catholics do not worry that much about the details, rather they worry about the quality of the life they have led. Maureen will wind up in Heaven, Hell, or Purgatory. Centuries ago, there was an unofficial presumption that most people went to Hell. Today, the assumption is that most go to Purgatory and ultimately to Heaven. No Catholic would hold to the very concrete descriptions of Heaven, Hell, or Purgatory today. Most realize that language fails when trying to describe eternity. While Catholics do not spend a lot of time discussing Purgatory (except once in a while with their parish priest), Purgatory is the unofficial heart of Catholic belief. In Purgatory, one knows that she will get to Heaven, but while she can do nothing for herself, she can help and pray for the living. The living, in turn, commonly pray for the deceased. An old Irish Monsignor once told the present writer: "we're none of us perfect, but with the help of God and the saints and each other, we will make it to the pearly gates." This was a good summary of Roman Catholic belief and practice.

Note

1. The only exception to this is that priests, even inactive priests, are anointed on the *backs* of their hands. This is a sign of respect for the most important anointing in his life: when a priest is ordained, he is anointed on the palms of his hands for the last time in his life. The only exception is if he were to be elevated to being a bishop, then he would again be anointed on the palms of his hand.

Selected Bibliography

Algerigo, Giuseppe, and Komonchak, Joseph A. (eds.) 2002. *History of Vatican II*. Maryknoll, NY: Orbis.

The Catholic Encyclopedia. 1912. New York: Appleton. 15 Volumes.

Chadwick, Owen. 1957. *From Bossuet to Newman: The idea of doctrinal development*. Cambridge: Cambridge University Press.

Friesen, Ilse E. 1999. Saints as helpers in dying. In *Death and Dying in the Middle Ages*, Dubruck, E. E. and B. I. Gusick, (eds.). New York: Lang.

Geary, Patrick. 1994. *Living with the Dead in the Middle Ages*. Ithaca: Cornell University Press.

Ignatius. 2003. *Letters*, in Ehrman, B. D. (ed.) *The Apostolic Fathers*. Cambridge: Harvard University Press.

Martos, Joseph. 1981. *Doors to the sacred*. New York: Doubleday.

Anonymous. *Martyrdom of Polycarp*, in *The Apostolic Fathers*.

McCarthy, Timothy G. 1994. *The Catholic Tradition: Before and after Vatican II, 1978–1993*. Chicago: Loyola University Press.

Tucker, Karen B. W. 2002. "Sick, liturgical ministry to" in *The New Westminster Dictionary of Liturgy and Worship*, Bradshaw, P. (ed.). Louisville: Westminster John Know Press, 2002.

United States Conference of Catholic Bishops. 2003. *General instruction of the Roman Missal*. Washington, DC: USCCB.

Study Questions

1. What four beliefs distinguish Roman Catholic Christians from other Christians?
2. Explain the meaning of the debate over Purgatory?
3. Why did the rite of Extreme Unction become Anointing of the Sick? When? What principles grounded this change?
4. How does her priest minister to "typical Catholic Maureen" during her illness and dying?
5. What rituals happen after her death, and what are their stated purposes?

CHAPTER 6

Death and Dying in Islam: "This Day Your Sight Is Made Keen"

Gisela Webb

Historical and Thematic Beginnings

Islam is the last of the major world religions, with over a billion Muslims across the globe. Islam is the second largest religion in the world and within the decade will be the second largest religion in the United States. Its historical beginnings were in 7th century Arabia, with the revelatory experiences of Muhammad, the Prophet of Islam. Within two centuries of the prophet's death, Islam had become a major religious and political force in the world, extending from (today's) Spain to Afghanistan, and well into regions of Africa and Southeast Asia.

The traditional accounts of the life of Muhammad contained in the collections of *hadiths* ("sayings" of the Prophet) and traditional biographies present Muhammad as a prayerful and sensitive person who had been orphaned at an early age, raised by his uncle Abu Talib within the traditions of the pre-Islamic Arabian tribal custom, and married to a widow and business woman named Khadijah, who supported him as he began his prophetic career. In 610 CE Muhammad began to have what he described as "revelations" (*wahy*), both aural and visionary, which continued over a 20-year period until his death in 632 CE. The core of the revelations criticized two major components of Meccan society: the worship of multiple gods and the plight of the needy, as the Meccan leadership gained wealth with not only the trade routes that passed through Mecca, but with the ancient pilgrimage site, the Kaaba, situated in Mecca, which housed the idols of the deities the Arabians worshiped. In those 20 years, Muhammad experienced both rebuke and attack from the Meccan elites, he made the historic *hijra*, or emigration to Medina, establishing the first Islamic community (and the beginning of the Islamic calendar), and he returned to Mecca, reclaiming the Kaaba, emptying the idols and re-establishing it as a symbol of submission to Allah, "the God." The revelations of Muhammad were experienced in a number of types of situations: some during prayer and meditation, some in times of community opposition to and persecution for his teachings, some in response to evolving social, political, and religious demands as the Islamic community grew. The revelations were memorized, written down, and collected by his followers and, according to tradition, put in the order prescribed by Muhammad (Esack, 78ff.). This collection of recitations/discourses, which consists of 114 chapters (*suras*), constitutes the Qur'an, the sacred text of Islam. For Muslims, the Qur'an has the status of "Word of God," comparable to the status of the Torah for Orthodox Jews or Christ (as *logos*) for Christians. The words and sounds of the Qur'an are experienced by Muslims not only as sources of religious knowledge, but of grace (*barakah*) and inspiration (*ilham*).

For Muslims, the Qur'an also contains the divine law, principles, and mandates for belief and practice in everyday life. The major duties are known as the Five Pillars, and are incumbent on all Muslims: 1. Recitation of the *shahadah* (the "witnessing"). Muslims must recite the two-part creedal statement, "*la ilaha illa Allah, Muhammadun rasul Allah,*" that Allah is one and transcendent and that Muhammad is the (final) prophet of God. Specifically required in this affirmation is the belief in the previous revelations, holy books, and prophets, the belief in angels, *jinn* (beings "created from fire"), and the final dispensation of divine justice, with consignment to Heaven or Hell, of all persons at the end time. 2. *Salat* (liturgical prayer). In this ritual of unity, submission, and remembrance of Allah, Muslims are enjoined to pray five times daily (morning, noon, afternoon, evening, night) facing Mecca. 3. *Zakat* (the 'poor tax'). As a symbol "purifying" one's wealth as well as one's commitment to help the poor, one promises a portion of their wealth to the needy. 4. *Sawm*. During the lunar month of *Ramadan*, Muslims are required to fast from food, liquid, and negative thoughts from sunrise to sundown as a means of engendering compassion for the poor as well as inner reflection and discipline. 5. *Hajj*. Muslims are to make the pilgrimage to Mecca at least once in their life as a symbol of their submission to God at the site (built by Abraham) representing the unity and transcendence of God as well as the center of the universal Muslim community. It is worth noting that during the pilgrimage, everyone is required to wear the *ihram*, the white shroud-like garment, as a symbol of the unity and equality of humankind as well as the preparedness for death.

The Qur'anic verses are described (in the Qur'an) as participating in, and "descending" from, the common source of all knowledge and wisdom available to human beings, the *umm al-kitab*, literally the "mother (or archetype) of the book," or "word" of God, which has been transmitted from the beginning of time through the prophets. It warns individuals and communities of their heedlessness and forgetfulness of the divine command to care for those in need, and criticizes their habitual return to idolatry. It makes particular criticism of the "reversion" of the Arabs from the [earlier] belief in the One God to polytheism, calling upon the idol worshipers in Mecca to restore the original function of the pilgrimage site of the Kaaba, which according to tradition was built by Abraham and Ishmael as a symbol of rejection of idolatry and submission to God.

The Qur'an discusses the times of trial, rejection, and persecution experienced by all the prophets, including Muhammad, and the guidance, wisdom, and hope given by God that sustained them. The Qur'anic stories of the Hebrew prophets (and others Arabian prophets not named in the Bible) do not include the full Biblical narrative (except for the story of Joseph and "the Pharoah") but function as summaries and examples of deeds of the ongoing legacy of God's mercy and revelation. Jews and Christians are described as "*ahl al-kitab*" "people of the book," that is, prior historical groups that had received authentic revelations. The Qur'an criticizes certain aspects of Jewish and Christian religion (political opposition and betrayal posed by some of the Jewish tribes, the divinity or sonship of Jesus, the "Trinity" of God), but it affirms others (the authenticity of all the Hebrew prophets including Jesus and John the Baptist, the miraculous birth of Jesus to Virgin Mary, Jesus' status as "prophet," "word," and "spirit" of God, and the role of Jesus at the end time, the role of Gabriel in revelation), clearly reflecting the not-distant past theological discussions in the early Christian church on Jesus' nature and function. In terms of the organization of the *mus-haf*, the written corpus of the Qur'an: the earlier revelations—short, highly evocative and "hymnal" in character, many having to do with the cataclysmic "end time"—are found at the end of the Qur'anic corpus. The later *suras* received by Muhammad are lengthier, more directed to legal, economic, and social issues in the emerging Muslim community; they are found in the beginning of the *mus-haf*, after the opening *sura*, the *fatihah*. In contrast to the prevailing ethos of the pre-Islamic Arabians, where ultimate loyalty belonged to the tribe, where fate, time, and destiny unalterably determined the course of one's life, the Qur'an affirmed that life had purpose; that events in human history and individuals are in the hands of a merciful and just God; and that death is not the end, but rather a passage to new and eternal existence. Moreover, the Qur'an puts extraordinary emphasis on the binding relationship between faith (*iman*) and practice, or righteous deeds (*a'mal al-salihat*) and with many specific references to caring for parents, relatives, orphans, the needy, wayfarers (*sura*, 2:215), it promises rewards for those who heed the message of the prophets and calamitous results in this world and the next for those who did not.

Developing Theologies on Death and Dying

Islamic belief and practices, theology and rituals, with regard to death and dying are best understood by seeing the interrelationship of three major Qur'anic themes: creation, revelation, and the end time. One can see in the developing theological reflection on Qur'anic creation themes that the goal and hope of individual existence is to return to an original state/time of unity with God, referred to as the "Day of the Covenant" (*al-yawm al-mithaq*). The revelatory experience of the prophet Muhammad, particularly Muhammad's "Night Journey" (*sura* 17, *Isra'*), interpreted in developing theologies and popular piety beginning in the 2nd century of Islam, would come to represent an interior, unitive state of "return" to God in this life. The "states and stations" of Muhammad's journey would become models for both the Islamic mystic's states and stations to God as well as for the experience of the individual at death, in the interim experience between individual death and cosmic death known as the *barzakh*. Finally, the many visually and orally powerful Qur'anic verses about the Day of the Resurrection (*al-yawm al-qiyamah*), when the cosmos itself reverses in a cataclysmic annihilation (*fana'*) and return to its origin, led to speculation about kind of knowledge and experience this would mean for the individual, at the end time, but also as an interior state about "death before death," wherein the individual is able to see "the truth of oneself" with the kind of clarity, honesty, and annihilation of the *nafs*/self that separates one from God.

I should caution the reader who is new to Islamic thought that, as with all religions, a critical examination of religion reveals, indeed, a history of reflection on the meaning and application of sacred texts, in this case, the Qur'an and *hadiths*. Islam is no different. Moreover, as with Judaism, in Islam there is not a central authority who pronounces official doctrine, but there are interpreters (*kalam*/theological, *fiqh*/juridical, *sufi*/mystical) and traditions that became accepted as "orthodox," or at least of lasting influence, in Muslim communities. A most cursory look at major divisions of thought in the Islamic world, Sunnism and Shi'ism represent the main "wings" of normative Islam, the major difference being in the special status, reverence and authority given by Shi'ites to the family and descendents of the Prophet as inspired transmitters and interpreters of law, theology, and grace/charism.

In terms of figures that represent the theological mainstream of Islam, the figure of al-Ghazali (d. 1111) is considered "orthodox." Not only was he prolific, but he functioned as an interpreter in several of the traditional Islamic sciences: theology, philosophy, law, and mysticism (*tasawwuf*). Moreover, he is considered by Muslims to be a "reconciler" between theological extremes, taking a "middle way" approach to such issues as whether and when one ought to read the Qur'an literally or symbolically, and whether *tasawwuf*/sufi/Islamic mysticism, with its language of union with God, can be considered compatible with "orthodox" Islam. His manual on what happens to the soul at death *al-Durra al-Fakhira* (The Precious Pearl), with its vivid description of experience awaiting the dead "in the tomb" and on the "Day of Resurrection" (*al-yawm al-qiyama*) reflects a lasting heritage in Islamic eschatological thought. (For more in depth study of the important varying traditions on these issues, see Smith/ Haddad, *The Islamic Understanding of Death and Resurrection*).

Creation

The Qur'an speaks of human beings, male and female, as being created from God's one 'nafs' (or "soul"). God asks Adam to "name" things. Adam could, whereas the angels could not (2:30), which Muslims read and elaborated in theology and poetry as a demonstration of the human capacity for creative knowledge. God "pulled from the loins of Adam" the souls of all future generations of human beings and asked them, "Am I not your Lord?" (7:172). The souls of all human beings answered yes, and this testifying to God's sovereignty was interpreted as indicating that human beings have within themselves the "reality" of a "pre-existent," "natural" state of "islam," submission to God, which human beings perennially forget. This primordial state of unity with God, testified to in their knowledge of, and submission to, their Lord, this "day of the covenant," *al-yawm al-mithaq*, would become a model, or goal of life itself, a "return" to that state of unity with God. (The language of "unity" with God would become highly nuanced in theological discourses in order to preserve the transcendence—unicity and unlimitability—of God). Adam and Eve disobey God in the Garden, but they repent and are forgiven, thus Islam does not teach a cosmic or ontological breech, or rupture, in the relationship between man and God, expressed in the doctrine of original sin. For Muslims, Adam's sin is an example of the tendency or stage of the human soul called the *nafs ammarah*, the "soul that commands evil." The Qur'an and its commentators also speak of the aspect or stage of the human "soul that is at peace with God," the *nafs al-mutma'inna*, as well as other "loci" in the human being for intimate knowledge and certitude of God, *qalb* (heart) and *aql* (intellect) (Schimmel, 25). The Qur'anic language of an innate/forgotten/ignored experience of man's primordial confession of God's lordship (*rububiyyah*) would be interpreted by theologians and mystics of Islam as signifying the possibility for future generations to actualize that state. The mystical interpreters would describe both the spiritual path in this life and in the hereafter as a gradual discarding of the veils of the human soul, the passions and inclinations of the body as well as those associated with ignorance and self-centeredness. The extent to which one is able to remember and live (epistemologically and ontologically) that primordial covenant is seen as determining one's experience at death.

Revelatory Experience of the Prophet

The Qur'anic verses of two of Muhammad's paradigmatic experiences, the descent (*anzala*) of the Qur'an to Muhammad and the ascension of Muhammad in the *isra'*, the "night journey" (*sura*, 17), provide models for deepened experience of "islam" in this world as well as for the experience that the soul will have in the interim period between the death of a person and the end time of the universe known as the *barzakh*. *Sura* 17 gives a brief reference of a night journey of the Prophet in which he traveled from "the sacred mosque to the farthest mosque," the latter interpreted as a journey from Mecca to Jerusalem. By the 9th century many versions of this story have come in the form of *hadiths*, which vary in version and degree of detail, describing the awakening of the Prophet by Gabriel (in some versions accompanied by the angel Mika'il) who then leads Muhammad on a night's journey from Mecca to Jerusalem, then through the heavens described in Ptolemaic astronomy to the Gates of Paradise, and finally to the Throne of God. Muhammad's journey always includes the vision of Hell and the "appropriate" punishment experienced by sinners who have committed various kinds of evils as well as a vision of the paradisal garden. The guide-angel of Muhammad acts as interpreter of the visions to which the Prophet is witness. At each stage of the journey Muhammad is blinded by the light, and Gabriel, in many versions is comforter and advisor, interceding with God so that Muhammad is granted a new vision. Gabriel is not allowed to go all the way to the Throne of God, signifying the theological understanding that the human creature has "higher" status than the angel, affirming the role of the human being as *khalifah*, vice-regent, of God, the possessor (potentially) of all the names and qualities of God. In various other traditions humans have higher status than the angels because they partake of both spirit and matter, body and emotions. By the 9th century the Mi`raj literature has developed side by side and in a sense become fused with Muslim eschatological literature. What the angel reveals to Muhammad in his journey becomes the prototype of the experience of the soul upon "physical" death, and the angel functions as both part of the hierarchy of being and revealer/interpreter of that hierarchy. By the 3rd Islamic century the theologian and mystic Bistami (d. 874), begins to use the Qur'anic term *fana'* which in the Qur'an refers to the "annihilation" of all things in God at the end time, as a reference to the spiritual pilgrim's own Mi`raj experience, the various stations and stages of inner transformation and attainment to the presence of God within this life.

Barzakh

Parallel to the development of Mi`raj literature are traditions that detail and interpret the process of death, the structure of Heaven, and the Day of Resurrection, the eschatological, or end time, themes. The descriptions of death found in such manuals on death as Ghazali's *al-Durra al-fakhira* and the *Kitab ahwal al-qiyama*, still dominate belief and practice in popular Islamic piety, although if one asks the question the events depicted are "literal" or "symbolic," the consensus seems to be they happen "in some real sense."

One could argue that the Qur'anic discussions on death and resurrection are aspects of the theme of the nature of divine justice, and that the symmetry of the heavens is a symmetry or perfection of justice, and indicates the emphasis in Islam on the notion of accountability: the notion that there are "natural" consequences to human deeds, both good and evil, and that there is ultimately no evasion from acknowledging and experiencing the configuration of one's *din* (faith).

The Qur'an makes numerous references to the categories of the "here" (*al-dunya*), the world in which human beings live for an appointed period of time (*ajal musamma*) which is known only to God, and the hereafter (*al-akhira*), which human beings enter at death.

> He it is who has created you out of clay, and then decreed a term
> [for you]—a term known [only] to him . . . [6:2]
> when the end of the term approaches, they can neither delay it by
> a single moment, nor hasten it. [10:49 tr. Asad]

The terms *dunya* and *akhira* are used with reference to both time and space as well as to two moral alternatives. The Qur'an cautions those who seek the *dunya* at the expense of the *akhira* (Esack, 158).

> To the one who desires a harvest in the life to come (akhira) we shall
> grant an increase in his harvest; whereas the one who desires [but] a
> harvest in this world (dunya), we [may] give something thereof—[but]
> he will have no share in [the blessings of] the life to come (akhira). [42:20]

The Qur'an describes an intermediary stage between the *dunya* and *akhira*: the *barzakh*, which is understood by Muslims as a period of in the grave, and much discussion in theology and in the traditional manuals on dying has focused on the nature of the experience (and the nature of the experiencer) in the grave/*barzakh*.

> [As for those who do not believe in the life to come, they go on
> denying] until, when death approaches anyone of them, he prays:
> O my Lord Sustainer! Let me return [to life] so that I may act
> righteously in whatever I have failed. Nay it is indeed but a [meaningless]
> word he utters; for behind those [who leave this world] there is a
> barzakh until the day when all will be raised from the dead. [23:99] (Esack, 159)

Traditional creeds mention the questioning of the soul upon death by the angels Nakir and Munkar and the punishments of the grave (*adhab al-qabr*) (Smith, 205). The works of Abu Hamid al-Ghazali's *al-Durra al-fakhira* (The Precious Pearl) and the *Kitab ahwal al-qiyama* represent the prevalence of manuals on death (still used today) that inspire commitment, hope, and fear by describing experiences undergone by the deceased at the time of death. The removal of the soul/spirit from the body is carried out by angels; God through the angels orders the time of the individual's death. We find the theme of the "recording angels," who in some narratives allow the deceased a glimpse of the Gates of Paradise. We see the theme of the recording angels removing the soul/spirit from the body, with differing degrees of ease, shock, or pain depending on the quality of faithfulness of the person in life. Once the person is in the grave and buried, he is asked by the angel, "Who is your Lord?" "What is your din?" "Who is your prophet?", as well as questions about the Qur'an, prayer, and right action (Smith, 35ff). The descriptions of the fate of the soul after death parallel the Mi`raj imagery, the overarching theme being the soul's immediate tastes of the fruits of their religious duties as it ascends on a journey—as in Mi`raj literature—with Gabriel acting as guide and interpreter for the soul as it ascends through the successive heavens.

The faithful soul's journey is through the (Ptolemaic) cosmological heavens to the "Throne of Mercy." The impious soul is described as trying to attempt the journey in the company of the angel Daqya'il, but is thwarted as Daqya'il flings the soul back into the body even as the corpse is being washed (Smith, 40). Another element in the eschatological manuals, related to Zoroastrian themes, are narratives describing the visitation of persons by beauty or ugliness, personifications of the dead person's good or bad deeds while on Earth.

The question of who or what experiences the events of the *barzakh* has been debated. But the majority of Muslims regard the experience of the tomb as a conscious experience of the deceased in the grave. Of course the literature is also seen as a way of speaking about an inevitable conscious reckoning of our life's works, that even as we die, the ease or hardship of the transition "takes the shape" of our life's deeds. Some commentators interpret this time in the grave and its punishments as a kind of purgation of sins, a means of divine mercy for the person whose deeds do not constitute "eternal" punishment. (One student told me that the angels beat you in the grave. I asked for how long. He answered that he was told that if you are chastised enough for your sins in the tomb/grave before the Day of Resurrection you will go to Paradise; if not, you go to Hell at the final hour, *al sa`a*.) Some suggest that all people have some deeds that need purgation. Another interpretation is that it warns the living, and finally that it serves as a bridge, a symbol of continuity between this life and the next, between our actions on earthy and the final dispensation of justice (Smith, 48).

Al-Yawm al-qiyama (Day of Resurrection) *and al-Sa 'ah (the Hour)*

The Qur'an speaks in vivid language of the signs of the arrival of the Day of Resurrection, *al-sa 'ah*, the [final] Hour. Ultimately, the end time is no less than a cataclysmic, transformative reversal of the world and our individual selves.

> When the sun is shrouded in darkness
> And when the stars loses their light
> And when the mountains are made to vanish
> And when the she-camel being with young, about to give birth, is left unattended
> And when all beasts are gathered together and when the seas boil over
> And when all human beings are coupled with their deeds
> And when the girl child that was buried alive is made to ask for what crime she was killed
> And when the heaven is laid bare
> And when the blazing fire is brought into view
> [on that day] every human being will come to know what he/she has prepared for him/herself. [81:1–14 tr. Asad]

The Hour is announced by the sound of a trumpet (usually associated with the angel Israfil), with human degeneracy and cosmic disintegration signaling the end of the world—and with that disintegration, only the unity of God will remain (Smith, 71).

Other signs of the hour include references to an "anti-Christ figure," *al-Dajjal*, the creatures *Yajuj* and *Majuj* (Gog and Magog), the eschatological *mahdi*, a savior figure (sometimes equated with Jesus, sometimes a separate figure), and the (second) coming of 'Isa/Jesus, [based on 4:158–159], the reckoning (*hisab*), or weighing of each person's deeds on a scale (*mizan*), the individuals' crossing a bridge (*sirat*) over Hell. But ultimately, all perishes but God.

> There is no Deity save Him; Everything is bound to perish, save his [eternal] Self. With Him rests all judgment; and unto Him shall you be brought back. [28.88 tr. Asad]

Commentaries on the Resurrection/Hour experience suggest several implications of the language: The first, as with the *barzakh*/grave experience, the notion of individual accountability is paramount. Moreover, the traditions emphasize the conscious recognition/awareness of the configuration of the *din*, the life of faith, during one's earthly existence (*dunya*), and the angel is the constant companion/agent/cognitive intermediary in the death process. The imagery of the Hour (*al sa 'ah*) however, seems to emphasize the moment when every human being is shaken to the foundations in a unique and unprecedented self-awareness of his/her deeds. "We have rent your veil so your sight today is keen" (*sura*, 50:22 in Rahman, 106). Modernist interpreter Fazlur Rahman suggests that it is indeed the quality of transparency of the heart that the Quran intends the human being to achieve. The events of both *barzakh* and the events of the Hour, point to the inevitable transparency of *oneself to oneself* as well as to God. The mystical interpreters took up the discussion of the Day of Resurrection, focusing on "the day when the Earth shall be transmuted into something else and the heavens as well" (*sura*, 14:48). Just as the sufis came to speak of piety in human life as an orientation toward the re-actualization of the "Day of the Covenant," the eschatological notion of the Day of Resurrection became the focal point and symbol of the supreme experience of the sufi path: the "recreation" of a new state within the human soul, the final overcoming of the struggle with the *nafs*, and a reintegration into the lasting presence of God. We see development in the mystical literature of the reciprocal action in which purification by God (symbolized here by the angel) is required for perception of spiritual truths, while discernment of the heart (*qalb*) and intellect (*'aql*) are those elements that lead back to purity of intention. Thus, creation, revelation, and resurrection are seen in Islam as cosmic events as well as interior ontological states that in a sense mirror each other, with the angel as constant symbol and "agency" of the divine power at work within the human personality.

Funerals and Burials, Care of the Body at Death

This discussion of Islamic burial customs will serve as a summary of those elements of Islamic death rituals that are typical and traditional for Muslims. It is true that there are local and unique customs in parts of the Islamic world, such as the Indonesian ritual of *selamatan*, the "religious meal" held by family and friends of the deceased at particular intervals after the death of someone, both to honor (and/or pray for the deceased) at the transition of death and to restore balance and peace in the household. However, I will refer to the guidelines given by the founder of a mosque community in the United States, Muhammad Raheem Bawa Muhaiyaddeen, for this community draws members from immigrant (and "born American") residents from the many geographic regions of the Islamic world to its regular congregational Friday prayers, which are conducted in the traditional Hanafi rite, one of the "orthodox" schools of Islamic law. The Bawa Muhaiyaddeen community also bought land outside of Philadelphia to be used for communal needs: to learn to farm, to create a cemetery for community members, and to build a *mazar* (shrine) in which Bawa was buried and which draws visitors for private reflection and prayers, family gatherings, and rituals to honor their *shaykh*/teacher. One should note that the care prescribed in the funeral, from the body washing to the burial assumes that the deceased is cognizant of the events, actions, and attitudes around them, and as such, the actions and intentions of funeral attendants have an effect on the comfort or distress of the deceased as they begin their transition.

The burial of a Muslim is to take place within 24 hours of death; embalming and cremation are not allowed. (Thus the cemetery, or burial grounds, must have the proper legal zoning. In the United States, Muslims will sometimes be buried in Jewish cemeteries because of this same requirement in Jewish law and custom.) Burials are not to be viewed as a business venture, and everyone in the community should assist in the funerals of its members. Normally, the funeral committee makes the proper arrangements with the mosque community's members.

The deceased must be purified (washed) and buried in a way that emulates the *sunnah*, or custom of the Prophet Muhammad. The body and hair must be washed according to guidelines of "sanctity, modesty, tenderness." Men attend to men, women to women. It is considered a grace for children to assist in the washing of their own parents. Prayers and *dhikr* (usually repetitions of the *shahada*, "*La ilaha illa 'Llah*") are gently recited during the ablution of the body. The body is enshrouded in several unhemmed, white cotton cloths of specific number and dimensions that are layered, cut, folded, and tied in the manner traditionally associated with Prophet Muhammad's burial. The deceased is "gently and lovingly" placed in a wooden casket and taken to the mosque for the congregational *janaaza* (funeral) prayer. The men in attendance carry the body to the burial site. It is suggested that women stay some distance from burial, out of concern for "the sensitive receptivity of their hearts." (Sometimes special exceptions are made.) The shroud is loosened and the body (without the casket) is lowered into the grave with the face toward the direction of Mecca. The deceased is laid to rest upon wooden slats. Wooden slats are also placed at the top of the burial chamber so that no Earth will bear down on the body. The atmosphere at the burial site should have composure, peace, tenderness, and compassion to protect both the deceased and the loved ones from extreme grieving and attachment that would prevent the deceased from moving forward in their journey. The grave is filled with Earth, small stones are placed as a cover of the burial mound. In this community wooden slats are stood upright at each end of the mound, symbolizing the scale (*mizan*) that weighs the balance of the deeds in one's life. The *muezzin* gives the traditional call to prayer (made to announce the five times prayers). The *talqin* is recited; that is, the men around the grave recite both the questions that God's angelic messengers will ask of the dead and the appropriate responses for the benefit of the deceased. The opening chapter of the Qur'an, the *Fatihah*, is recited and a supplication is offered on behalf of the dead. According to tradition, when the last person has taken seven steps from the grave, the angels Munkir and Nakir begin their questioning within the grave of the departed soul. In the evening following the burial, members of the community are invited to the mosque to recite, in congregation, the Qur'anic chapter, *Ya Sin*, the subject matter of which expresses the essence of one's final self-understanding of the one's life, purpose, and ends, namely a return to the unity of God.

Some Issues of Contention

There are a number of controversial issues in Muslim views and practices relating to death. These are: the finality of Hell, the cult of saints, prayers for the dead, paradisal virgins and other sensual language, jihad, suicide bombing, and martyrdom.

The Qur'an speaks of two alternatives for each individual in the *akhira* (here), *jannah* (Paradise) or *jahannam* (Hell). Hell is a place of fire, scorching wind, and suffering and, according to most commentators, eternal separation from God. Some 20th-century scholars, such as Fazlur Rahman and Muhammad Ali (Ali, 1990, 229–231) have suggested that Hell is remedial as well as punitive, calling attention to Qur'anic verses and the *hadith* stating that "God's mercy overrides his wrath" and that "eventually" Hell will be emptied of all its inhabitants (Esack, 163).

Does Islam approve of praying for the dead? Does Islam approve of praying to, or venerating, the dead, e.g., saints, holy people? These have been debated questions in the past and still are. In conservative schools of thought, such as the Hanbali of Saudi Arabia, there is a strict interpretation of Qur'anic verses against attempts to intercede (*shafa'a*) on behalf of the dead. Some verses in the Qur'an indicate that such attempts are useless (2:48, 6:51). On the other hand, it is a common practice, and verses are cited that leave room for the possibility that the prayers or intercession, particularly of Muhammad, will be answered (e.g., 47:19, 20:107). One can see in some of the death and burial manuals that Muhammad said not to mourn excessively and to limit praying for the dead. But in many parts of the Islamic world, it is considered a duty for family members to pray at the grave, (in fact some *hadiths* indicate the son should pray for the father at the latter's death and give alms on behalf of the father). The traditional *selamatan* meals on behalf of the dead—to aid them in their transition—in the largest Muslim country in the world, is an example of the prevalence of this sentiment. In many Islamic countries including Egypt, Morocco, Indonesia, India, and Syria, visiting and praying the grave of a *wali* ("friend of

God") to attain grace, or *barakah*, or to ask for help or healing, is considered to be a normal part of the cultural religious traditions. It may be disapproved of by "modernist-conservatives" trends or "Saudi/*wahabi*" influenced groups, but popular piety prevails.

Paradise is described as an abode of gardens, rivers flowing, peace, abundance, and joy. The language of Paradise in some references seems particularly sensual and materialistic, and "which does not always appeal to the more noble instincts of men" (Esack, 163). This is especially the case with the description of males attended by "wide-eyed companions," the *hur*. The majority of traditional commentators have maintained that these are "parables" for an experience that can only be hinted at through sensual language. Muslim woman scholar Amina Wadud suggests that the materialistic references appear in the earlier Qur'anic revelations, appealing to the *imaginaire* of the harsh Arab desert life, the need of which changed as the Muslim community and understanding of the message matured (Wadud, 1999).

One final note in regard to contemporary issues: the bombing of 9/11 by terrorists and the ongoing violence in the Middle East have raised questions about the term *jihad* (often translated as "holy war") as used by Muslims (and non-Muslims). In addition, the terrible political struggles for human rights, land, and security in Israel/Palestine—and the adoption of suicide bombing by young Muslims as weapon of political resistance—have raised the question of martyrdom and suicide in Islam. There are several resources that deal with these questions (Esposito, 22ff.), but in summary the following can be said: the term *jihad* is used in the Qur'an to mean "striving in the way of God," without exclusive reference to war. However, war, or fighting, is allowed under certain conditions and with certain rules (if one has been attacked or oppressed, and if one does not injure civilians or even the environment). In a verse received after several years of persecution by the Meccan leaders, Muhammad would declare the possibility of "just" war. "And fight in the way of God with those who fight with you, but aggress not: God loves not the aggressors . . . [but] persecution (or "oppression") is more grievous than slaying" (*sura*, 2:217). However, *jihad* interpreted as mandate for suicide bombing is a new phenomenon in Islam. While vigorously denounced by the majority of Muslim leaders and scholars, it is clear, terrible, but true that hopelessness and the experience of oppression and attack, are being interpreted as a call to resist. With the recent establishment of the Muslim Peace Fellowship, Muslims Against Terrorism, and other groups searching for "peace with justice and justice without violence," Muslims attempt to address the interpretations of martyrdom and *jihad*. However, the on-ground perception of a Western dominated (with right-wing Christian and Jewish supporters) "oppressive" foreign policy, makes the task daunting.

Selected Bibliography

Asad, Muhammad. 1980. *The messenger of Islam*. Gibralter: Dal al-Andalus.

Bowering, G. 1980. *The mystical vision of existence in classical Islam*. New York: Walter De Grayter.

Corbin, Henri. 1978. *Spiritual body and celestial Earth: From Mazdean Iran to Shi'ite Iran*. Princeton: Princeton University Press.

Esack, Farid. 2002. *The Qur'an: A short introduction*. Oxford: Oneworld Press.

Esposito, John. 2002. *Unholy war: Terror in the name of Islam*. Oxford: Oxford University Press.

Khalidi, Tarif. 2001. *The Muslim Jesus: Sayings and stories in Islamic literature*. Cambridge: Harvard University Press.

Nasr, Seyyed Hossein. 2000. *Ideals and realities of Islam*. Chicago: Kazi Publications.

Rahman, Fazlur. 1980. *Major themes of the Quaran*. Minneapolis: Bibliotheca Islamic.

Schimmel, Annemarie. 1975. *Mystical dimensions of Islam*. Chapel Hill: University of North Carolina Press.

Sells, Michael. 2001. *Approaching the Qur'an: The Early Revelations*. Ashland, Oregon: White Cloud Press.

Smith, Jane I., and Haddan, Yvonne Y. 2002. *The Islamic understanding of death and resurrection*. Oxford: Oxford University Press.

Wadud, Amina. 1999. *Qur'an and woman: Rereading the sacred text from a Woman's perspective*. Oxford: Oxford University Press.

Study Questions

1. How do Muslim ideas of "creation" and the "pre-existent state" express ideals of human nature?
2. What is Muhammad's "Night Journey" and how has it influenced Islam's view of death?
3. What is the Day of Resurrection in Islam?
4. What is barzakh? What happens there?
5. What are the principle burial practices for Muslims?

CHAPTER 7

On Death and After in Brahmanic Hindu India

William Cully Allen

Introduction

Hinduism is a diverse family of related religious traditions, including agnosticism, monism, dualism, monotheism, and polytheism. Hinduism is indigenous to India. Archeological evidence of its roots extends back to prehistory, and its textual roots, the Veda, are traceable to at least the second millennium before the Common Era (c. 1200 BCE). Nevertheless, traditional Hindus believe the Veda is a beginningless and authorless text. There are over 900 million Hindus in India alone. Over the past century and a half, Hindus have immigrated in large numbers to various parts of the world, including Southeast Asia, Indonesia, Europe, North America, Africa, the Middle East, and Australia. Although forms of Hinduism are widely diverse throughout India and the world, the Sanskrit Brahmanical tradition constitutes a cultural core in relationship to which alternative forms of Hinduism identify themselves, some rejecting and others affirming the Vedic legacy of the Sanskrit Brahmanic tradition.

Death in Brahmanical Hinduism is inseparably related to sacrifice and creation. Sacrificial ritual is central to Brahmanic Hinduism. Sacrifice entails death. According to one of the oldest Upanisads, the philosophical portion of the Veda, death precedes creation:

> In the beginning there was nothing here at all. Death alone covered this completely, as did hunger; for what is hunger but death? Then death made up his mind: Let me equip myself with a body. (Oliville, 7)

Death is an essential dimension of sacrifice, and by means of sacrifice the universe is created and sustained. Life depends on death. According to one of the oldest and particularly well-known Vedic creation hymns, the entire universe is the self-sacrificial act of the Cosmic Person, the Purusha (Hopkins, 22). This Purusha is further identified with the entire cosmos itself. The Purusha, in an act of creative self-sacrifice, dismembers itself in death, creating the world out of its own body. For example, the hymn declares the four social classes of traditional Hindu Brahmanic society are formed from distinct parts of the Purusha's anatomy. The mouth became the priestly class (Brahmins, hence Brahmanic Hinduism), symbolizing the importance of sacred Vedic Sanskrit speech in the performance of rituals; the Purusha's arms became the soldiers and administrators; the thighs became the producers, symbolic because of their proximity to the reproductive organs but more importantly because agricultural and commercial productivity uphold and support all classes of society; the feet of Purusha formed the common laborers, upon whose humble services the entire body of society depends. Among the oldest Hindu Brahmanic conceptions and visions of the origin of the universe, we find the centrality of sacrifice and the essential role of death in the creation and maintenance of the cosmos. The hymn further explains that the Cosmic Person, Purusha, is identical with the sacrifice and both the Purusha and the sacrifice are identical to the universe. In short, the Purusha is the universe which is continually re-enacting the drama of self-sacrifice (Flood, 48). Death, in this ritual context, is meaningful because it is essential to sacrifice, the movement, and meaning of the universe itself.

Life Journey Rituals: *Samskaras*

In spite of its rich diversity, a set of life journey rituals comprise a common core of Hinduism. This schedule of life journey rituals has its roots in Brahmanic Sanskrit texts and traditions. The rituals punctuate a person's passage through various stages of life. These life journey rituals are called *samskaras*, a word that literally means "construction," "accomplishment," "perfection," and "refinement." Periods of transition from one stage of life to another are considered precarious and dangerous. Therefore, *samskaras* are performed to celebrate the completion of one stage of life and to accomplish a successful passage from one stage of life to the next (Lipner, 264). They are rituals to purify and thereby refine, accomplish, and ultimately perfect or complete the life-body's journey through its innumerable embodiments en route toward *moksha*—the soul's final liberation. It is a circuitous route to *moksha*. A common core understanding about the nature of death and what happens to the life-body beyond death has persisted in India, with some adaptations and modifications, from ancient times to the present (Knipe, 111). This chapter describes contemporary Sanskrit Brahmanical rituals and beliefs surrounding death, and beyond.

A *samskara* is the ritual advancement of a life-body from its moment of conception to immediately beyond bodily death. The majority of the rites take place before a child reaches the age of six months, including the performance of several rituals even before the umbilical cord is severed. One of the main reasons for the performance of *samskaras* is the refinement of the life-body by the elimination of impurities. For this reason, much attention is given to the person's previous life-body, especially its dangerous passage from body to body. *Samskaras* mark an orderly and meaningful passage from conception through childhood, initiation into studenthood, marriage, death, and beyond.

At Death

The final *samskara* in the journey of the life-body is the ritual disposal of the material body after death. The final *samskara* is called *antyesti*, which literally means "final sacrifice." This final *samskara* is itself a ritual sacrifice in which the deceased person is the sacrificial offering. This final *samskara* has the same purpose as those previously performed. The *samskara* celebrates the completion of a stage of life; the *samskara* performed at death is a celebration of the completion of a particular life-body. It refines the life-body by eliminating impurities and rendering the entire material body into ashes or Earth. It also constructs another body for another birth in the long course of recycling.

Preparing the deceased's body for cremation or burial has therapeutic and consoling effects on the bereaved. The face of death is unveiled. Bodies are not usually embalmed or cosmetically beautified. The viewers see the true face of death, the face of the deceased as it was at the moment of death. It is an occasion on which many Hindus reflect on death and face the fact of their own death. Preparations for the disposal of the dead body express a deep debt the living owe to the dead. Preparations are performed by the living in anticipation of a continued reciprocal relationship of mutual dependence with the deceased. On the day a Hindu dies, the Hindu is brought home and laid on the floor inside the house or on the ground immediately outside the house. In either case the floor or ground is first smeared with cow dung, a sacred purifying agent. While family members and friends witness, a designated family member ceremonially sprinkles the corpse with water and wraps the dead body in a shroud of new clothes. Friends and family adorn the corpse with garlands of flowers. The body is also anointed with a sandlewood paste, which both helps the body burn and emits a pleasant aroma suppressing the odious smell of burning flesh. By these ritual gestures, the deceased is purified and empowered for the impending postmortem journey, and the bereaved feel good for helping prepare their loved one for it.

The dead body is then placed on a bamboo ladder or a rope bed, hoisted upon the shoulders of loved ones, and carried feet first to the place of cremation, usually a river bank, or to a burial ground. The procession is typically led by the eldest son, followed by the corpse after which trail the family and friends, but no women; the women stay at home where they continue to mourn. According to tradition, there can be no crying at the cremation ground because the deceased may involuntarily ingest the polluting effects of tears and mucus expelled by mourners. The processioners chant incessantly throughout the march: *Ram nam satya hai* (Rama's name is the truth). If the corpse is taken to a cremation ground, the feet are usually dipped in a sacred river on the banks of which most cremation grounds are located. A special class of people constructs the funeral pyre with wood, especially with fragrant smelling sandalwood for the wealthy. Family and friends help lay the corpse on top of the pyre with the feet facing south, the direction of Yama, the god of death, and the head facing north, the location of the god of wealth. The chief mourner, usually the eldest living son, lights the fire. When a man is cremated, the fire is lit at his head; when a woman is cremated, the fire is ignited at her feet. When the body is nearly burned up, the chief mourner smashes the skull with a bamboo stick. Cracking open the head punctuates the moment of ritual death and releases the newly formed thumb-sized body into the air where it takes up its new residence for the next 10 to 13 days. Immediately after the body is burned, mourners take a ritual bath in the river and return home without looking back. Of course there are wide ranging variations of this pattern from region to region, but the basic structure of ritual procedure outlined above is discernable in death rites practiced all throughout India today.

After Death

In Brahmanic Hindu India death is a social event. This is made dramatically evident in the numerous rituals performed by family and friends on behalf of the dead body. Death is a social event because one is not alone in death. The journey the soul resumes with cremation or burial of the gross body is a journey the soul makes with the support of its living descendents. The soul never exists apart from a body of some sort because the soul is the one who experiences, and there can be no experience without a body.

The cremation or burial simultaneously destroys the gross material body and constructs a new subtle body, also physical though less gross than the material body which is destroyed by the final *samskara*. Upon death, after cremation or burial, the individual takes recourse to the new ritually formed subtle body. This subtle body is only a temporary and transitional body which takes the form of air. It is the size and shape of a thumb and is wisped about in the wind. As such it is subject to heat and cold and suffers the experience of extreme temperatures. Without a body there can be no experience (Michaels, 138). For this reason there is no stage in the repeated process of birth and death in which the individual exists without a body of some type.

For the period of 10 days (13 in some regions) immediately following the disposal of the gross physical body, rituals are observed in order to destroy the thumb-sized air body gradually and simultaneously recreate yet another body the size and shape of a forearm called a *preta*, literally "one who has passed away." The *preta* body also must eventually (in some regions one year after death, in other regions 10 or 13 days after death) be destroyed to create the celestial body of a glorified father (*Pitr*) in which to enjoy the pleasures of Heaven. These rituals to transform the thumb-sized body of air into the *preta* and the *preta* into a glorified father (*Pitr*) entail the offering of balls of rice. Each day for 10 to 13 days after death, rice cooked in milk is fashioned into a tennis ball sized lump which both represents and nourishes the deceased ancestor. Each day a new lump is fashioned and placed on a hand-made altar of Earth and worshipped with flowers and incense. A mixture of water and sesame seed is poured onto the rice-ball each day, adding an additional cup of water and sesame seed each day until the final day when 10 or 13 cups are poured out to complete the construction of the new *preta* body.

This ritual to destroy the airy body and create the *preta* body is essential. If the ritual is not performed, or not well-performed, the deceased person is believed to remain in a body of air, suffering from extreme temperatures and wreaking havoc on the lives of those living relatives who failed to perform the necessary rituals properly. This is a particularly dangerous transitional period during which the rituals performed by the survivors on behalf of the airy embodiment determine the soul's success or failure to pass into the next progressive stage of life's journey. In other words, a dead ancestor who is not successfully transformed into a *preta* allegedly becomes a ghost, a malcontented spirit, believed to inhabit the atmosphere or trees and make life miserable for the living relatives who failed to perform the required rites of respect and bodily transformation. The same destiny awaits the unwed or those who die untimely or inauspicious deaths, unless of course they are divinized or declared immortal for their heroic acts. There is a recent trend to hasten the transformation of the airy body into the *preta* as soon as possible after cremation or burial, and to expedite the creation of the glorified *Pitr* body to the 10th or 13th day formerly designated for acquiring the *preta* body.

Once established as a glorified father (*Pitr*), for the next three generations the ancestor is eligible to receive the numerous offerings in yet another round of monthly (or in some regions daily) sacrificial rituals performed in reverential commemoration and supplication of the departed ancestor who has finally attained a position of cosmic power accessible and available to the living. There is a reciprocal relationship between the dead and the living. The exalted fathers are only made and maintained as exalted fathers by virtue of the living who perform rituals on their behalf. On the other hand, the living invoke their exalted fathers to help assure good fortune and the fulfillment of ordinary human interests in every day life. The dead are grateful because they are established and sustained by their survivors, and the survivors, in turn, depend on the grateful dead for health, wealth, and wish fulfillments. In this economy there is an exchange of merit. The merit necessary to establish a *Pitr* is engendered by means of the performance of sacrificial rituals; the merit generated by the ritual performance of the living on behalf of the dead empowers the *Pitr* with grace to help descendents in times of need.

Each time a father dies and successfully undergoes the various transformations and passages into new bodies and new realms concluding in the final accomplishment and construction of the *Pitr* body, the eldest member of the company of the *Pitr*, i.e., the great-grandfather, graduates, as it were, out of the company of the fathers into a new association of the three preceding generations referred to as the "remote dead." The "remote dead" are distinguished from the more "recent dead" who are more immediately accessible and potentially helpful to the living. Ritual invocations refer to the "recently dead" as those with "faces of tears," while the "remote dead" are described as those with "faces of joy." After graduating beyond the three generations collectively known as the "remote dead with faces of joy," ancestors dissolve into thinner altitudes from which they are reincarnated.

An exchange of power between the living and the dead is generated by the ritual performance of sacrifices by the living on behalf of the dead. These rituals both establish the dead ancestors as exalted Fathers (*Pitrs*) and empower them to intervene in the fulfillment of the interests of the living. The dead are quite alive. But for how long? The Rig Veda left open the question of what becomes of the exalted Fathers once they have passed beyond the two tripartite companies of Fathers. The *Upanisads* filled the gap with the doctrines of *karma*, *samsara*, and *moksha*.

Reincarnation: *karma, samsara,* and *moksha*

The idea of reincarnation makes its first scriptural appearance in India around 800 BCE in one of the oldest Upanisads, the philosophical section of the Veda. The doctrine of reincarnation is introduced in the context of questioning what happens to the soul at bodily death. According to the Upanisadic sage,

> It is like this. As a caterpillar, when it comes to the tip of a blade of grass, it reaches out to a new foothold and draws itself onto it, so the self, after it has knocked down this body and rendered it unconscious, reaches out to a new foothold and draws itself onto it. (Olivelle, 64)

The idea of *karma* first appears in the very same passage. It is introduced to give an explanatory account of the process of reincarnation.

> What a man turns out to be depends on how he acts and on how he conducts himself. If his actions are good, he will turn into something good. If his actions are bad, he will turn into something bad. A man turns into something good by good action and into something bad by bad action. (Olivelle, 65)

Karma, in this context, refers only to human volitional action. The word *karma* comes from a Sanskirt verbal root meaning "to make" and "to act." *Karma* entails the idea that to act is to make consequences. Furthermore, the doctrine insists that the person who performs a given action must live, somewhere, somehow, sometime to face and experience the consequences of those actions. Some actions produce consequences experienced immediately, some later in life, and some actions produce results which can only be experienced after the death in a new life-body; hence the doctrines of *karma* and reincarnation arose together. *Karma* is the principle of causality applied to the moral dimension of human life. All willful human actions produce results and the agent of the action must live to experience those results, whether for good or bad. This view places the responsibility for human problems and predicaments squarely on the shoulders of each individual. Karma should not be confused with fate or predestination. *Karma* is conceived by Hindus as an impersonal ethical principle, not the law of God, but a principle operative in shaping the nature and destiny of human beings. Human beings, by means of *karma* (volitional actions which produce results) determine their own being. In other words, commensurate with one's karmic conditioning (habitual patterns of thought and action), human beings make themselves whatever they become.

Samsara is a Sanskrit word meaning "to flow together." The word *samsara* envisions the process of birth, death, reincarnation and re-death, etc., as a cyclical syndrome. *Samsara* refers to the potentially endless process of birth, death, rebirth, and re-death. This cyclical syndrome is a predicament. It is not ultimately desirable to those who seek *moksha* above all else. *Moksha* is the Hindu term for liberation, not of the soul from the body, but liberation from the otherwise endless syndrome of repeated births and deaths. *Samsara* is not limited to earthly life. The various postmortem embodiments through which the departed soul experiences pleasures in Heaven or suffers torments in Hell are also part of the *samsaric* cyclical syndrome. The departed soul's experiences of Heaven and Hell are not eternal. Hell is endured only as long as the person's past actions warrant; the same is true of the soul's delights in Heaven. When the karmic consequences for good actions previously performed on Earth have been fully experienced in Heaven, the departed soul's time in Heaven expires, and the soul must transform into yet another body suitable to another environment commensurate with the consequences of previous human actions. In this way the life-body is recycled through the universe in an endlessly recurring syndrome of birth and death unless and until the soul attains *moksha*—release from the rounds of birth and death here, there, and everywhere.

Putting Moksha in Perspective: Four Aims and Four Stages of Life

While *moksha* is the ultimate spiritual aim of life, it is not necessarily the most pressing or urgent personal ambition of every Hindu. Hindu tradition has long recognized four legitimate aims worth pursuing in life, and four stages of life. These four aims and four stages provide an orientation toward life. The four aims include: 1. Pleasure, especially aesthetic, erotic, and sensual enjoyment; 2. Success, particularly economic and social; 3. Duty, social responsibilities, and obligations; and finally 4. *Moksha*, liberation and release from birth and death and all embodiments. The four stages of life are: 1. Student, 2. Householder, 3. Forest Dweller, and 4. Sunyasin—enlightened renunciant.

Many Hindus see life as a movement from aim to aim and stage to stage. Not all aims are appropriate to all stages. For example, celibacy is enjoined for all but the Householder. The Householder stage commences soon after Studenthood and is characterized by the concerns of marriage, career, and family. During the Householder stage the first three aims of life (pleasure, success, and social obligations) have much greater importance than the pursuit of *moksha*. Brahmanic Sanskrit Hinduism has produced sacred literature which provides advice on the pursuit of erotic and aesthetic pleasures; Hinduism has also produced sacred Sanskrit texts providing council for how to achieve material success in the pursuit of personal, economic, and social interests. There are far more Hindu rituals performed in the interest of an ordinary Householder's life in this world than for transcending this world in the interest of *moksha*. Most Hindus are normal people interested in the pursuit of pleasure and success in this world. The pursuit of *moksha* is extraordinary. There-fore, most Hindus do not have a life-denying pessimistic assessment of the *samsaric* syn-drome. Why should they? For most, the pursuit of pleasure and success within the limits of culturally prescribed morality is a meaningful life.

Renunciation of these pursuits is an exceptional ideal; it is not for just anyone, any-time. It is only an appropriate pursuit for those who have already satisfied their appetite for success and pleasure. However, because the world is so full of possibilities for the enjoy-ment of pleasure and success and because there are potentially innumerable lifetimes dur-ing which to experience it all, most Hindus are in no hurry for *moksha*. Nevertheless, for those who are in a hurry because they cannot bear the thought of enduring yet another round of birth and death, there are direct and immediate Brahmanic spiritual methods for procuring *moksha* at death. One such expedient way to *moksha* is to die in Banaras. Each year thousands of people make pilgrimage to Banaras, Hinduism's most ancient and sacred city, in anticipation of dying there because many believe that those who die in Banaras will go directly to *moksha* (see Justice, 1997; also Parry, 1994).

Historically, the Forest Dweller stage arose in order to accommodate asceticism while simultaneously discouraging it until old age. The renunciation of pleasure and success are rare ideals, only appropriate to those of retirement age. The Forest Dweller stage is an option rarely exercised by Hindus in India today nor was it ever a popular option in the past. It is a stage of life which, according to Brahmanical norms, a person may not begin until a son and grandson have been produced. After a person has fully discharged his debt to society in the production of a son and grandson, the Brahmanical tradition provides the option for one to renounce all social obligations, family relations, and possessions in order to retreat to the forest (or a retreat house in the city) and practice austerities and other spiritual disciplines in pursuit of *moksha*.

The one who is absolutely committed to realizing the final and ultimate aim of life, *moksha*, enters the final stage of life called *sunyasin*, literally "one who has completely abandoned." Entrance into this stage is marked by a *samskara* which entails the ritual per-formance of the renunciant's very own funeral. The one who enters the final stage con-structs an effigy of himself and performs the final death rite *samskara* on the symbolized self. This ritual performance of the *sunyasin's* own death frees the surviving relatives from the obligation to perform death rites when the *sunyasin's* body finally dies. The *sunyasin*, having fully renounced all social identities, roles, and responsibilities, wanders about as a symbolic embodiment of social transcendence. When the *sunyasin's* body dies, it is never cremated. There is no need to purify the one who has completed the final stage of the jour-ney. There is no need to construct another body since there are no unfulfilled aims for the *sunyasin* to pursue. When *sunyasins* die, they are often buried head up in a seated medi-tation posture.

However, asceticism is neither the only nor the most popular form of spirituality and religious life in Hindu India. There are ways to *moksha* without going to and through the forest. Devotional theism is the most popular form of religious practice throughout India today and has been from ancient times. Devotional theistic spiritualities have absolutely no use for the Forest Dweller stage of life. It is utterly unnecessary because devotional theisms have numerous and diverse ways to attain *moksha* without retreating from the business of everyday life in the world of family relationships and social obligations. For many Hindu devotional theists, *moksha* is even attainable by God's grace through faith.

There are numerous alternative visions of what *moksha* entails. For some *moksha* is the enjoyment of bliss in the presence of God; for others, it is analogous to deep, dreamless sleep in which there is no sensory activity, hence no pain or suffering, but only pure unconscious peace. For still others, *moksha* is envisioned as the experience of pure consciousness, the mystical direct awareness of the profound infinite depth of one's own being. Various versions and visions of *moksha* abound in Hinduism, and there are perhaps just as many, if not more, different paths to *moksha* as there are versions of exactly what *moksha* is.

The Question of Dualism Regarding Soul and Body

According to Samkhya, the oldest Brahmanic Hindu tradition of systematic reflection on the Veda, there are two dimensions of reality. Systems of thought which maintain belief in the existence of two separate dimensions of reality are called dualist. Although Samkhya is atheistic, its dualistic understanding of reality in general and human nature in particular deeply influenced all subsequent Brahmanic Hindu understandings about human nature. The Samkhya tradition asserts that there are two beginningless and endless principles of reality. One is called *purusha*, from the Rig Vedic creation Hymn, the other is called *prakrti*. Before translating these two terms into approximate English equivalents, a few observations about their relationship to each other may help clarify their distinction from each other. *Purusha* is not *prakrti* and *prakrti* is not *purusha*. They are absolutely distinct and different from each other. They have nothing whatsoever in common. Moreover, according to the Samkhya view, the confusion of *prakrti* with *purusha* is the fundamental cause of the human predicament. Human beings constantly mistake *prakrti* for *purusha*. So *prakrti*, whatever else it may or may not be, is not *purusha*; it masquerades itself as *purusha*, beguiling and deceiving itself into believing itself to be the *purusha*. Whatever is not *purusha* is *prakrti*; there is no room for anything else. These two categories constitute a comprehensive world view. *Purusha* is Pure Subject without an object; it is the Pure Self as it is in and of itself. According to the Samkhya tradition, this Pure Self is pure consciousness, conscious only of itself. This is the Pure Self of each human being.

Purusha is usually rendered "spirit" in English and *prakrti* is translated as "matter or nature." This is a bit misleading, however, because *prakrti* includes many things more readily associated with spirit than matter. For example, the entire psycho-physical human being is composed of *prakrti*, not *purusha*. All mental phenomena, including thought, imagination, memory, intuition, and all emotional moods and states of mind are always and only *prakrtic*; they are never characteristics or actions of *purusha*. *Purusha* has no need to act. Human beings act to fulfill aims and desires. Desires presuppose lack. *Purusha* is a Perfect Person because in *purusha* there is no lack. Action entails movement while movement presupposes a gap between where one is and where one wants to be. There is no such gap for the *purusha*. Yet *purusha* acts, motivated neither by unfulfilled desire, nor to bridge a gap between where the Pure Self is and where it wants to be. The *purusha* acts in accordance with its essential nature as the Cosmic Self-Sacrificing Person, who is none other than the infinite universe itself, spontaneously and ritually re-enacting its own self-sacrificial nature.

So *purusha* is pure consciousness; *prakrti* is unconscious matter. According to Samkhya, various human states of awareness are cases of false consciousness because they are rooted in *prakrtic* existence, and do not participate in *purusha* at all. *Purusha* is completely disconnected and disassociated from all *prakrtic* activity, including ordinary and extraordinary states of human awareness. So *prakrti* is matter, provided matter is understood to include all the activities of the psycho-physical human being. Insofar as it has become commonplace to think and speak of the human brain as "grey matter," it should not be difficult to understand why the Hindu classifies the mind as matter (*prakrti*), and not spirit (*purusha*).

The term Samkhya, which gives its name to this ancient Hindu philosophy, literally means "discrimination." Discrimination is the key term of this philosophy because Samkhya aims at discrimination between two selves: one self is changing and not eternal while the other self is changeless and eternal. The changing self is composed entirely of *prakrti*, materiality. This material (*prakrtic*) self is a superficial self, a pseudo-self, a socially and psychologically constructed self. It is the personality of an individual, the embodiment of memories, impressions, dispositions, proclivities, inclinations, tendencies, habits of thought, imagination, and deliberate action. In short, the *prakrtic* self is a character always in the process of being shaped and reshaped, largely by the habituation of intentional patterns of action.

The *purusha* is the Pure Self, the profound innermost core of one's being. The Pure Self is not constructed. It is neither born nor does it die. It is, according to Samkhya philosophy, pure consciousness, the Pure Self knowing itself as it is in and of itself. It is Pure Subject without an object. It is the unique case where the subject who knows is simultaneously the object known. Yet in this case the self allegedly knows itself, not as an object to itself, but as itself, immediately, mystically. Samkhya's method entails the primacy of knowledge as an instrumental means to enlightenment, the discovery of the profound innermost self, by practicing meditative disciplines aimed at discrimination, discerning and distinguishing between the profound innermost self (*purusha*) and the individual personality (*prakrtic* self) that is not *purusha* but which has a perpetual tendency to pass itself off as *purusha*. This Samkhya philosophy of dualism between the psycho-physical, mind-body complex on the one hand, and the profound innermost self, utterly detached from any participation in the mental or physical activities of the *prakrtic* self on the other hand, is foundational to the emergence of *jnana* yoga, a discipline for discriminating self knowledge from mispredicated identity.

The existential predicament of human beings is an identity crisis. The superficial self continually mistakes itself for the profound innermost self, *purusha*. In other words the pseudo-self, composed of materiality—including the physical body, mind, and senses—erroneously imagines itself to be the nonphysical eternal, unchanging self, called *purusha*. The aim of Samkhya philosophy is to "discriminate" between the changing personality of an individual whose body is formed and transforms, and the changeless, birthless, deathless, infinite self, *purusha*.

The dualism of Samkhya provided the philosophical framework for Classical Yoga, meditational techniques for gradually realizing the complete, total, and final separation of *purusha* from *prakrti*, the true self from the imposter. Classical Yoga arose in part to answer the question, "How can the *purusha* realize itself by means of the *prakrtic* self?" Since the mind and all its mental actions, and the body and sense organs are all part of the *prakrtic* self, and the *purusha* is totally other to the *prakrtic* self, how can a *prakrtically* constituted person do anything at all to realize *purusha?* The distance and difference between *purusha* and *prakrti* signals an infinite gap, but neither Samkhya nor Classical Yoga is interested in bridging that gap. Discrimination is for the sake of separation. Classical Yoga introduced specific psycho-physical techniques for a person to progressively withdraw and isolate the operations of the *prakrtic* self, including breath suspension, self-induced sensory deprivation, shutting down all operations of the mind, eventuating in the alleged mystical encounter of *purusha* itself.

At the opposite end of the spectrum on Hindu views about human nature and reality is the Hindu Tantric tradition. Tantrism, as an identifiable religious movement, began in India during the 4th century of the Common Era, though its textual roots are traceable to the Veda, and its archeological roots are prehistoric. Tantrism turned the dualistic terms of Samkhya (*purusha* and *prakrti*) upside down and backwards. Tantrism, appealing to the same Brahmanic Vedic authority as Samkhya, declares that the two dimensions of reality are not dual, but non-dual. In keeping with the Rig Vedic vision of *purusha* as the Cosmic Person who creates the universe through an act of self-sacrificial death and dismemberment, Tantrism sees the human body as a microcosmic version of the macrocosmic universe. In this way *purusha* and *prakrti* are essentially identical, not different.

Tantrism identified *purusha* with *Siva*, the male principle of the universe, and *prakrti* with *Shakti*, the female principle of the universe. Whereas the traditions of Samkhya and Classical Yoga and other Brahmanic spiritual disciplines aim at discrimination and isolation of *purusha* from *prakrti*, Tantrism aims at the unification and integration of purusha (*Siva*) and *prakrti* (*Shakti*). This had radical implications for Tantric Hindu attitudes toward the role of sexuality in spiritual discipline. Instead of ascetic abstinence from sexual intercourse, some Tantric spiritual practices entailed the ritual performance of sexual intercourse, a symbolic re-enactment of the union between Siva and Shakti. Not a form of hedonism, Tantrism also developed various forms of meditational, devotional, and even ascetic practices in pursuit of *moksha*, which for Tantrism is symbolized in the union, not separation, of *purusha* (*Siva*) and *prakrti* (*Shakti*).

Since *Shiva* and *Shakti* represent a unity, not a duality, many Tantric disciplines aim at destroying the discriminations people ordinarily make between apparent dualities. For example, in order to destroy the dualistic understanding about life and death, some Tantric ascetics use a hollowed out human skull as a begging bowl and eat their food from it. Some also practice meditative techniques while seated on a dead corpse in a graveyard. Others even scavenge and eat the decomposing flesh of abandoned corpses. Mother Kali, a favorite Tantric goddess, is often iconographically depicted with a garland of skulls around her neck symbolizing the interdependence of life and death.

Conclusion

Death does not always kill. The dead live on somewhere, somehow. In Brahmanic Hindu understandings of death, the body is very important. Without a body there can be no experience. The Brahmanic death rituals both destroy one body while simultaneously creating another, and another, and perhaps yet another. The options are diverse. Once a person dies the person takes recourse to a thumb-sized and shaped subtle body inhabiting the air. From this airy embodiment one may either become a ghost vexing the surviving descendents or one may become a *preta*, the forearm-shaped body in which form one may slip into Hell or a *preta* may be successfully transformed into a celestial body to experience the pleasures of Heaven for a season. One may even be divinized or declared immortal, but unless and until a person attains *moksha*, release from the otherwise endless syndrome of birth and death, no one goes anywhere forever. Eventually, life-bodies are reincarnated on Earth as plants, animals, or human beings according to the consequences of actions performed in previous human embodiments. Hence, the route to *moksha*, the final aim of life, is circuitous for most, but a straight path is also possible by way of dying in Banaras, by the grace of God, by way of the *sunyasin* (the one who renounces all social relationships and responsibilities, and who abandons possessions and personal identity in pursuit of *moksha*), and by any one of a myriad of other devotional, ritualistic, and ascetic disciplines.

Brahmanic Hindu death and post death rituals in India demonstrate a persistent concern for patrilinear continuity between generations. This is especially evident in the roles afforded to the eldest surviving son in the performance of important ritual gestures. Women's identities in death are in association with their husbands, so women who die unmarried are subject to become ghosts. Death is a social event because the dead continue a mutually dependent relationship with their survivors. The living perform rituals which create, sustain, promote, and empower the continued embodiments of their ancestors. In turn, the survivors hope their ancestors will bless them in the fulfillment of socioeconomic interests. For Brahmanic Hinduism, death is meaningful in the context of sac-rificial ritual. It is a ritual economy of mutual exchange between the ancestors and their survivors, linking the present to the past, and the living to the dead.

Glossary of Sanskrit Terms

karma: Willful human actions which produce unavoidable consequences.

moksha: Release from the otherwise endless rounds of birth and death.

pitr: The body of a glorified father in Heaven.

prakrti: In Samkhya philosophy materiality including the body, senses, mind, and all its functions.

preta: Departed ancestor in a subtle body the form and shape of a forearm.

purusha: In Samkhya philosophy the pure self, the pure subject, the deep innermost self.

samsara: The potentially endless cycle of birth and death.

samskara: Life-journey rites of passage from conception to immediately beyond death.

Sanskrit: The sacred language of the Brahmanic Hindu tradition.

Selected Bibliography

Flood, Gavin. 1996. *An introduction to Hinduism.* Cambridge, UK: Cambridge University Press.

Hopkins, Thomas. 1971. *The Hindu religious tradition.* Belmont, CA: Wadsworth Publishing Co.

Justice, Christopher. 1997. *Dying the good death: The pilgrimage to die in India's Holy City.* Albany: State University of New York Press.

Knipe, David M. 1977. *Sapindikarana:* The Hindu rite of entry into Heaven. In *Religious Encounters with Death,* eds. Frank Reynolds and Earl Waugh. University Park: The Pennsylvania State University Press.

Lipner, Julius. 1998. *Hindus: Their religious beliefs and practices.* London: Routledge.

Michaels, Axel. 2004. *Hinduism past and present.* Princeton: Princeton University Press.

Olivelle, Patrick. 1996. *Upanisads.* New York: Oxford University Press.

Parry, Jonathan. 1994. *Death in Banaras.* Cambridge, UK: Cambridge University Press.

Study Questions

1. Describe the cyclical process of bodily transformations after death to the next birth in reincarnation.
2. How do the four aims of life and four stages of life provide a map or blueprint for living?
3. Explain the relationship between *karma* and *moksha*. What is the role of *karma* relative to *samsara* and *moksha?*
4. Define *purusha* and *prakrti*. How are these two different from "soul" and "body"?
5. Why is the body important in Brahmanic Hinduism?

CHAPTER 8

Tibetan Buddhist Views on Death: Compassion and Liberation

Eve Mullen

An Introduction to Buddhism

The main topic of this chapter is Tibetan Buddhist perspectives on the ideal death and relatedly on the ideal life. Before jumping into Buddhist views and practices in the Tibetan culture, however, it is helpful to establish some basics within the Buddhist religious tradition in general. The story of Buddhism best begins with the figure of the Buddha himself, considered to be the founder of Buddhism in all variations of the religion in the world today, whether in the Tibetan Vajrayāna, Japanese Zen, or any of the other myriad of Buddhist traditions in existence across the globe.

Siddhartha Gautama was the man known as "the Buddha." This is not to say that he is the only Buddha in history; he is simply regarded by Buddhists as the founder of Buddhism, as the first compassionate teacher of the truth. Siddhartha Gautama was a prince in what is today the region of northern India or Nepal. Born to King Shuddhodana and Queen Maya of the Shakyas in the 6th century, BCE, the young prince is said to have declared even while still an infant, "For enlightenment I was born, for the good of all that lives. This is the last time that I have been born into this world of becoming" (Conze, 36). The first part of his life was spent in palace luxury under the watchful eye of his father who, frightened by a prediction at his son's birth that Siddhartha would not become king but would instead become a great teacher, provided his prince with a life that would discourage curiosity about the outside world, a life in which suffering was hidden. But the prince's curiosity prevailed, and upon seeing the world outside the palace walls, a world filled with sickness, old age, and death, Siddhartha became an ascetic and began his journey to discover the truth of the universe and the end to suffering. He operated within a context assuming *karma*, "action" or the law of justice in the universe, and *samsara*, the *karma*-driven world of death and rebirth. One can think of this Indian-origin worldview as a great, cosmic engine of life: if *samsara* is the engine of birth, death, and rebirth, then karmic action is its fuel. All actions, good or bad, must return to the individual who performed them. Thus, it is *karma* itself that causes rebirth. Siddhartha Gautama, then, sought an end to rebirth. The assumptions are not very different than those found in Hindu thought, but the man who would become the Buddha would draw dramatically different conclusions about the nature of the self than did his Hindu counterparts.

The teachings of the Buddha, collectively called the *dharma*, are also known as the "Middle Way," an acknowledgment that extremes do not illumine truth. A life of royal luxury—one extreme—did nothing to lead the seeking prince to any truth, nor did a life of severe asceticism reveal reality to him. Between the extremes of luxury and severity, Siddhartha Gautama gained enlightenment. His title, "Buddha," comes from the Sanskrit word for "to awaken." The Buddha is thus one who has "awakened" to the truth, one who possesses a deep insight into reality itself. The fruits of his meditations upon the nature of reality are the Four Noble Truths, the most fundamental of Buddhist teachings. They begin with an assertion. First, life is suffering. That is to say, life in *samsara* is fraught with unhappiness, and even when one has found something pleasurable in life, that enjoyment only leads to further displeasure. For when we wrongly assume that the pleasure will satisfy, we find it only fades away. The second truth is that of craving or desire. The craving one feels for further pleasures is worsened by the fact that no pleasure is lasting. As a result, we wander hungrily from one thing to the next, or one idea or person to the next, searching for happiness that does not come in lasting form. Third, the Buddha tells us that there is an end to suffering, *nirvana*. *Nirvana* is a "blowing out" from *samsara* and refers to an end to rebirth, to life itself. Thus, there is a way out of the suffering, a liberation from the life of craving and desires. The path to *nirvana*, the end of life, is the Eightfold Path to enlightenment, the fourth truth. Author Walpola Rahula likens the Buddha to a physician who diagnoses an illness and prescribes a cure: the symptom of life is pain, suffering; the diagnosis or cause of this pain is craving. The prognosis for us is good, however. The Buddha assures us that there is an end to suffering; he prescribes a mode of living that minimizes the earning of more *karma* and that can eventually lead to *samsara's* end. The eight prescriptions are right understanding, right thought, right speech, right action, right livelihood, right effort, right mindfulness, and right concentration. This Eightfold Path reflects three major virtues for the person to cultivate: right understanding and thought lead to wisdom. Right speech, action, and livelihood lead to correct ethical conduct. Right effort, mindfulness, and concentration lead to honed mental abilities vital to the primary Buddhist religious practice, meditation. It is through meditation that the Buddhist practitioner can focus on reality, cut through the illusions of craving and desire, and find enlightenment and liberation.

Key to the Buddhist view of reality are the concepts of impermanence, emptiness and *anatman* or "no-self." Impermanence and emptiness describe the state of the world. Nothing lasts. The tallest of mountains will crumble, and the mightiest of rivers will change course and become dry. All things then are empty of inherent existence. What exists is only a series of connected moments in time, all in flux and possessing no stability or permanence. In Buddhist thought, attempting to find a thing in itself, such as a chariot to use the early Indian Buddhist adept Nāgārjuna's classic example, results in the realization that the thing does not exist inherently. A chariot exists on a conventional, mundane level only: we see a chariot and can climb into a chariot. We can attach a chariot to a horse and ride away. But the Buddhist emphasis is that we cannot define the chariot via its parts, shape, or collection of parts. Analysis shows only parts, themselves impermanent, and a shape that does not itself define the object, for a shape of a chariot could be simply a drawing of a chariot, not a functional chariot. In short, Buddhist analysis concludes that all is emptiness.

The self, perhaps the most difficult "object" for a person to deconstruct in this way, is also empty. "No-self" is then the Buddhist truth about the human being. We are impermanent. There is in actuality no "I," no "me." Instead, identity is defined in five constituents of mind and body, what the Buddha called the five *skandhas*, or "aggregates." These are form, feeling, mental discrimination, consciousness, and conditioning factors that include the emotions. Like the parts of a chariot, these parts of a person are changing, impermanent, and empty of inherent existence:

> Where all constituent parts are present,
> The word "a chariot" is applied.
> So likewise where the *skandhas* are,
> The term a "being" commonly is used. (Conze, 149)

In ignorance, we allow ourselves to believe that the self is enduring, perhaps even eternal, when in fact the self is nothing more than a perceived continuity of moments in shifting time. The illusion of self or ego must be overcome, for it is this illusion that wrongly motivates the individual to a life of craving and desire. The Buddha's teachings urge one to find liberation from suffering by recognizing that there is no self to satisfy. There is no ego to feed. To find release from rebirth, one needs only to become enlightened to this basic truth. Meditation is the tool for deep realization of no ego. Looking inward to search for the self reveals that the self does not exist; the attainment of this truth is, again, the highest goal of the Buddhist practitioner.

From this foundational *dharma* of the Buddha, the great diversity of Buddhist traditions is born. Mahāyāna "Great Vehicle" Buddhism is the Buddhism that spread to Tibet, China, and Japan, among other global locations, and Theravāda "Way of the Elders" Buddhism is that which grew from Indian roots to Sri Lanka, Burma, Thailand, and Southeast Asia in general. While the institutions of these cultures may vary, the basic Buddhist tenets do not. Within the Mahāyāna is the Tibetan Buddhist tradition, the Vajrayāna, the "Diamond Way," or "Lightning Bolt Way." Due to its unique tantric character, some scholars and Buddhist practitioners place it in a category all its own.

Buddhism in Tibet

Buddhism found its way onto the isolated plateau of Tibet via silk trade routes stretching between India and China. The slow diffusion of Buddhism from India into Tibet was punctuated by several historical-legendary figures and events. In the 7th century, King Songsten Gampo, influenced by his Buddhist wives from Nepal and China, provided Buddhism with royal patronage, officially sanctioning the tradition and proselytizing for Buddhist truth and practices in Tibet. In the 8th century, the great teacher Padmasambhava, a charismatic yogin according to Tibetan sources, came to Tibet from India and helped to further establish Buddhist doctrine in the formerly animistic culture. In the 15th century, Buddhism had become an integral force in Tibetan education, seen in the establishment and success of the great monasteries, many with thousands of monks, or *lamas*. The monasteries were large, dynamic universities, learning centers for all of Tibet. Also in the 15th century, Buddhism became forever intertwined with Tibetan political history with the appearance of the first Dalai Lama. The Vajrayāna cosmos, like those in other Mahāyāna schools of Buddhism, contains a multitude of *bodhisattvas,* or enlightened beings who are purposefully reborn into *samsara* in order to lead others compassionately to liberation. The long line of Dalai Lamas, the political and spiritual leaders of Tibet, is a bodhisattva lineage. All Dalai Lamas are considered to be one *bodhisattva*, the enlightened Avalokiteshvara, also known in the Tibetan tradition as Chenrezig, who returns out of compassion again and again to the Tibetan people. It is this same line of authority that is embodied today in Tenzin Gyatso, the 14th Dalai Lama who is the head of the Tibetan government in exile now in India.

The line of Dalai Lamas comes primarily from the Gelugpa, or "Yellow Hat" school, one of four main sects of Tibetan Buddhism. The Gelugpa trace their origins to the 15th century and the teacher Tsong Khapa, himself considered to be an incarnation of Avalokiteshvara. Despite the power the Gelugpa enjoyed, it was in reality the latest sect to be founded. The Kargyupa and Sakyapa sects both originated in the 11th century, and the Nyingmapa, or "Ancients," trace their line of authority to an 8th-century yogin. It is to a work attributed to Padmasambhava, the *Bardo Thödol*, that we now turn.

The *Bardo Thödol*: A Tantric Text

Tibetan Buddhism, or the Vajrayāna, is a tradition characterized in part by the esoteric. The word *tantra* comes from the Sanskrit root verb meaning "to extend" or "to spread" and refers to an esoteric way to reach liberation. Tibetan Buddhist tantric practices include an eroticized, ritualistic element. Wisdom and compassion, two prerequisites for Mahāyāna enlightenment, are represented metaphorically by female and male figures, the female embodying wisdom, the male embodying compassion. In Tibetan Buddhism, wisdom and compassion are inseparable virtues, and in Tibetan Buddhist art this nonduality is symbolized by sexual intercourse. Tibetan art forms, often used as tools for meditation, are infused by such strong symbolism. Deities and demons inhabit temporary *mandalas* of sand or butter, or adorn painted silk *thangkas*, all colorful maps of the meditator's imagined path and mind. Some spirits are helpful; others are terrifying monsters who, representing hate, lust, or other hindrances in the person, must be defeated in a metaphorical battle against one's desires. The deeply rich symbolism found in the Vajrayāna points to the same teachings in all Buddhist cultures: there is no self, and desires attached to the imagined, illusory self must be overcome in order to achieve release. The meaningful symbolism of male and female united in sexual intercourse is one to keep in mind, for it is an essential element in the *Bardo Thödol*, the Tibetan Book of the Dead.

It is traditionally held that the *Bardo Thödol* was created by Padmasambhava in the 8th century and rediscovered in the 14th century by a Nyingmapa monk, Karma Lingpa. This makes the *Bardo Thödol* a *terma*, a hidden text in the Tibetan tantric tradition. Its content and ritual function are seen in its name: *bardo* means "between two," or "between state," and *thödol* is "liberation through hearing." The work's title thus refers to a teaching to be heard by those in the intermediate state between one life and the next rebirth, between past and future. But as Tibetan Buddhologist Ngawang Jorden points out, insofar as all lives in *samsara* are between past and future, the *Bardo Thödol* is a teaching for all. While the work is considered uniquely Nyingmapa, it is exemplary of Tibetan tantra in general. In the Nyingmapa and Kargyupa sects of Tibetan Buddhism, the text is part of an extended funeral ritual lasting seven weeks. The teachings are read aloud by a monk to the lingering spirit of a deceased person, but those who are living can listen and benefit, as well.

According to the *Bardo Thödol* the period of 49 days from the moments of death and after is a time of vital importance. In this time the deceased will either find liberation from rebirth or enter *samsara* once again. The words of the *Bardo Thödol* are instruction and comfort through this most difficult rite of passage. The reader does not abandon the dead person: he continues to read as if the deceased has not yet found liberation. The readings from the *Bardo Thödol* guide the dead through three states within the seven-week period; liberation is possible in all three. The states of transition are the *Chikhai Bardo*, the *Chönyid Bardo*, and the *Sidpa Bardo*.

The *Chikhai Bardo* is the "moment of death" state in which consciousness separates from the body slowly. This stage can last up to four days, and traditional Tibetan funeral rites dictate that the body cannot be disposed of before this period ends so that the consciousness may free itself properly from its physical fetters. The ideal method of body disposal is cremation: the finality of this method of disposal leaves no traces of the physical to which the dead person can still be drawn. One rarer, additional method is more dramatic in its lessons of nonattachment and impermanence: the corpse can be butchered and fed to forest creatures and carrion birds, accomplishing body disposal, a visceral education in impermanence, and the earning of good *karma* through the compassionate action of feeding animals. At the very least, yet still in keeping with the effort to discourage attachments to the corpse, the body is placed in a white cloth and left untouched until final disposal by burial or other means. Lamentations over a body are also considered dangerous for the deceased person, as he or she may be confused by the show of attachment in grief and the consciousness may not separate from the body.

In the *Chikhai* state, it is said that a great, clear light shines within an empty void. The light appears bright and strong to the dying or dead person:

> and now thou art about to experience it in its Reality in the Bardo state, wherein all things are like the void and cloudless sky, and the naked, spotless intellect is like unto a transparent vacuum without circumference or centre. At this moment, know thou thyself; and abide in that state. (Evans-Wentz, 91)

The reality referred to here is the clarity of mind that can set the Buddhist practitioner free. Reality is likened to the focused, "spotless" mind and is seen in the empty void of the *Chikhai* stage. It is a void lacking boundaries and is representative of absolute, Buddhist nondualism: there are no boundaries between "self" and other. If the person recognizes this opportunity for liberation, then movement into the next stage will not occur. The end to rebirth will be achieved: "Like the sun's rays . . . dispelling the darkness, the Clear Light on the Path dispelleth the power of *karma*" (Evans-Wentz, 100). The light is true reality of no-self. When no-self is recognized, nonattachment is achieved and *karma* is no longer earned. When *karma* is no longer earned, there is no need for rebirth.

The second stage is the *Chönyid Bardo*, or state of experiencing "supreme reality." The *Chönyid* can last up to 14 days. In this stage, the luminosity of the clear light persists. But powerful images appear. First come the visions of peaceful deities, transforming into frightening, threatening figures. The dead person is instructed to remember these words:

> May I recognize whatever [visions] appear, as the reflections of mine own consciousness;
> May I know them to be of the nature of apparitions in the *Bardo:*
> When at this all-important moment [of opportunity] of achieving a great end,
> May I not fear the bands of Peaceful and Wrathful [Deities], mine own thought-forms. (Evans-Wentz, 103)

The appearing deities are projections of one's own true nature, fears, and desires. The belief is that we make our own heavens and hells from our emotional states and from our minds in general. The dead person is urged, "Be not daunted thereby, nor terrified, nor awed . . . Recognize it" (Evans-Wentz, 104). Despite the distracting visions, enlightenment is possible on this level. The individual can see the visions, pleasant or wrathful, as emanations from his or her own mind and thus recognize the perfections that exist and the faults that must be overcome. The person can conquer the projected images, or the person may call upon enlightened Buddhas for rescue from the horrors and confusions of this state. Liberation is an inwardly achieved goal in most of the Buddhist schools and sects, but here we find that a faithful practitioner asking for grace from the enlightened powers is also a sound option:

> May the Buddhas, exerting the force of their grace,
> Cause not to come the fear, awe and terror in the *Bardo* . . .
> May the assurance of fearlessness be obtained and the *Bardo* be recognized.
> (Evans-Wentz, 149)

The *Chönyid* section of the *Bardo Thödol* states that the lessons of this *bardo* are "the essence of all doctrines" (Evans-Wentz, 152). Clarity of mind is necessary for liberation. All hindrances to this clarity must be removed. As such hindrances are caused by one's own illusions of ego and, relatedly, by one's own desires and perceived temptations, the illusion of the ego is that which ultimately must be conquered. Defeating the hallucinations of the *Chönyid* stage is defeating one's own selfish nature.

The *Sidpa Bardo*, or "becoming" state, lasts for about three weeks. In this stage, the person is drawn to *samsara*, the luminosity of the clear light is faded, and the chances for liberation are greatly decreased. The deceased is "becoming" again and searches for a body. The lama reads to the person who is surely tempted to return to his or her old life:

> Even though thou couldst enter thy dead body nine times over—owing to the long interval which thou hast passed in the *Chönyid Bardo*—it will have been frozen if in winter, been decomposed if in summer, or, otherwise, thy relatives will have cremated it, or interred it, or thrown it into the water, or given it to the birds and beasts of prey. (Evans-Wentz, 165)

The frustration of not finding one's body results in one kind of misery in the *Sidpa* state. Another comes at the appearance of two sides of the person, the good and the evil, who in turn count one's good and evil deeds in life. This is a judgment in which *karma*'s influences and one's next life are determined. Yama, the lord of death in this judgment scenario, appears as a fierce, terrifying executioner, perhaps hacking the person into pieces in his ruling. The *Bardo Thödol* guides the person through this anguish. The dead person is assured once again that the visions seen in the *Sidpa* state are only projections from one's own intellect. The person cannot be hurt, as there is no physical reality here, only emptiness: "Apart from one's own hallucinations, in reality there are no such things existing outside oneself as Lord of Death, or god, or demon, or the Bull-headed Spirit of Death. Act so as to recognize this" (Evans-Wentz, 167). The horrors emanating from the illusion of ego, then, continue to plague the deceased.

Yet near the end of these hallucinations in the *Sidpa* state there is one last glimmer of hope for liberation, even as the person is spiraling down toward *samsara*. Searching for a "womb-door" from which to be born again, the individual sees couples engaged in the act of procreation that allows rebirth into the world for those spirits not yet liberated.

The reader of the *Bardo Thödol* uses this opportunity to guide the person toward a recognition of a father and mother not as an entryway to a womb but as a symbol of enlightenment:

> at this time thou wilt see visions of males and females in union. When thou seest them, remember to withhold thyself from going between them. Regarding the father and mother as thy Guru and the Divine Mother, meditate upon them and bow down; humbly exercise thy faith; offer up mental worship with great fervency; and resolve that thou wilt request [of them] religious guidance. By that resolution alone, the womb ought certainly to be closed . . . (Evans-Wentz, 177–78)

The "guru" and "Divine Mother" in this passage are open to interpretation but are traditionally understood as male and female aspects of the Buddha. In Tibetan Buddhist symbolism, the *yab-yum* image is then brought to mind: the *yab-yum*, or male and female coupled divinities, symbolizes the union of compassion and wisdom. Again, compassion and wisdom are inseparable virtues necessary for a clear, enlightened mind, and the symbol for this nonduality is a male and female in sexual intercourse. This is also the last image seen by the deceased person who has not found liberation in the three stages of death. The cycle of life from conception to death then comes full circle, also within the Tibetan Buddhist symbolic world: as death transforms into life, the very process of entering the world of rebirth can hold the sought-after escape from it. If the dead person sees a *yab-yum* in the figures once considered to be future parents and realizes the Buddhist virtues it represents, then the end of rebirth can be attained.

Still, the chances for liberation from *samsara* are only slight in the *Sidpa* stage. If liberation was not found in the first two stages of death, it is assumed that any person entering the "becoming" state will indeed become reborn into the world of suffering and will be at the mercy of the law of *karma* once again.

Tibetan Traditions in the West

Over 131,000 Tibetan immigrants and transnationals, as well as Tibetan refugees from the Chinese occupation of Tibet, live in exile outside of Tibet's geographical borders. Approximately 4,000 live in western countries such as the United States, Switzerland, and Canada. The Buddhist tradition they bring with them is affected by their new host cultures. Regulations on body disposal, lack of available monks for carrying out rituals, and other issues influence the practice of funeral rituals in the new Tibetan communities. Another impact upon Tibetan tradition comes from western attention. Since Oxford anthropologist W. Y. Evans-Wentz first translated the *Bardo Thödol* into English in 1927, many westerners have taken a keen interest in the *Bardo Thödol*. Exemplary of this interest is the Living and Dying Project in San Francisco, California. The Living/Dying Project, founded in 1977 by Stephen Levine, is now under the direction of Dale Borglum who founded a self-described "spiritually-based" hospice in Santa Fe, New Mexico. The Living/Dying Project offers support for people facing life-threatening illness and for their caregivers. The programs within the Project draw upon sources from many religions, including the Tibetan Buddhist *Bardo Thödol*. In the mission statement of the Living/Dying Project, the focus and main goals of the programs are made clear: the Project encourages and cultivates facing death without fear and using life-threatening illness as an opportunity for spiritual growth. The Tibetan tradition seems ideal for these aspirations, and the text is often read to patients in the Project. The *Bardo Thödol* offers comfort, guidance, and one Buddhist perspective on the human individual's place in a samsaric world of rebirth.

In his commentary on Evans-Wentz's translation of the *Bardo Thödol*, the great psychologist Carl Jung wrote that the *Bardo Thödol* provides an "ultimate and highest truth," namely that "even the gods are the radiance and reflection of our own souls" (xxxix). For Jung, the soul, a western religious concept absent in Buddhism, was shown in the pages of the *Bardo Thödol* to be ultimate reality itself. Jung perhaps can be forgiven for his references to a human soul in an analysis of a Buddhist text, for he likens the concept to mind, or "one's own consciousness," the human psyche. Jung's work greatly influenced further psychological interpretations of the *Bardo Thödol*, most of which emphasize the occurrence of projections from the mind's subconscious: fears, desires, and repressions manifest as demons, deities, or other creatures. But as D. G. Dawe has pointed out, it would be a mistake to conclude that the religious hierarchies of demons and deities found in Tibetan Buddhism can be reduced to mere apparitions or explained away in psychological terms. In the Tibetan Buddhist view, the beings that help define the Vajrayāna tradition's character do not diminish in power or reality when they are recognized as one's inner, true nature and deep-seated flaws. The deities are part of reality and must be dealt with earnestly via ritual and religion, not just by rational analysis, be it psychological or other.

Conclusion: The Tibetan Buddhist Ideal Life and Ideal Death

A story common to all Buddhist traditions is that of Krisha Gotami and the mustard seed. Krisha Gotami was a woman who was overcome by grief at the death of her child and approached the Buddha to beg him to bring her child back to her. The Buddha instructed her to go into the village and return with a mustard seed from any household that had not experienced death. The hopeful woman ran from house to house, looking for the ingredient that would allow the Buddha to perhaps work a miracle for her. But soon the Buddha's lesson became clear: no person, no family is untouched by death. Death is a reality for all. When the woman returned to the Buddha with this realization, she asked him to teach her about life and death. He replied, "If you want to know the truth of life and death, you must reflect continually on this: There is only one law in the universe that never changes—that all things change, and that all things are impermanent." Sogyal Rinpoche, author of *The Tibetan Book of Living and Dying,* cites this story about death and grief as a vital lesson for life: "A close encounter with death can bring a real awakening, a transformation in our whole approach to life" (29). Tibetan Buddhists view death as a chance for awakening to the Buddha's teachings and the reality of no-ego, and as an opportunity for enlightenment, the ultimate awakening. Confronting death also cultivates a joyous appreciation for life. It is as a human being that an individual can best learn of spiritual matters and engage in meditation because human beings have the greatest capacity for focus and concentration. Out of all the existences that can be one's fate in the world of rebirth, human existence is best. And given the infinite possibilities for rebirth, the Buddhist must assume that an enemy in this life was a loved one in another. Thus, even one's enemies are to be treated with kindness and patience. This is particularly meaningful for Tibetans today. Since the occupation of Tibet by China, it is estimated that over one million Tibetans have been killed. The current Dalai Lama calls for Buddhist values in this situation. He exemplified the Buddhist compassionate attitude in his acceptance speech for the 1989 Nobel Peace Prize:

> The basic meaning of compassion is not just a feeling of closeness, or just a feeling of pity. Rather, I think that with genuine compassion we not only feel the pains and suffering of others but we also have a feeling of determination to overcome that suffering . . . I tell our generation we are born during the darkest period in our long history. There is a big challenge. It is very unfortunate. But if there is a challenge then there is an opportunity to face it, an opportunity to demonstrate our will and our determination. So from that viewpoint I think our generation is fortunate (Gyatso, 1990).

The Dalai Lama's words point to opportunity in crisis. One's enemy, or more accurately in Buddhist terms, one's hate, bitterness, or fear toward an enemy offer something beneficial: the opportunity to practice Buddhist values and grow toward enlightenment. The virtuous life for a Buddhist is one of wisdom and compassion: living a life of wisdom according to the Buddha's dharma and of compassion for all living beings. Death's presence can be the impetus for grasping and attaining such virtues in life. As Glenn Mullin writes:

> Once one has developed a solid appreciation of the human potential, it is important to take up meditation upon impermanence and death. In the Atisha tradition coming from Guru Serlingpa of Indonesia, this means practicing meditation upon three subjects: the definite nature of death, the uncertainty of the time of death, and the fact that at the time of death nothing except spiritual training is of any real value. (53–54)

The meditations on death are known as "the three roots" in Buddhism. These foundational meditations have tangible fruits: they force the meditator to confront the reality of death and in turn cultivate an appreciation for our lives as precious opportunities for improvement and, ultimately, for enlightenment.

Those unfamiliar with Buddhist assumptions about rebirth often find the concept of nirvana baffling. Why is the goal of Buddhism an end to life? Would not another chance at life be desirable? But in Buddhism, life in *samsara* is one of repetitive suffering. Would a college student find continual enrollment as a freshman desirable after repeated years in school and repeated graduations? The idea of becoming trapped in such recurring lives is not attractive. Freedom from rebirth is the unmistakable goal. Buddhists do not, however, treat life with disdain. Life is valuable and to be celebrated. This can be seen in the face of the Buddha: typical representations of the Buddha are not of a morose, emaciated figure with contempt for life but of a healthy, vital figure with a smiling, peaceful visage.

In sum, the ideal Tibetan Buddhist life is one led in an acknowledgement of death: all are subject to death, and thus all are equal in death's certainty. Compassion for others flows naturally from this knowledge and is to be extended to all living beings. Wisdom and compassion together comprise the Tibetan Buddhist worldview: life becomes meaningful through practicing kindness and living in the light of the Buddha's noble truths. A good death is one of calm awareness of potential. In a religious tradition of no-self, death is not an end to an individual person but an opportunity for selfless wisdom and compassion, and for liberation, as well.

Glossary

anatman: (Sanskrit) "No-self," or "no-ego." In Buddhism, *anatman* is the denial of a lasting soul.

bardo: (Tibetan) "Between two," or "between state." An intermediate plane of existence between death and rebirth.

bodhisattva: (Sanskrit) In the Mahāyāna Buddhist tradition, the ideal personhood. An enlightened being who remains in *samsara* to guide others.

Buddha: (Sanskrit) An "awakened" being who has attained enlightenment.

dharma: (Sanskrit) The Buddha's teachings. This word refers to "duty" in the Hindu tradition.

karma: (Sanskrit) "Action." The law of justice in Indian-origin religions.

lama: (Tibetan) A monk of the Tibetan Buddhist tradition.

nirvana: (Sanskrit) "Blow out." The end to life in *samsara* and the ultimate goal of Buddhism.

samsara: (Sanskrit) The world of rebirth defined by suffering.

skandhas: (Sanskrit) "Aggregates." The individual person in Buddhism is regarded as five aggregates or parts, themselves changing. This supports the doctrine of *anatman.*

terma: (Tibetan) A hidden text from the Tibetan Buddhist tantric tradition, considered to be authored by a great teacher and rediscovered later.

Selected Bibliography

Conze, Edward, trans. 1959. *Buddhist scriptures.* London: Penguin Books.

Dawe, D. G. 1989. Bardo Thödol. In *The Perennial Dictionary of World Religions*, Keith Crim, ed. San Francisco: Harper and Rowe.

Evans-Wentz, W. Y., trans. 1960. *The Tibetan Book of the Dead*, with a Psychological Commentary by C. G. Jung. London: Oxford University Press.

His Holiness the Fourteenth Dalai Lama, Tenzin Gyatso. 1990. "The Nobel Evening Address." Stockholm, Sweden: The Nobel Foundation.

Mullin, Glenn H. 1998. *Living in the face of death: The Tibetan Tradition.* Ithaca, New York: Snow Lion Publications.

Study Questions

1. The word "Buddha" comes from the Sanskrit for "to awaken." How did Siddhartha Gautama "awaken"? To what knowledge or insight did he awaken and become enlightened?

2. Define *nirvana*. Is *nirvana* a place? Why is the goal of Buddhism to escape *samsara*? How does the Eightfold Path aid one in the escape from *samsara* and from the workings of *karma*?

3. *Anatman* is the Buddhist concept of no-self. How is *anatman* related to Buddhist attitudes and beliefs about death? What lessons do the story of Krisha Gotami and the mustard seed teach us about *anatman* and impermanence?

4. What are the states of transition found in Tibetan Buddhist beliefs about the period between the time of death and rebirth? In what stage is the opportunity for enlightenment best, and why? When is it least likely to occur, and why?

5. How has the Tibetan Book of the Dead been employed in the West? Why has it become so popular and successful?

CHAPTER 9

The Chinese Experience of Death: Continuity in Transition

Amy Weigand

From ancient times until the present, the Chinese people have viewed death as a transition from one mode of existence to another. The transition is a drastic but nonetheless natural event, at least when it closes out the life of a mature woman or man who has married, raised children, and perhaps seen the birth of grandchildren. Fundamentally, the traditional rituals which accompany death mark the transformation of the deceased from a living member of the family to a revered ancestor. The relationships between the deceased and the living change, but continue on. At all times, these relationships are characterized by reciprocal obligations and caring; both the living and the dead continue to depend upon one another for their well-being. There is continuity as well between the world of the living and the realm of the dead. The souls of the deceased inhabit a world which looks and functions very much like the one they left behind.

The theme of continuity in transition also applies to the development of Chinese thinking and ritual practice regarding death and the afterlife. These have been shaped and modified over centuries by changing philosophical, religious, and historical trends. This essay will explore the forms which Chinese ideas and practices with respect to death and the afterlife take in the present, recognizing their roots which reach into thousands of years of Chinese history.

The discussion begins in Part I with an introduction to the four major religious and philosophical strands interwoven over the centuries into Chinese ritual life: "popular religion," Daoism (Taoism), Confucianism, and Buddhism. Each will be briefly described within its historical context. (Of course, Communism is another philosophy which has had a tremendous impact upon Chinese funerary, burial, and post-burial practices—and to some degree upon the beliefs which inform these practices. But given Communism's relatively recent arrival, it will be treated separately in the final section.) Part II will explore the major concepts and concerns which find expression in traditional death-related ritual practices. These practices themselves are described in Part III, with attention to some of the significant regional variations. Finally, in Part IV we turn to the contemporary scene in the People's Republic of China (PRC).

119

Part I: The Religious and Philosophical Traditions of China

The four religious and philosophical systems which have played the most significant role in Chinese history up to the Communist era (1949 to the present) of the PRC are "popular religion," Confucianism, and Daoism—all indigenous to China—and Buddhism, which was imported from India but inscribed with a distinctive Chinese character. Some Chinese people practice other religions, including Christianity and Islam, and some ethnic minorities are Muslim or have their own particular religious forms. But it is the four major traditions which, through mutual influence upon one another over the course of over 2,000 years, have created the ritual expressions of the Chinese experience of death.

The complexity of the interaction of these four traditions has several implications. First, many Chinese people who are not ordained or initiated practitioners of a particular religious group do not identify themselves as "Buddhist," "Daoist," and so forth. They typically engage in practices associated with each of the traditions, according to the purposes to be served, and are not concerned about possible doctrinal inconsistencies. Furthermore, within the traditional funeral ritual of a given Chinese community, it is common for there to be elements which might be identified as Buddhist, Daoist, Confucian, and "popular." Therefore, I will discuss each tradition separately in this section only; elsewhere, specific concepts and practices will be identified with particular traditions only if their origin is relatively clear and if such attribution will make them more readily understandable.

The least well-defined of the traditions of China is the collection of practices and beliefs often referred to for convenience as "popular" or "folk" religion. These may be seen as having origins in religious or philosophical thought which predate the earliest of the established schools, but as continuing to change and develop in interaction with those other traditions. Some ideas which are dominant in the "popular" sphere have ended up as elements of one or more of the formal traditions; this may have been the case with the incorporation of yin/yang[1] as fundamental principles of Daoist cosmology. Likewise, elements from each of the other traditions have made their way into the "popular" religious imagination; the Buddhist notion of rebirth appears to be an example of this dynamic. In practice, it appears that any idea or ritual which shows widespread currency and is not specifically associated with any formal system is designated part of "popular religion."

With respect to funerary, burial, and post-burial practices in China, "popular religion" supplies the general framework of ritual and many of the ideas that inform that ritual. Among the elements of this framework are the general continuity between the world of the living and the realm of the dead, and thus the continuing reciprocal obligations of deceased ancestors and their living descendants. The notion of a dual soul (discussed in Part II) also stems from this "popular religious" source, as do the prevalent ideas about ghosts and the dangers they pose to the living. In addition, some of the "specialists" we will discuss in the next section, including the geomancer (who knows how to assess and manipulate for positive effect the cosmic energies circulating in a given area), the local "funeral advisors," and the spirit mediums might be considered part of the "popular religious" structure.

The spirit world deeply permeates the material existence of the living, according to the traditional Chinese view. Offerings and communication of significant events reflect the importance of such "popular" deities as the god of the stove (who oversees a particular household) and the local Earth god. It is common for a dangerous ghost, such as that of a child, a drowning victim, or a person who died violently, to be managed through deification; i.e., offerings are made, protection is requested, and if the new deity manifests power on behalf of an individual or community, his or her cult begins to grow. The two general methods of communicating with the spiritual realm have ancient roots in "popular" practice: divination is used not only to determine auspicious dates and times for important events, but to consult deities and deceased family members regarding significant decisions or trouble that has befallen the family. Other Chinese interactions with the dead and with specific deities, especially in southern China and Taiwan, feature communication through mediums and "spirit writing."

Confucianism bases its teaching on the actions and ideas of Master Kong (traditionally 551–479 BCE), known in the West as Confucius; he was a teacher who aspired to restore order and harmony to a chaotic political scene through mindful adherence to the behavioral ideals of the golden age of the Zhou (Chou) Dynasty (c. 1040–770 BCE). Although he lived during the 6th and 5th centuries BCE, Master Kong's teachings were not accepted by rulers and high officials of his day. However, beginning during the Han dynasty (206 BCE–220 CE), soon after the reunification of China by the short-lived Qin dynasty, Confucianism as it had been developed by generations of philosophers became the official ideology of the Chinese state. It maintained this status throughout many of the subsequent dynasties, until the fall of the last emperor in the early 20th century. One indication of the extent of the influence of Confucianism and its later expression as Neo-Confucianism is the fact that the examinations which determined eligibility for government positions at all levels were based on books associated with Confucian teachings. This meant that, until 1905, all well-educated citizens were extensively trained in Confucian and neo-Confucian thought.

Master Kong himself is reported to have avoided such questions as the nature of spiritual beings (*Analects*, 7:20), and death (*Analects*, 11:11). His concerns lay entirely with the goodness of an individual's life and the harmony and well-being of the community. However, this does not mean he had nothing to say about how rituals surrounding death and ancestors should be handled. For example, a person exhibits filial piety (an important Confucian virtue) through his or her conduct upon the death of a parent:

> When parents are alive, serve them according to the rules of propriety. When they die, bury them according to the rules of propriety and sacrifice to them according to the rules of propriety. (*Analects* 2:5; Chan's translation, 23)

He also stressed the importance of sincere emotion and attentive participation in the conduct of funerals and offerings to one's ancestors (*Analects*, 3:4,12).

On a very basic level, Confucianism gave special significance to the family as the fundamental unit of society. Who you are is defined not so much as an individual person, but according to your relationships and roles. As we shall see in the discussion of what ritual practices accompany whose deaths, this notion has had a tremendous impact upon how the dead are treated.

Daoism has undergone a much more complex development, and the origins of Daoist thought cannot be traced back to any particular person. The early foundational texts include the *Dao De Jing* (*Tao-te Ching*), also known by the name of its purported but legendary author *Laozi* (*Lao-tzu*), and the *Zhuangzi* (*Chuang-tzu*). There is some debate about the dates of composition and the authorship of both books, but the *Dao De Jing* was probably compiled by 250 BCE, and the *Zhuangzi* during the 2nd century BCE. There are also several less well-known texts which are grouped with the others as articulations of Daoist philosophy. During the 2nd century CE, the first of a number of Daoist religious movements was founded. Today, two of the major groups remain active, especially in Taiwan, where their operation was not affected by the repression of the Communist era in the PRC. The Daoist priests who commonly preside over certain funeral rituals may be affiliated to one degree or another with these religious organizations.

The Daoist classics illustrate clearly the ancient Chinese attitude toward death, which was one of relatively tolerant acceptance; death was viewed neither as unnatural, perverse, nor as punishment by divine mandate. The tale which is almost universally cited as the paradigm for a Daoist response to death is one of many on this theme found in the *Zhuangzi*. After Master Zhuang's wife died, his friend Hui Shi went to visit him, and was shocked to find him squatting on the ground pounding on a pot and singing. When Hui Shi reprimanded him for insulting the memory of his wife, Master Zhuang replied:

> Not so. When she first died, how could I not grieve like anyone would? But on looking back into her beginnings, I saw that she originally had no life, and not only was she without life, she had no bodily form, and not only was she without bodily form, she had no *qi* [*ch'i*]. Scattered amidst the muddle and confusion, a change occurred and there emerged her *qi*, the *qi* changing, she emerged in bodily form, and her bodily form changing, she emerged alive. Now, she has changed again, and has died. This is but to travel together with the passage of the four seasons from one to the next. When she was on the point of taking her repose in the great mansion of the world, I was in a state, trailing after her and howling, but it then occurred to me that this was a failing on my part to understand her circumstances, so I gave it up. (Zhuangzi, 18; Ames' translation, 67)

China first encountered Buddhism just before the beginning of the Common Era, but Buddhist ideas and practices had not pervaded the lives of the common people until the 7th or 8th century. The well-developed Buddhist teachings about "judgment," punishment in a number of hells, and rebirth in one of several realms were integrated into existing beliefs in a way which preserved the general structure of Chinese ritual. Pure Land Buddhism, one of the two Buddhist traditions developed in China and still being practiced today, contributed another possible destination for the soul of a deceased person. It is widely thought that Buddhism owes its survival in China to the Buddhist emphasis on performing rituals for the dead, whether recently deceased ancestors or the forgotten dead. As we shall see in Part III, Buddhist monastics commonly conduct rituals at specific intervals following a death, and also during the Ghost Festival, one of the most important festivals of the Chinese year.

Part II: Key Themes and Concepts

Longevity and Immortality

Long life, prosperity, and an unbroken line of descendants have been the three primary goals of the Chinese since ancient times. In addition, the image of the *xian* (*hsien*) (commonly translated "immortal" or "transcendent") was invoked starting in the Zhou period (800 BCE) to express a longing for some state beyond a long life—and even beyond the earthly realm altogether. Lyvia Kohn, a scholar of Daoism, delineates the two senses which the character *xian* represented: one was long life, even to the point of avoiding death, and the second was a release from conventional life, perhaps through withdrawal into a mountain wilderness or in an ecstatic state (622). The wide range of ideas about what the status of *xian* involves and how one may achieve it includes: the prevention of old age, illness, and weakness, leading to long—and even eternal—life without loss of vitality; a state of mind associated with mystical insight into the *Dao* (*Tao*), source of all that is, and achieved through practices which refine the physical body until it consists only of lighter-than-air *qi*; liberation of the immortal soul through destruction of the physical body by fire; escape from unbearable life circumstances—social and political; a spiritual state in a world beyond death; and rising to Heaven after death (see Kohn, 623–25).

Was the concept of the *xian* and the goal of immortality in tension, or even conflict, with the Daoist ideal (expressed in *Zhuangzi*, for instance) of accepting death as simply one more transformation of things? At any rate, those who sought immortality or transcendence did so through physical and/or psychological practices. Alchemy was a common physical technique, which required the preparation and ingestion of a substance (often poisonous) which would, in theory at least, render the person a *xian*. One might take this step, for example, in response to a summons to assume an official position in the heavenly bureaucracy. Other practices include modification of diet (including abstinence from grains), exercises, regulating the breath, and sexual techniques.

The other category of practice aimed at achieving long life and, ultimately, immortality, works psychologically through meditation and visualization activities. These practices create a tranquil mental state, especially toward one's own death. They may also result in an experience of oneness with *Dao* as the root of all, of joining the cosmic inter-play of *yin* and *yang*, or an altered consciousness, ecstatic flight to other realms, and the joyous transcendence of the limits of both body and mind (Kohn, 631).

The physiological and the psychological aspects of achieving the state of a *xian* are not mutually exclusive. Success in alchemical efforts required attention to one's psychological or spiritual state as well as to the physical transformations of substances. (Indeed, the practice of material alchemy eventually was superseded by the practice of "inner alchemy," a technique of visualization.) Likewise, meditation practice went hand-in-hand with diet, fasting, and physical exercises. An inscription from 329 CE by Daoist practitioners on Mt. Wangwu illustrates the interaction of these efforts. It sketches the steps for refining the body into breath, pure breath into spirit, and finally, pure spirit to union with *Dao*. It also outlines the stages of mystical progress:

> the recognition of the delusions that make up one's everyday consciousness, the attain-ment of a concentrated mind, the arising of insight, and the bodily union with the Tao, which results in eternal life. (Kohn, 627)

As immortality became an obsession during the last century before the Common Era among some segments of the populace, including a number of Han emperors, health and longevity continued to be foundational ideals of Chinese life. Indeed, one could not hope to become a *xian* unless one lived a long life in very good health. In the end, Daoists came to understand the *xian* as one who lived out his or her full natural life span and achieved a psychological experience of immortality through some version of practice. The result would not be avoidance of death, but ascension into a heavenly realm after the body had been shed at death. Thus the theme of immortality within Chinese culture represents a longing for both a particular psychological state in this world and a transcendent state in a paradise realm. The figure of the *xian*—riding on the wind, drinking the dew, pacing the constellations—pervades Chinese literature and imagination. But as we shall see in the following sections, this type of immortality does not appear in the rituals surrounding the deaths of ordinary mortals.

The Dual Soul

The simplest way to describe the traditional Chinese conception of the human soul is as a combination of two portions, called the *hun* and the *po* (*p'o*). They are commonly referred to in English as "souls," but this is not meant to suggest that an individual's iden-tity is "split" on the spiritual level. Rather, the *hun* and *po* are best viewed as two aspects of the person's nonphysical being. The view of the *hun* and *po* forming a "harmonious union" within the body during an individual's life, then separating upon death, became widespread on both the popular and elite levels of society during the Han dynasty (see Yu, 1987).

The *hun* represents the *yang*, active, male aspect of the soul. It directs actions by intention, channels intellectual energy, and experiences the spiritual dimension of life. As a light substance, the *hun* is believed to rise quickly when it leaves the body, and so represents that part of the soul which journeys to the underworld for judgment. It is the *hun* which is eventually reborn into another body.

In contrast, the *po* is identified as the *yin*, receptive, female aspect. It regulates the physical body, including the senses, and is responsible for the movement of all body parts. Because the *po* consists of heavy *yin* substance, it sinks slowly when it leaves the body. This makes it the most dangerous aspect of the deceased, and the community goes to great lengths to insure that the *po* stays with the corpse as it is removed and buried, rather than going astray and causing trouble for the living. It seems fairly clear that the *po* soul would receive the offerings made at the grave during the annual *Qing ming* festival. What is less obvious is which aspect of the soul might be considered to reside in the ancestral tablet (discussed below).

Existence after Death

From as long ago as the Shang Dynasty (traditional dates 1751–1112 BCE), the Chinese have envisioned a conscious existence after death; however, to the ancient mind, this was not an eternal existence. Eventually, the soul would dissipate into primal *qi* and lose its individual identity. Several factors were implicated in the survival of the soul after death: the level of health and nourishment enjoyed by the person when alive; the extent to which the soul's daily needs were met by offerings from its living descendants; and the amount of time it took for the body of the deceased to decay (see Yu, 1987, 378ff.).

Traditional practices up to the present time reflect this sense that the soul is subject to disintegration and that it can be sustained by food offerings as long as the body is intact. For instance, the system of offering food to ancestors is designed to provide them with needed sustenance in the underworld. In addition, some families continue to adhere to the Zhou regulation limiting offerings to ancestors by common people to two generations back (parents and grandparents); alternatively, offerings may be maintained only for ancestors still remembered by living family members. These practices may at one time have been tied to the assumption that the souls of more distant ancestors have already dissolved. Those ancestors who have lost their individual identity are honored collectively on particular holidays.

Although belief in an afterlife has formed part of the Chinese outlook since ancient times, the nature of that existence has changed rather dramatically over the centuries. The earliest descriptions of a realm of the dead picture it as a type of royal court, inhabited by the souls of kings and lords, which survive longer than less prosperous souls. This image then developed into a dark and miserable subterranean destination called the Yellow Springs.

During the Han dynasty, the Chinese government was organized into a vast multilevel structure of departments and officials who administered all the governmental functions of the empire. Accordingly, by the end of the Han, the underworld had been transformed into a counterpart to the imperial bureaucracy. It was composed of four departments of celestial officials whose duties were to keep records of the deeds of the living and to process information regarding the dead. As Buddhism became more generally accepted, the officials of the underworld acquired another function: judgment and punishment of the souls under their jurisdiction. The Chinese adopted the Buddhist idea of a number of courts in Hell; however, those deserving of punishment could be ransomed by offerings of the family to the responsible underworld officials. Souls which were not under a sentence of punishment, along with those who had been ransomed, resided in an underworld realm which mirrored the world of the living (see Watson and Rawski, 180–202).

Rebirth had also by now achieved widespread acceptance, and the soul's stay in the underworld was considered temporary. One of the objectives of the funeral rituals was to ensure a favorable rebirth. According to some, the soul was not reborn until the living no longer had a memory of the deceased (Watson and Rawski, 192). Thus the idea of rebirth was incorporated in a distinctive way by the Chinese, leaving intact the afterlife in the underworld, and the presence of the soul in the tablet and at the grave.

There are a relative few whose destinies do not play out in the manner described above. These are individuals of exceptional merit, who are escorted to the "Western Paradise" or "Pure Land" of Amida Buddha either directly from the first court of Hell or after some period of time in the underworld. These fortunate few will no longer be reborn in a realm of suffering, but will instead progress steadily toward awakening as a Buddha. Messages of condolence, grave flags, and banners carried in funeral processions frequently refer to the hope that the deceased will go to the Western Paradise, and funerals might include rituals by Buddhist nuns or monks designed to usher the deceased into the Western Paradise. However, anthropologist Myron Cohen notes that mainstream "popular religion" operates on the implicit presumption that there is no "salvation" in the form of a paradise or Heaven for the vast majority. This presumption forms the basis for many of the traditional "popular" funeral practices and offerings to ancestors (Watson and Rawski, 187). The family tries to help the soul on its journey to the underworld and through the various courts of Hell by offering food and "spirit money" (paper money of no value to the living, but used in underworld transactions). They also hire Daoist priests to obtain from the gods written orders for the soul's release. In addition, they provide the deceased with objects needed for a comfortable underworld existence, such as clothing and a furnished house. These items are created in exquisite detail out of paper and then burned, along with money for the soul's use.

We now turn to a more comprehensive look at the rituals performed at traditional Chinese funerals in modern times, burial practices, offerings to ancestors, communications with the deceased, holidays involving the dead, and activities designed to deal with the harmful conduct of ghosts.

Part III: Ritual Practice

Many of the descriptions of funeral, burial, and post-burial rituals offered below are taken from anthropological field work in small Chinese communities of mixed economic status. The examination of these topics is limited by the fact that detailed studies of villages in Taiwan and Hong Kong are far more numerous than similar work in the PRC, and most of the fieldwork upon which all of the studies are based was completed in the 1960s and 1970s. Furthermore, it is impossible to generalize about Chinese funerary, burial, and post-burial practices. Discrepancies can be found from one region to the next, not to mention from one village to the next. The most salient differences appear between north and south/southeast China (especially the Cantonese region), and between each of these and Taiwan and Hong Kong. Within the PRC, traditional practices have dramatically declined in urban areas, and have been somewhat curtailed in some rural communities; however, Guangdong province is one region where one might still observe the traditional funeral rituals.

Who receives the full set of funeral and post-burial rituals? Generally, adults who have been married, and often young unmarried men. In some areas, the wealthy are expected to hold lavish funerals, in terms of the number of priests, musicians, and other attendants hired for the funeral, the abundance and type of food offered to the deceased and served to those in attendance, and the elaborateness of the house and other paper items constructed and burned for the benefit of the deceased. An extravagant funeral not only enhances a family's status, but demonstrates filial piety and a focus on the continued well-being of the deceased. On the other hand, poor families frequently cannot afford a tomb, and may resort to leaving the coffin or urn at a temple or other location. Unmarried women often receive a scaled-down version of the rituals, and the death of a child is commemorated with very little ritual.

Regardless of geographical region or historical period, the main concerns represented in traditional Chinese funeral, burial, and post-burial rituals are the same: 1) to show appropriate respect and care for the deceased and to provide for his or her needs in the afterlife; and 2) to protect the living from the immediate dangers posed by the corpse and the newly released soul, as well as from the problems which could result from a dissatisfied ancestor or an unfortunate ghost.

Anthropologist James Watson outlines a general uniform set of funeral rites performed through the late imperial period of China (the turn of the 20th century) and carried on today in Taiwan, Hong Kong, some rural areas of the PRC, and in some overseas Chinese communities (see Watson and Rawski, 3–19). Elements of this set of rites include the use of white to signify death (red is the color of life and luck); white banners are often hung outside the home of the deceased, and mourners wear white clothes, shoes, and head coverings made out of hemp or sackcloth. The fabric and style worn depends upon the specific relationship of the mourner to the deceased. Bathing the corpse—either fully or just symbolically—and dressing the body are also common. Traditional funerals always include the burning of spirit money and paper miniatures of daily objects and even people (servants) for the deceased to use in the underworld. Likewise, offerings of food—especially rice and pork—are universal; the deceased takes in the "essence" of the food and the mourners then feast on it. The burning of incense completes the offerings. Additionally, there is always music—particularly drums, but also pipes or even Western-style brass bands—which serves to settle the soul and to accompany and guide it through the ritual. The corpse is placed in a heavy, airtight wooden coffin, which is then sealed with nails and even caulking. Presumably this assures that decay will be as slow as possible. Finally, the coffin is removed from the village to the burial ground at an auspicious time determined by an expert. The connection of non-family members with the deceased formally ends when the procession passes the limits of the neighborhood or village.

A normal part of the traditional funeral is the creation of an ancestral tablet where the soul will reside. This tablet is a small wooden plaque on which the posthumous name of the deceased is written; after the funeral, the tablet is set on the altar in the home of the deceased. (In modern times, since grown children are more likely to live in a separate home from their parents, the tablet may go to the home of the son or daughter responsible for making the offerings.) Less commonly, tablets are installed in a hall maintained by families of common lineage. An ancestral tablet is not prepared for everyone; for example, children (with exceptions) and strangers who have wandered into the community are not entitled to any offerings, and so do not get tablets. Furthermore, even those who have tablets do not always receive the ritual treatment given to a full-fledged member of the family. This is particularly true of unmarried women; had they married, they would typically have left their birth family to join their husband's family, so they are not considered part of their family of birth. Therefore, their tablet is usually not placed on the altar, but rather in some out-of-the-way corner or in a temple or convent which will accept it.

Traditional funerals require the participation of certain types of specialists, due to the highly technical nature of the rituals and the high stakes involved for the family and community should something go wrong. One category of specialists are paid professionals, such as the priest (Daoist or other) who presides over the funeral; the diviner/astrologer and geomancer who choose appropriate dates and times for the rites and decide on the proper burial site and orientation; the musicians; and in Cantonese funerals, the corpse handlers. The other category consists of unpaid "consultants." These include: local scholars familiar with Confucian doctrine regarding ritualized wailing and other formal behavior expected of mourners, mourning clothing, offerings to the deceased, rituals for giving and receiving condolences, and so on; and elders looked upon as funeral specialists, who keep an eye on the progress of the funeral rituals, offer advice, and correct any mistakes they perceive (Watson and Rawski, 62–63, 117).

Written descriptions of 19th and 20th century funerals in north China include additional elements (see Naquin in Watson and Rawski, 37–68). Not only is news of the death communicated to the local community, but a delegation of mourners goes to inform the local gods as well. After the coffin is sealed, ideally on the third day after the death, a set of rituals is performed to ensure that the soul remains with the body rather than roaming about wreaking havoc. The removal of the coffin from the house is often followed immediately by burial, but not always. If the family has the means to store the coffin, it may choose to do this—even for decades—perhaps to find a suitable burial site, or for the convenience of burying spouses together. At the gravesite following burial, the family makes offerings of food and incense to the deceased and to the god of the soil for that location.

One additional category of specialist is mentioned in the accounts of northern funerals: Buddhist monks and Daoist priests are traditionally called upon to perform rituals to benefit the *hun* soul. They come to the house of the deceased to "do the sevens," chanting scriptures every seven days for up to 49 days after the death. It is hoped that this practice will ease the soul's suffering and guide it through the Hell realm. If monks or priests are not available (which is a common situation in many areas of the PRC today), people seek assistance from lay Buddhists or Daoists living in the community.

One major distinction between northern and southern China (including Taiwan, Hong Kong, and the Cantonese generally) is the southern practice of second burial. The body is sealed in the coffin initially (although in some areas the seal is broken before burial to facilitate decomposition) and then buried. After seven to ten years, the skeleton is exhumed, and the bones are cleaned and arranged in a ceramic pot. The pot is placed either at the original grave site or elsewhere; it may or may not be reburied in a permanent tomb.

A distinctive feature of the Cantonese approach to death is the intense concern with death pollution, generated by contact with "killing airs" released by the corpse. Although death is seen as a natural event in many instances, one of the consequences of death is the release of "vital biological forces," which are dangerous if not controlled by reabsorption into the flesh of the living (Watson and Rawski, 114). If this does not happen, the soul of the deceased will never be at peace. These "killing airs" come from the flesh, which is *yin*, and not from the bones, which are *yang*. Men are considered most endangered by exposure to a corpse, as this harms their *yang* energy and results in increased susceptibility to debilitating disease. For this reason, men only attend funerals when required to by family obligation. Women, on the other hand, being imbued primarily with *yin*, are relatively immune to the permanent effects of death pollution, and so are usually the ones who attend funerals on behalf of their families.

Cantonese communities send family representatives to participate in funerals. These individuals, along with the relatives of the deceased, are responsible in part for absorbing the dangerous vital forces from the corpse. But because the mourners as a group cannot take on all this pollution, the family pays others to accept it; in the eyes of ordinary people, this is one function of ritual professionals like the priest, musicians, and corpse handlers. (Of course, these specialists do not accept that interpretation of their exchange of services for money.) Therefore, Cantonese funeral specialists endure varying degrees of marginalization by the communities which employ them. The most unfortunate are the corpse handlers, who wash and prepare the body for burial. They are employed directly by the coffin shops, where they often live and eat together, since they are completely ostracized and frantically avoided by everyone else (see Watson and Rawski, 112–14, 124–26).

People in all regions of China honor their ancestors by offering food and burning incense and spirit money on particular days throughout the year. These occasions include the anniversary of death and the *Qingming* (literally "clear and bright") festival. Offerings made on the anniversary, like other offerings presented on the altar in the home or in the ancestral hall of the lineage, consist of cooked foods which the people ordinarily eat, although perhaps with more meat and delicacies. After the offering ritual, the family and guests share the food among themselves. The practice of making offerings to ancestors is intended to convey respect, to provide for the needs of the ancestor in the underworld, and to insure the continued good will of the ancestor toward his or her descendants. It is said that an ancestor who is dissatisfied with the treatment he or she receives may resort to instigating trouble, such as illness or misfortune, in order to get attention.

On the springtime holiday of *Qingming*, families go together to the graves of their deceased relatives. There they weed, rake, and sweep the site before making offerings of dried foods (mushrooms, tofu, noodles, meat, or fish), and perhaps steamed buns and cakes, as well as burning incense and spirit money. Explanations for the difference in the food presented at the grave in relation to the domestic altar vary. Anthropologist Emily Ahern theorizes that the greater the difference felt to exist between the living and the being to whom food is being offered, the less like ordinary cooked food the offering will be. Since the soul at the grave is associated with the corpse, which is feared even when confined in the Earth, the feeling of familiarity and safety which characterizes offerings in the home or hall is absent at the grave (167–74).

The rituals we've discussed up to this point have presupposed that the person who died was a married adult with offspring who would provide for his or her well-being after death. Obviously, not everyone who dies fits this description, and there are various methods and ritual practices designed to address these situations and limit the potential for harm to the living. One common practice for adult men who do not have any children is to "adopt"—preferably a son—by bequeathing property or money to a nephew or another individual in the next generation in return for a promise to make offerings to him (and his wife) as an ancestor. Such "adoptions" can even be done posthumously. At any rate, families often support childless couples with offerings; this recognizes their other contributions to the family and the fact that they had the potential to produce descendants for the lineage. They receive offerings with other ancestors on certain holidays, such as the New Year.

Of those who die without descendants, children and unmarried women are least likely to receive offerings from the living. An infant or small child who dies is presumed to have been not a true child of the parents, but a malevolent spirit or the reborn soul of someone to whom the parents owed a debt. This "creditor" lives off the family until the debt has been satisfied, then dies. The family at that point has no further responsibility to the soul of the child. If, however, some misfortune is interpreted as caused by the deceased child, the family will be inclined to recognize the child as one of their own, and thus a proper recipient of offerings (if a boy) or of some form of appeasement (if a girl).

An unmarried woman may receive offerings once in a while from her family. If her tablet is housed in a temple, she may also partake of the offerings of patrons. One other method some Chinese communities have developed to prevent the souls of their dead female children and unmarried daughters from becoming hungry and homeless ghosts who may disrupt the health or prosperity of the living is to arrange a marriage for them after they die. A living bridegroom is found either by the offering of a substantial dowry, or by other forms of "persuasion" by the deceased bride herself (e.g., the ghost may inflict illness upon her chosen spouse or a member of his family). The nature of the ghost's wishes is often conveyed through a medium. When the typically reluctant groom agrees to the arrangement, a modified traditional wedding ceremony is performed, sometimes with a figure dressed as a bride representing the ghost. None of the usual ties between the families of married couples follow from "spirit marriage," and the husband is free to marry a living woman if he has not already done so. The purpose of the wedding is to create an obligation for the groom's family to place the deceased bride's tablet on their domestic altar and make offerings to her as an ancestor (see Jordan, 140–55).

The special time of year dedicated to providing for the multitude of wandering ghosts of the uncared-for dead comes in the 7th lunar month, during which all souls are released by the underworld authorities to enjoy the offerings given by the living. The high point of the month is the 15th day, the Feast of the Hungry Ghosts, when people offer an abundance of food both to their ancestors and—outside their homes—to the hungry ghosts. The ghosts' food consists of uncooked grains, raw fruits and vegetables, and uncooked meat. Large community events are common on this day; these feature chanting and rituals by Buddhist or Daoist priests, the burning of incense, spirit money, and paper clothing for the ghosts, and opera performances.

How do the living know what ghosts want? Many Chinese today continue to employ longstanding techniques for communicating with the dead and even visiting the underworld. For instance, when a person experiences an unexplained illness or suffers a reversal of fortune, he or she may take the problem to a local medium, through whom a deity or a dead relative may be consulted. This is one way to learn that a child who died a generation ago is insisting upon recognition as a family member, or that a deceased unmarried daughter is demanding a husband. In Taiwan, a common technique for such consultations is the "divination chair." Two men, who are illiterate, grasp the legs of a small chair, and the deity or ghost who is sought takes control of the chair and quite emphatically traces written characters on the surface of a table. Each character is read by a designated person, assisted by observers. A correct reading is confirmed by the chair striking the table once.

Another way to make contact with the realm beyond death is to visit the underworld or send someone on your behalf. Skilled individuals can induce a trance in other persons and guide them to the underworld, where they may seek out relatives or souls whom others have asked them to check on. The living often want to see their parents or a family member who died prematurely. Only those remembered clearly by the living are encountered in the underworld, since otherwise they are viewed as having reached their time of rebirth (Ahern, 236–37).

Part IV: Rituals for the Dead in the People's Republic of China

The traditional Chinese rituals and ways of approaching death have undergone dramatic revision since the beginning of the 20th century, and especially since the 1949 revolution and institution of the Communist government of the PRC. (See Whyte in Watson and Rawski, 289–316.) The Communist Party's attitude toward "popular" and Daoist religious expressions has been one of suspicion toward what it terms "superstitious" beliefs and practices. The government complains about the wastefulness of traditional funeral and burial practices in terms of land for burial, wood for the heavy coffins, manufacturing capacity dedicated to producing incense and spirit money, and the like. As a result of government campaigns which forced Buddhist and Daoist monastics back into lay life, especially during the Cultural Revolution, there is a relative absence of these ritual specialists in many areas of the country.

In place of traditional funeral rites, the Communist Party's preferred way of dealing ritually with death is for family and friends to pay their last respects to the deceased (in a room set aside in the hospital or at the funeral home) and then to attend a "memorial meeting" before or after cremation of the body. A memorial meeting consists of an audience assembled in a hall in the funeral parlor, where attendees listen to eulogies in honor of the deceased, usually delivered by leaders in the deceased's work unit. These should stress the contributions he or she made to society. After the eulogies, those attending stand in silence, then bow and file out—perhaps stopping to express condolences to the immediate family. There are no references to spirits, ghosts, or the hereafter, no food offerings and no burning of ritual items; expenditures are minimal (Watson and Rawski, 295).

The ritual of the memorial meeting shifts the emphasis away from the deceased's place in the family lineage, and instead focuses on who the individual person was and what he or she had accomplished. What is important is no longer gender, marital status, whether one has any children, and thus what one's status in the afterlife will be, but rather the contribution one has made to society, especially through the workplace. Also, under this ritual framework, the work unit replaces the family as the fundamental organizational unit of urban society (Watson and Rawski, 309).

How successful has this aspect of ritual reform been? A change in practice is much more evident in urban areas than rural. However, while rural funerals are typically still traditional, they have been simplified to a large degree. Some city-dwellers hold private religious rituals in their homes to honor the deceased. They may maintain some form of ancestral shrine where offerings of food, incense, and paper items are made on holidays and anniversaries. Most, however, simply commemorate the dead as officially called for, rather than engaging in ritual offerings.

Disposal of the body is another focus of reform in the PRC. Cremation has met with varying degrees of official and popular acceptance or rejection since it was introduced as an option by Buddhism. At the beginning of the Song dynasty (960–1297), for example, cremation was outlawed for the first time, and there is evidence that it had become by then a common practice across China. It cannot be inferred, however, that cremation has ever been preferred rather than simply accepted as an alternative to burial. The poor, especially those in cities, seem to have opted for cremation more readily than the affluent, probably because they could not afford land. Wealthier families sometimes chose cremation, again for practical reasons such as the difficulty of burying coffins in some regions, or because relatives had died far from home and transportation of the body would be too burdensome. Those who had a choice might opt for cremation of a childless relative, who would not have been the focus of offerings by descendants, but choose to bury their own parents. Confucians denounced the practice of cremation from the outset, calling it unfilial and a barbaric desecration of the body (See Ebrey, 1990).

The government policy in the PRC advocates cremation while actively discouraging burial. Again, this policy has been more influential in the cities; some contributing factors include the general absence of coffin shops in urban areas (a consequence of the Cultural Revolution), the unavailability of burial land, and the difficulty and cost of transporting a body some distance for burial. But only cities and county seats normally have cremation facilities, so only city-dwellers, suburbanites, and others in the vicinity of a crematorium have that option in the first place (Watson and Rawski, 304).

The ashes of a cremated body are either buried in a cemetery, taken home, or deposited in a funeral parlor or cemetery, from which they will be disposed if not claimed within several years. For the *Qingming* festival, relatives often visit the cemetery or request the ash boxes they have left in repositories, in order to observe a moment of silence or place flowers next to them. Offerings of food, spirit money, or incense were frowned upon (Watson and Rawski, 296). However, since the government reform movement of the late 1980s, it is reportedly much more common for traditional gravesite rituals to be performed before the remains, wherever they may be.

In modern-day China, especially in the PRC, continuing traditions exist side-by-side with relatively rapid transformation in the ways people think of and deal with death. And in just the way that the *yin* begins to ascend at the moment that the *yang* reaches its peak, it seems as if the old traditions may be reviving among a generation of Chinese who have known only the newer rituals. We have observed how the Chinese culture has for many centuries adapted to and integrated new ideas about death and the afterlife, while continuing to uphold the fundamental goals of longstanding practices: to show respect and provide for the well-being of the ancestors while maximizing the prosperity and vitality of the family. Along the way, the Chinese have developed ritual responses to a variety of perceived problems generated by death itself, the status of the deceased, and the circumstances of the souls in the underworld. Time alone will tell how the more recent transformations brought on by the Communist Revolution and the current emergence of the PRC into global prominence will impact either the rituals surrounding death or the ideas which inform and shape them.

Note

1. Chinese words and names are romanized here according to the *pinyin* system. For those terms which are widely familiar in their Wade-Giles version, that form is given in parentheses after the first mention of the word. All Chinese terms are listed in the glossary.

Glossary

hun [the *u* is pronounced like the *oo* in "hood"]: the *yang* aspect of the soul; it departs quickly from the body and goes to the underworld, where it is judged, then resides until its eventual rebirth.

po (*p'o*): the *yin* aspect of the soul, which remains near the body and under certain circumstances may become a troublesome ghost.

qi (*ch'i*) [pronounced *chee*]: In its primary sense, the breath, energy, vital substance, or life force which permeates the cosmos, circulating through and around all living beings.

Qingming [pronounced *chingming*]: The Clear Brightness festival, celebrated two weeks after the vernal equinox (usually around April 5). It features visits to the graves of family members for sprucing up and offerings.

xian (*hsien*) [pronounced *shee-en*]: immortal or transcendent being.

yin/yang: From ancient times, two of the principle energies of the cosmos, whose cyclic, complementary action generates the seasons; *yin* is associated with the dark and cold, and *yang* with the light and warm. During the Han (1st century BCE) the pair became linked with gender terms (*yin*/female, *yang*/male) in hierarchical relationship (*yang* superior), and then came to correspond to a set of other polar terms, such as weakness/strength, death/life, and yielding/firmness (see Raphals, Ch. 6).

Selected Bibliography

Ahern, Emily M. 1973. *The cult of the dead in a Chinese village*. Stanford, Stanford University Press.

Ames, Roger T. 1998. Death as transformation in classical Daoism. In *Death and Philosophy*, Jeff Malpas and Robert C. Solomon, eds. London and NY: Routledge.

Chan, Wing-tsit. 1963. *A source book in Chinese philosophy*. Princeton, NJ: Princeton University Press.

Ebrey, Patricia. 1990. Cremation in sung China. In *The American Historical Review* 95(2) (April):406–428.

Graham, A. C. 1989. *Disputers of the Tao*. Chicago: Open Court.

Jordan, David K. 1972. *Gods, ghosts, and ancestors: The folk religion of a Taiwanese village*. Berkeley: University of California Press.

Kohn, Livia, ed. 2000. *Daoism handbook*. Leiden, The Netherlands: Brill. Eternal life in Taoist mysticism. In *Journal of the American Oriental Society*, 10(4) (Oct.–Dec. 1990):622–640.

Loewe, Michael. 1982. *Chinese ideas of life and death*. London: George Allen & Unwin.

Orzech, Charles. 1996. Saving the burning-mouth hungry ghost. In *Religions of China in Practice*, Donald S. Lopez, ed. Princeton, NJ: Princeton University Press.

Raphals, Lisa. 1998. *Sharing the light: Representations of women and virtue in early China*. Albany: State University of New York.

Stepanchuk, Carol, and Wong, Charles. 1991. *Mooncakes and hungry ghosts: Festivals of China*. San Francisco: China Books and Periodicals.

Watson, James L., and Rawski, Evelyn S., eds. 1988. *Death ritual in late imperial and modern China*. Berkeley: University of California Press.

Wolf, Arthur P., ed. 1974. *Religion and ritual in Chinese society*. Stanford: Stanford University Press.

Yu, Ying-Shih. "O Soul, Come Back!" A Study of the Changing Conceptions of the Soul and Afterlife in Pre-Buddhist China. *Harvard Journal of Asiatic Studies* 47(2) (Dec. 1987):363–395.

"Life and Immortality in the mind of Han China" *Harvard Journal of Asiatic Studies* 25(1964–1965):80–122.

Study Questions

1. What are the traditional goals or concerns of the Chinese when it comes to handling death, and how do particular practices meet those goals?
2. Describe the relationship between the world of the dead and that of the living.
3. Chinese funerary rituals provide for a variety of possible after-death experiences. Describe several of these, and explain how the living try to help the deceased with regard to each experience.
4. Why do problems with ghosts arise, and what steps might a Chinese family or community take to deal with them?
5. How have the policies of the Communist system affected what people in the People's Republic of China do when someone dies?

CHAPTER 10

Death and Dying in Japan

Pamela D. Winfield

Introduction

In order to understand Japanese views of death and dying, one must first understand the synthetic nature of Japanese religion as a whole. Japan has traditionally prided itself as Asia's great synthesizer; combining Taoist, Buddhist, and Confucian influences from the Asian continent with its own Shintō naturalism. Later, waves of Euro-American missionary activity added Christianity into the mix. The result is a hodge-podge of cultural forms that is simultaneously derivative of the mainland and unique to the island archipelago. Japanese beliefs in heavens and hells, for example, are consistent with continental ones, but ghost stories involving the fallen warriors of the Heike clan are noteworthy for their classically Japanese flavor.

On the surface, this combination of Shintō, Taoist, Buddhist, Confucian, and eventually also Christian thought may appear to be confusing, or at the very least, self-contradictory. Shintōism technically abhors any impurity or pollution associated with death. Religious Taoism however, strives toward immortality and the incorruptibility of the deceased. Buddhism officially teaches that there is no soul (*anātman*) that survives death. Confucianism, however, teaches that one should revere one's ancestors long after they are in the grave. How then, can these religious ideals co-exist in one place or in one individual? How can one reconcile a religion that detests the defilement of dead bodies with another that immortalizes and even mummifies the body? How can one reconcile one religion that cremates the body with another that buries and reveres the dead ancestor's body? And how can any of these co-exist with Christian doctrines about the soul's heavenly afterlife?

To answer these questions, we must remember several factors. First, we must relax our strict definitions of what it means to be religious in Japan. To paraphrase a proverbial saying, the Japanese see no problem blessing their babies at Shintō shrines, getting married in Christian churches, and then burying their dead in Buddhist temples. It is fine for each religion to function differently at different stages in life. Moreover, as we shall see, different religious ideas about death and dying have been popular at different times in history.

high above the city lights. The exact meaning of these burning outlines has been lost over time, but some speculate that they speak to the medieval fusion of Shintō and Mahāyāna Buddhist thought in Japan. This is known as *ryōbu shintō* (both Buddhism and Shintō) or the *honji suijaku* system (in which source bodhisattvas are considered to be the "original ground" for the *kami's* "local manifestation." During Obon the spirits are entertained with several days of specially prepared vegetarian foods (*shōjin ryōri*), the company of reunited families, and *Bon-odori* dancing in the town square every evening. After three days of celebrations, the annual visit by one's departed ancestors is over. The bonfires are lit again to signal the end of Obon, and spirits are ritually seen off so they can happily return to the abode of the dead. In some areas, this involves the enchanting spectacle of floating paper lanterns at night. Each family prepares a reed and paper lantern with the ancestor's *kaimyō* posthumous Buddhist name written on it. A candle is placed inside to help light their way back to the ancestral realm, and the lantern is carefully launched down a stream or river. The miniature flotilla of hundreds of glowing lanterns, each representing an individual ancestor, drifts out to sea accompanied by traditional *taiko* drumming and soulful flute music. Obon is a perfect example of how Buddhist, Confucian, and Shintō elements in Japan have combined over time to help honor the dead.

Into the Modern Period (17th Century–Present)

The modern period saw the continued presence of these religious views about death and dying. Buddhist monks continued to perform the typical three- to four-day Japanese funeral, chanting *sūtras* for the deceased, conferring the *kaimyō* name for the *ihai* memorial tablet, overseeing the cremation of the body, and interring the remains in the family grave after 49 days. The priests continued to make house calls to home altars or *butsudan* to perform memorial services on the death anniversaries of the departed ancestor, and families continued to pray before the *butsudan* every morning, placing flowers and lighting candles and incense before a Buddha statue and (in the modern period) a photograph of the deceased. They continued to demonstrate the Confucian virtue of filial piety every year at Obon by cleaning the family grave and praying in the ancestor's presence for the continued health and well-being of family members. Life and death continued as they had for centuries, with a few notable exceptions. These were namely the resurgence of Neo-Taoist immortality beliefs and the exposure to Christian beliefs about the resurrection of the body.

In the early modern Edo period (1600–1868), Neo-Confucian thought was declared to be the official state orthodoxy. In remote mountain areas such as Mt. Haguro, however, a significant number of extraordinary mountain ascetics called *yamabushi* practiced a combination of Buddhist and Neo-Taoist austerities. Their ideal was to emulate Kūkai's perpetual *samādhi* and become living buddhas (*sokushinbutsu*, alternately pronounced *miira*). In order to obtain such incorruptible, immortal bodies, they abstained from eating the five grains, lived only off of dew and what the trees provided (*moku-gyō*), subjected their bodies to extreme temperatures, chanted *sūtras* under freezing waterfalls (*taki-gyō*), and voluntarily suffered a wide range of other rigors. They essentially became walking corpses, even wearing the traditional white pilgrim's outfit to signal that they were dead to the world (white, or the absence of color, marks death in Japan). Years of self-denial and strict asceticism dessicated their bodies to such an extent that they were already well-prepared for self-mummification. Today the shrunken remains of their 'incorrupt-ible' bodies can still be seen seated in meditation posture, dressed in Buddhist robes, enshrined in the Mt. Haguro/Dewa Sanzan mountain complex. They continue to be wor-shiped there as 'living buddhas' to this day.

Life everlasting was also packaged to the Japanese in a different form by proselytizing Christians as well. When the Jesuit missionary St. Francis Xavier first landed in Japan in 1549, he initially converted many *daimyō* lords to Christianity in the southern island of Kyūshū. His success undoubtedly resulted as much from his promises of trade with Europe as from his promises of the resurrection of the body and life everlasting at the right hand of the Father. Soon, however, news that Catholic Spain had completely colonized the Philippines made the Japanese authorities nervous. They thereafter began to crucify Chris-tians intermittently from 1597 onwards, and finally prohibited Christianity outright in 1640. It is not known whether the self-styled Christian martyrs of this period requested crucifixion or if it was a cruel joke on the part of the *bakufu* government. Regardless, they are the only known cases of crucifixion in Japan, though many others were killed by other means if they refused to apostatize (usually this was determined if they refused to trample on a bas relief *fumie* image of Jesus).

Throughout this early modern period, many underground "hidden Christians" (*kakure kirishitan*) continued to practice their religion in secret. They baptized their babies and buried their dead with modified Christian prayers even as they conformed on the surface to government laws requiring everyone to register with their local Buddhist temple. These registry temples (*dannadera*) were instrumental in constructing the modern role of Japa-nese Funeral Buddhism since most family members preferred that their ashes be buried in the family plot on the cemetery grounds of the temple where they were registered. The grave itself was leased in perpetuity from the temple that owned the land. If the family line died out, the land would revert to the temple and be turned over to a new family to lease. This added to the Confucian pressure on women either to produce progeny or let the entire family down. In the modern period, many women have eschewed this pressure, regardless of the costs involved. At the time of writing, a typical grave plot in Tokyo roughly costs $25,000 to lease. Depending on the size, style, and grade of stone used, grave markers in Tokyo can range from roughly $16,000 to $90,000.

Meanwhile the isolationist policy and strict government laws during the Edo period began to cause societal strains, especially as the economy worsened. Inevitably and on a daily basis, people were confronted with the classic conflict between external duty and internal feelings. Now the old samurai ideal of committing suicide in the face of uncom-promising conflict resurfaced in dramatic form. Chikamatsu Monzaemon's 18th-century

Love Suicides at Sonezaki, for example, tells the tragic tale of two lovers—a *chōnin* merchant and a *geisha* entertainer—whose secret liaison traps them between duty and love. Like Romeo and Juliet, death is the only way for them to remain together forever. As they kill themselves, the characters apologize to their families for their unfilial behavior but chant the *nenbutsu* in the hopes of being reborn together in the Pure Land. Chikamatsu's *bunraku* puppet-play turned Kabuki-drama was so wildly popular at the time that it inspired many desperate couples in real life to kill themselves as well. These copy-cat double love suicides became such a national crisis that the *bakufu* government eventually had to censor the play entirely. *Ukiyo-e* woodblock images of the play, however, were all the rage. *Ukiyo* is originally a Buddhist term that designates 'the floating world,' and images (*-e*) showing this illusory world of life and death were mass-produced to meet the demand during the Edo period.

The grisly reality of such deaths has been routinely glossed over and romanticized throughout history. In addition, the idealized honor of the samurai's ritual suicide by *seppuku* persisted well into the modern period, as individual aficionados of Japan's past attempted to sustain and extend its anachronistic appeal. General Nogi committed *junshi* (following one's lord to the grave) when the Emperor Meiji died in 1912; his *seppuku* is immortalized in Sōseki Natsume's novel *Kokoro* and his shrine still stands in downtown Tokyo today. The spectacular deaths of young, bright *kamikaze* pilots during World War II were likened to *sakura* cherry blossoms in the Japanese wartime propaganda, and the sado-masochistic novels of Yukio Mishima elevated the beauty of death to unprecedented degrees. His astonishing suicide by *seppuku* in 1970 protested the softening of young Japanese forces after their defeat in World War II. Akira Kurosawa's samurai movies have been extremely successful in romanticizing the honor code of Japan's medieval warrior. This idealized image is currently being revised, however, and many now acknowledge that the majority of samurai were indigent mercenary swords-for-hire who would rather flee or try to switch allegiance than take the extreme measure of ending their own lives.

Conclusion

We have seen how cultural expressions of death and dying have historically developed in Japan. Successive waves of foreign religious influence have mixed and melded with indigenous Shintō practice—as well as with one another—to produce a fascinating constellation of funerary practices and beliefs about the afterlife. The combination of Shintō, Taoist, Buddhist, Confucian, and Christian elements throughout Japan's early, classical, medieval, and modern periods has forged a multi-faceted approach to the universal experience of death and dying.

The contradictions still abound; today, it is still not common practice to tell the patient that he or she has cancer; yet families will openly discuss what kind of *butsudan* they want installed in the home after they're gone. Christians are a distinct minority in Japan, yet there are crosses and explicit resurrection imagery in popular modern Japanese *anime* such as Evangelion. Ancient Chinese cosmological notions of the square Earth and round Heaven are long past, but the continued belief in ghosts and the efficacy of spirit pacification still remain. For the average Japanese person, however, the contradictions among or even within religious traditions is of little concern. The theoretical inconsistency of Buddhists believing in spirits or reborn souls is not as important as practically dealing with death when it arrives. In a sense, therefore, the Zen ethos of living in the moment truly has taken hold in Japan. In a sense, we too might consider realistically acknowledging the inevitability of death so as to live life more fully here and now. For as Ikkyū rhetorically asked,

> Since the world is but a brief dream,
> Ought we be surprised at man's evanescence? (Sanford, 204)

Selected Bibliography

Bodiford, William. 1993. *Soto Zen in medieval Japan. Studies in East Asian Buddhism no. 8.* Honolulu: University of Hawaii Press.

Cowell, E. B. (ed.). 1969. The larger Sukhavati-vyuha. In *Buddhist Mahayana Sutras.* New York: Dover Publications.

Hall, John Whitney. 2000. *Japan: From prehistory to modern times.* Rutland, VT: Charles E. Tuttle.

Hisamatsu, Shin'ichi. 1974. *Zen and the fine arts.* New York and Tokyo: Kodansha.

LaFleur, William. 2000. *Liquid life: Abortion and Buddhism in Japan.* Princeton, NJ: Princeton University Press.

Mason, Penelope. 1993. *History of Japanese Art.* New York: Harry N. Abrams.

McCullough, Helen Craig, trans. 1990. *Tales of the Heike.* Stanford: Stanford University Press.

Ohnuki-Tierney, Emiko. 2002. *Kamikazes, Cherry Blossoms, and Nationalisms: The Militarization of Aesthetics in Japanese History.* Chicago: University of Chicago Press.

Reader, Ian. 1991. *Religion in contemporary Japan.* Honolulu: University of Hawaii Press.

Reischauer, A. K., trans., 1930. Genshin's Ojo Yoshu: Collected essays on birth into paradise. In *Transactions of the Asiatic Society of Japan,* 2nd series, 7(1930):16–97.

Sanford, James. 1981. *Zen-Man Ikkyū.* Chica, CA: Scholar's Press.

Scott-Stokes, Henry. 2000. *The life and death of Yukio Mishima.* Lanham, MD: Cooper Square Press.

Tsunoda, Rusaku, Wm. Theodore de Bary, and Donald Keene. 1958. *Sources of Japanese Tradition.* New York: Columbia University Press.

Additional Suggested Works

Fiction

Endō, Shusaku (trans. William Johnston). 1981. *Silence*. Parkwest Publications.

Sōseki Natsume (trans. Edwin McClellan). 1996. *Kokoro*. Regnery Publishers.

Chikamatsu Monzaemon (trans. Donald Keene). 1988. Love suicides at Sonezaki. In *Anthology of Japanese literature from the earliest era to the mid-nineteenth century*, Donald Keene, ed. Grove Press.

Niwa, Fumio (trans. Kenneth Strong). 2000. *The Buddha tree*. Rutland, VT: Charles E. Tuttle, Inc.

Films

Hideaki Anno. 1997. *Neon Genesis Evangelion: Death and Rebirth*.

Hideaki Anno, and Kazuya Tsurumaki. 1997. *The End of Evangelion*.

Juzo Itami. 1987. *The Funeral (Osō-shiki)*.

Masaki Kobayashi. 1964. *Hara-kiri*.

Akira Kurosawa. 2002. *Four Samurai Classics: The Seven Samurai, The Hidden Fortress Yojimbo, Sanjuro*. Criterion Collection.

Study Questions

1. What religious traditions in Japan have influenced death and post-mortem rites? What does each tradition say about the afterlife?
2. Itemize some mythological and historical examples of Shintō death pollution.
3. Describe the basics of the Pure Land attitude toward death. How does this differ from Zen views of life and death?
4. How do the dead and the living continue relationships? What rituals and ceremonies ensure that they do?
5. Describe Japanese attitudes toward suicide.

CHAPTER 11

The Life of the Dead in African and Africa Diasporic Religion

Terry Rey

Je ne sais en quels temps c'était,
je confonds toujours présent et passé.
Comme je mêle la Mort et la Vie—
un pont de douceur les relie.

L. S. Senghor

The dead live in African and African diasporic religion. They are very near to the living and intervene in our lives, sometimes as sustainers, sometimes as annoyers. Everything that we are originates in the ancestors, who gave us life and established how we are to live, thereby making a full, orderly, and dignified human existence for us possible. To them, we are thus deeply indebted, and as such the dead require and expect our veneration. They also require our food, our water, and, as we'll see, our children. Meanwhile, they pester and harm us when we neglect their veneration or commit breeches in the moral order, of which they serve in this fashion as guardians. This reciprocal relationship of living-dead service is central to most of the "traditional" religious cultures of East, West, Central, and Southern Africa, and to the extraordinary African-derived religious traditions of the Americas that not only survived the transatlantic slave trade but thrived and in some cases continue to spread, like Brazilian Candomblé, Cuban Santería, and Haitian Vodou. In this chapter, we will explore notions of life, death, and dying in these religions, describing selected core African religious beliefs and practices and illustrating how they were creatively adapted in the New World.

Sub-Saharan Africa is home to nearly 2,000 distinct ethnic groups, each with its own dialect and culture, thus the risk of generalization that we run in this chapter is unavoidable. To be sure, there are certain ethnic groups who do not venerate the living dead and whose spiritual lives revolve much more around, say, cattle and spears than the ancestors and the spirits that are the focus of cultic life of the vast majority of other African and

153

African-derived religious cultures. The Nuer of Sudan, for example, do not traditionally conceive of the dead as living near to them and/or frequently intervening in their lives. In his classic ethnography of this people, E. E. Evans-Pritchard (1956: 154) writes that in Nuer religion one finds an "almost total lack of eschatology. . . . they neither pretend to know, nor, I think, do they care, what happens after death." When pressed, the Nuer simply explained to the great British anthropologist that the dead return to God (*Kwoth*) from whence they came, and God now owns them, end of story. Ancestor cults are thus largely non-existent in Nuer religion, making it an exception to the general rule that, as Ogbu Kalu (2000: 54) explains, "(t)he reality of the dead-among-the-living attracts so much religious devotion that in many African societies the ancestors occupy more devotional attention than God/Supreme Being."

For the sake of concision, in the first part of this chapter we will analyze ancestral spirituality in the context of the cosmologies and related ritual traditions of two African ethnic groups: one from Central Africa, the Kongo; and one from West Africa, the Yoruba. In light of the broad and transatlantic parameters of this chapter, there are two very good reasons for choosing to focus on Kongo and Yoruba religious cultures: 1) there is extensive scholarly literature available on each; and 2) no other African cultures have been more influential on New World African religion than these. We will further sharpen our focus in each subsequent discussion: for the Kongo case, on cosmology; for the Yoruba, on ancestral performativity. The second part of the chapter then discusses several beliefs and rituals related to death and the dead in New World African religions that are deeply rooted in Yoruba and Kongo worldviews.

The Two Worlds of Kongo Cosmology

The Kongo people (pl. *baKongo*) are one of the largest and historically most powerful ethnic groups of the western region of Central Africa. Today they number roughly three million in an area stretching along the Atlantic coast south to north from Angola to Gabon and eastward across the Kwango River. From roughly 1390 until its fracturing in the 19th century, the Kingdom of the Kongo unified the *baKongo* as one of the greatest "national" communities in Central African history. In 1482, life for the *baKongo* would begin to radically change with the arrival of Portuguese explorer Diogo Cão, who brought, among other things, the Catholic faith. Soon the king of the Kongo, Nzinga a Nkuwu, converted to Catholicism, as did his court, his influential dynastic heir to the throne, Afonso I, and eventually the better part of the population. This mass conversion to Catholicism did not, however, lead to the demise of traditional forms of Kongolese religion, which thrived, on the contrary, in creative synthesis with the imported religion. Key structural similarities between Catholicism and Kongolese religion, including several that are relative to notions of death, made this synthesis especially fluid. For example, Catholic doctrine holds that there is one God who created the universe; Kongolese religion likewise features a monotheistic cosmogony, as *Nzambi* (God) alone created all that exists. And, for another, Catholic ritual practice features a rich stock of ritual paraphernalia (e.g., rosaries, crucifixes, icons, incensories, etc.), as does Kongolese tradition, with its abundant use of amulets, charms, statues, ropes, beads, and the like.

For the purposes of this chapter, the most important structural similarity between Kongolese tradition and Catholicism is that both religions teach that the dead live on in another realm, and that some of the dead (saints in the Catholic context; ancestors in the Kongolese) remain very near to us and can and do intervene in our lives. Given the strength and nature of the indigenous Kongolese ancestor and *bisimbi* (Earth and water spirits) cults and the cosmology that frames them, Catholic saints, who like ancestors are dead and white and would have to traverse waters were they ever to visit the world of the living, resonated quite harmoniously with traditional Kongolese religious notions. Consequently, as Wyatt MacGaffey (1994: 257) explains, for the *baKongo* baptism into the new religion brought by the Portuguese "was understood as an initiation into the powers of a new and improved version of the cult of local spirits," including ancestors.

Kongolese cosmology posits that the universe is divided into two worlds, the world of the living (*nza yayi*) and the world of the dead (*nsi a bafwa*). These worlds are divided by a river (*nzadi*), which humans cross when they die from *nza yayi* to be born as ancestors in *nsi a bafwa*, and which they cross again when they are born (often from *nsi a bafwa*) as the living in *nza yayi*. MacGaffey (1986: 62) refers to this as a "reciprocating universe" wherein "death is seen as a passage in space and time." As in many traditional African cultures, Kongo religion thus features a system of reincarnation. [1] It should be noted here, however, that African systems of reincarnation differ radically from Hindu and Buddhist understandings of *samsara* in that African views on rebirth are not predicated upon any fundamentally negative assumption about the material world; quite contrary to Buddhist and Hindu soteriologies, in which the avoidance of rebirth in this world is the ultimate religious objective, African systems of reincarnation understand this, *nza yayi*, to be the best of all possible worlds, and rebirth here is a very good and highly desirable thing. As A. O. Echekwube (1987: 19) puts it, the African "understanding of reincarnation cannot be regarded as negative, promising nothing but an endless and hopeless cycle of life. Instead, it is full of meaning and it is purposeful."

The cycle of one's life, death, and rebirth are symbolized in Kongolese religious thought as the 24-hour cycle of the sun's and moon's risings and settings, which, once traced, form a complete circle uniting the counterclockwise motion of the sun and the moon. The rising sun symbolizes our birth in this world, *nza yayi*, which in equatorial Africa happens throughout the year at or around 6:00 A.M. As we mature toward adulthood, having undergone at some point initiation into maturity, which is the most important rite of passage in African religion, we reach high noon. Here we are at the peak of our physical strength as human beings in *nza yayi*; as such, ideally we now own and till land, hunt and/or fish, are married, and have children. Then we become elders, beginning our inescapable descent toward sunset, our death out of this world. Here we cross the river, at 6:00 P.M., to rebirth as ancestors in the land of the dead, *nsi a bafwa*, this rebirth symbolized by the rising moon in the new evening sky.

Though located across the river from our world, the dead live in a land that is spatially and temporally conflated with *nza yayi*. There is a vague understanding among the *baKongo* that the dead awaken at night while the living are asleep, occupying the same worldly space, hence the world of the dead is a dark world that is colder and far less comfortable than the warm, light realm of *nza yayi*. It is for this reason that morning mists in the Congo are sometimes referred to as the smoke from the extinguished "cooking fires of the dead" (MacGaffey, 1986: 48), who, when the living in the morning awaken, retreat either into the forest or under or across the water to return to their own sleep.

Whether in the forest or across or under the water, the ancestors are white, and the color white is used to symbolize their world, *nsi a bafwa* (also called *kalunga*), which the *baKongo* sometimes simply call *mpemba*, "chalk," because of this whiteness. The river, meanwhile, is symbolized by the color red, the color of blood as well as the sky at the transitional moments between life and death at sunrise and sunset. A classical case of the African color triad of white, red, and black is rounded out by virtue of the fact that the reborn ancestor in *nza yayi* sheds her white skin—like a snake, as is said in Africa—and takes on new black skin like everyone else alive in *nza yayi*. [2]

Upon entering *nsi a bafwa*, one who just died is literally reborn as an ancestor but remains an integral member of the community of the living, though now from the other side of the river. From this 6:00 P.M. moment of death from *nza yayi* to birth in *nsi a bafwa*, the ancestor begins a decent toward midnight, which is the peak moment of her existence in the hereafter. At this point any one of five things can happen: 1) through the veneration of the living, the ancestor can begin to make her way back toward the river and a 6:00 A.M. death as an ancestor and rebirth as a living member of the community in *nza yayi* (This is the most desirable of the five possibilities.); 2) the ancestor can simply cease to exist, in large part due to a lack of descendants in *nza yayi* or a lack of veneration among her living descendants (This is the least desirable of the five.); 3) a neglected and angry ancestor can become a flying insect or small winged animal who torments ungrateful or immoral descendants in *nza yayi* by raiding the village at night and eating the souls of children; 4) a human ancestor can become a lizard; or 5) the dead can die again in *nsi a bafwa* and thereby be transformed into water or Earth spirits (*simbi*; pl: *bisimbi*) in *nza yayi* (MacGaffey, 1986: 77).

Ancestors invariably desire to return to *nza yayi*, and they are almost entirely dependent upon the living to get back here. For one thing, it is our veneration of the ancestors— in speaking about them, in decorating and maintaining their graves, in feeding them, etc.—that keeps them alive. And for another, doors through which the ancestors can return are only opened when we have children. Here is another way in which African systems of reincarnation differ radically from Buddhist and Hindu systems, in which a soul transmigrates into a variety of life forms, including the animal and the vegetal. In African systems, generally speaking, a departed human soul (or part of the soul or one of an individual's two or three souls)[3] can only reincarnate into a human body; furthermore, the human soul only reincarnates into a human body of its own lineage or kinship group. This explains physical resemblance of children to ancestors: they look like a deceased great-great grandfather or great-great aunt because *they are those persons* reborn. Certain African peoples sometimes name children accordingly; e.g., two common Yoruba names are "Mother (i.e., a female ancestor) Has Returned" (*Yetunde*) and "Father (i.e., a male ancestor) Has Returned" (*Babatunde*). This means of course that the living have a deep spiritual obligation to procreate, for the more children that we have, the more opportunities there are for ancestors to return to *nza yayi*.

In developing its master symbol, the matriarchs and patriarchs of Kongo religion drew a circle to illustrate the cycle of life-death-rebirth and the symbolically correspondent risings and settings of the sun and moon in a 24-hour period. Sunrise (6:00 A.M.) and sunset (6:00 P.M.) are connected by the river (*nzadi*), and a line is thus traced from the center of the right side of the circumference of the circle to the center of the left side. A second line traverses this with perpendicular precision inside the circle, connecting noon and midnight, the most spiritually potent moments of day and night. The *baKongo* call this cruciform symbol *yowa*, an encircled cross known to them for generations prior to the arrival of Christianity at the end of the 15th century.

Yoruba Ritual Performance of the Dead

Like the *baKongo* in Central Africa, the Yoruba people of West Africa have a long history of contact with exogenous religious traditions; longer as regards Islam, which first arrived in Yorubaland in the 14th century; while shorter as regards Christianity, which missionaries from Britain brought in the 19th. One of West Africa's oldest identifiable ethnic groups,[4] the Yoruba today number upwards to 25 million and live mostly in Nigeria, with smaller populations in Benin, Ghana, Sierra Leone, and Togo. Although most of these people are today Christians and Muslims, "traditional" Yoruba religion, *esin ibile*, is still widely practiced in Yorubaland and has recently witnessed an impressive resurgence, inspired in large part by *esin ibile's* remarkable survival and spread in the African diaspora and beyond. Yoruba religion is similar to Kongo religion in its recognition of a single creator deity, Olodumare, and in its ancestor and spirit (*orisha*) cults, though spirit cults do play a much larger role for the Yoruba in their more structured religious system, as does divination. Yoruba religion is also similar to Kongo religion in featuring a belief in the reincarnation of the ancestors among the living (which the Yoruba refer to as *yiya*, or "branching") and a belief that ancestors establish and officiate the ethical standards to which the living are expected to adhere. Adjuring the living in this regard and cleansing the living community of the consequences of its ethical transgressions are two of the key purposes of the dramatic *egúngún* masquerade festival among the Yoruba, one of Africa's most theatrical communal rituals pertaining to death.

The *egúngún* festival (*odun egúngún*) is an important communal and performative feature of ancestor veneration in Yoruba religion. Traditionally, the annual festival is held for seven days and tied to the yam harvest—often during the month of June, though this can vary from local community to local community. *Egúngún*, who are elaborately masked and costumed dancers representing the dead, sometimes also appear a few days following a funeral, chanting the name of the deceased into the town and village air and visiting the recently departed's household with news of her or his arrival in the other world, which the Yoruba conceive as being located in the sky, hence the ancestors are called "people of the sky" (*ara orun*). Living residents of the household feed the *egúngún* and give them messages to take back to their deceased loved one. During the annual festival, meanwhile, the elaborately robed and masked *egúngún* parade through the streets both day and night, dancing out symbolic commentaries, criticisms, and dictates for the living audience, who keep their respectful distance from the dancers, as the *egúngún* must never be touched. It is a dramatic performance meant to frighten and invigorate the living into recognizing their wrongdoings, atoning for them, and recommitting firmly to the communal morality that the ancestors have established for them. It matters little that the living, for the most part, recognize that the masqueraders are in fact living humans disguised as the dead returned; to use the language of Émile Durkheim (1995: 9), in ritually inspiring "collective effervescence" among practitioners of *esin ibile*, the *odun egúngún* nevertheless quite effectively evokes "collective representations that express collective realities . . . whose purpose is to evoke, maintain, or recreate certain mental states."

Widely varied in their individual manifestations, the *egúngún* represent in sound and vision not only the departed ancestors but also characters from a corpus of Yoruba mythology,[5] some of which are animals, like the chameleon and the monkey. The monkey, or more specifically the Patas guenon monkey, for example, derives from a myth about the origins of *egúngún* performance, and in Yorubaland some masks are thus constructed in part of real monkey skulls (Drewal, 1992: 91–93). Margaret Thompson Drewal (1992, 92) describes the appearance of such *egúngún* as follows: "Like the Patas monkey, *alaba*-type masks are tall, predominately red, and have horizontal black and white bands across their faces and top knots on their heads. A mantle of long cloth at the back of the costume can trail on the ground like a long tail or can be gathered up around the back of the neck like the monkey's fur ruff." Lest the reader have in mind an image of the mask as if on display in a museum, it is important to visualize the sometimes frenetic motion of the masks, which are worn by dancers animated by the pulsating drumming that accompany the entire festival. Hence, "like the Patas monkey, who walks on the ground upright on its hind legs, the masked performers appear in troupes and are playful, agile, and acrobatic."

For further illustration, and to provide just one example of an anthropomorphic *egúngún*, we may consider here William Gilliland's (1960: 122) description of *Eshishe*, "whose masks usually consist of woven or knitted mesh decorated with cowries," and whose entire body is covered with "finely split palm leaves" in such a way that *Eshsishe* has the appearance of a "walking haystack":

> Unlike Egúngún in other areas, Eshishe does not talk, even in the usual disguised voice. But he sings and whistles and has an odd way of calling 'Frr-rrh-rrh! Ho! Ho! Ho! Ho! . . . Hhi-a, hhi-a, hii-a!' He often carries a long, slender whip (*atori*). Sometimes he uses an irritative shrub (*esinsin*) to strike individuals who show disrespect. He is very athletic, running from house to house, jumping ditches and walls, and brandishing his whip.

Needless to say, this communal ritual is a lively affair.

The relative infrequency of the *odun egúngún* festival does nothing to weaken its vital and vitalizing relationship to the permanent ancestral shrines that most practitioners of *esin ibile* keep in or near their homes. "Although the entire performance is play in Yoruba terms, involving drumming and dancing, it also includes invocations to the deities and blood sacrifices, usually performed at *Egúngún* shrines in the morning of the masks' public appearance. Indeed, *egúngún* masks themselves are shrines in motion, composed of the ingredients that constitute the stationary shrines inside devotees' compounds" (ibid., 94). In this way, *egúngún* function to (re)infuse the ancestral shrines of the living with the living power of the dead, and to keep the living mindful of their spiritual obligation to serve the dead and to live in accordance with the moral precepts and wisdom that the dead have bequeathed to the living.

African Ancestral Spirituality in the Americas

Few chapters in the human religious story are more remarkable than the survival, adaptation, and spread of African religious traditions in the Americas and beyond. Despite racist prohibitions against the practice of their ancestral traditions, enslaved Africans in the New World managed to creatively preserve the religious spirit of the Mother Continent, which in the ensuing 500 years would not only persevere but grow into a veritable "world religion"—one of the only world religions to do so, we should add, without the aid of missionaries or militaries. Given its central place in African religion, ancestor spirituality unsurprisingly remains integral to New World African religion. There are abundant examples of this, but here we will limit ourselves to brief discussions of three: 1) the *tambe* and *axexê* funerary rituals in Brazil, birthplace of the African-derived religion of Candomblé; 2) *muertería* séances in Cuba, where Santería took root as the island's predominant Afro-Caribbean religion; and 3) the *fet Gede* celebration of Haitian Vodou. In each case, we will see that for Africans and their descendants in the New World, the experience of slavery resulted in collective trauma that "not only changed older ways of thinking about self and the world by offering alternative meanings, it also encouraged different memories about the past" (Greene 2002: 7). All the same, the core beliefs about the life, death, and our existence in the universe that underlie Kongolese cosmology and the Yoruba *engúngún* cult remain the baseline for New World African beliefs and practices related to the dead.

Funerary Rites in Brazilian Candomblé

From 1532 to 1888 Brazil received more enslaved Africans than any other colony/nation in the Americas (over 3.5 million in all), many of them *baKongo* and Yourba. Not surprisingly, there is thus ample evidence of the influence of both Kongolese and Yoruba religious notions on Afro-Brazilian religious understandings of death and dying. For one example from the colonial era we may take the *tambe* funerary ritual. James Sweet (2003: 176) describes *tambe* as "an elaborate funeral ceremony to insure the comfortable passage of the dead person's soul to the other world." Although *tambe* ceremonies were generally forbidden by the colonial Portuguese authorities, as were virtually all African religious practices in New World slave societies, by night Africans would retreat into the deep recesses of the plantations, on which by day they labored, in order to gather for drumming and dancing ceremonies on behalf of the newly deceased. These ceremonies, which closely resembled those described in the historical record of Central Africa, involved a great deal of eating and drinking, and rumors of sexual licentiousness at the gatherings soon caught the attention of the local Catholic clergy. Unsurprisingly, the clergy railed against them as superstitious rites of the uncivilized and sought more forceful legislation to suppress them. However, as Sweet (ibid.: 179) continues, "the deeper meaning of the *tambes* should not be lost behind the priest's moralistic clamor. Central African slaves required these elaborate funeral ceremonies to appease the spirits of the deceased. Otherwise, angry spirits would return, spreading more of the death, disease, and suffering that were already rampant in most slave communities."

Meanwhile, in contemporary Candomblé, despite the predominance of Yoruba influences on the religion, "the role of the *egúnngún* ancestor as moral arbitrator and guarantor of social harmony unfortunately failed to be reproduced in Brazil," as Reginaldo Prandi (2008: 438) explains. In Candomblé, as in Santería, the dead are simply called *égun*, though this should not be taken to mean that the *odun egúngún* ceremony has been widely preserved in the Americas, for it has not. Yet, whereas *egúngún* ceremonies have, with a few notable exceptions, declined in Candomblé, other African-derived rituals associated with death and dying have thrived, such as the *axexê* funerary rite. Perhaps a New World adaptation of a Yoruba funerary rite for deceased hunters, "(t)he *Axexê* that occurs in Brazilian Candomblé can be conceived of as a grand *ebó* or offering of sacrificed meat to the spirit of the dead" (ibid., 441), in which the spirits (orishas) of Yoruba religion—like Oyá, the female orisha who is guardian of both the marketplace, cemeteries, and change, and Eshu, the male orisha of gateways and crossroads—play an important role. Prandi (ibid., 443) breaks the ceremony down into five stages:

1) music, chanting, and dance; 2) possession, with at least the presence of Oyá; 3) sacrifices and diverse offerings to the *egún* and the *òrìsàs* ritually linked to the person, with Eshu being always the first to be praised and the one to take the *ebó*, obviously, and the ancestors praised by that group; 4) destruction of ritual objects of the dead person (*igbas*, beads, cloths, implements, etc.) . . . ; and 5) the sending away of the "broken" sacred objects, together with the offerings and objects used during the ceremonies, such as the musical instruments specific for the occasion or mats.[6]

A key point of comparison with the *tambe* ritual from the colonial era should be made as regards the motivation of *axexê* rites: in the Afro-Brazilian religion of Candomblé past and present serve both to ensure a respectful, safe, and comfortable transition for the departed person from the world of the living to the world of the dead, and to establish a harmonious relationship between the two. As is the case for practitioners of Africa traditional religions, Candomblé adepts consider such funerary rites to be of profound importance to the living as they are to the dead, all of whom are members of the human community. To neglect them is to tempt peril.

Muertería *Séances in Cuban* Santería

Among the African-derived religions of the Americas, none exhibit stronger Yoruba influence than Santería.[7] Like its sibling religions Candomblé in Brazil and Vodou in Haiti, Santería emerged out of the confluence of African traditions and their practitioners' negotiation of Catholicism. Part of this negotiation entailed the selective adaptation of Catholic ritual notions or symbols to help fill the gap that was left when originally African rituals proved impossible to recreate intact in the New World, including of course those pertaining to ancestor veneration. In addition to Catholicism, a second stream of European influence helped shape Santería funerary culture, *Espiritismo*, a Spiritualist religious practice rooted in the writings of the 19th Century French medium Alan Kardec, which focuses centrally on communication with the dead. This influence is reflected in Joseph Murphy's (1988: 57) description of a feature in a Santería cult house (*ilé*) in New York City:

> Before leaving the *igbodu* [ceremony room], I almost overlook a small niche in the wall serving as a shrine to the *egun*, the deceased members of the *ilé*. Their presence is symbolized by seven glasses of water, crosses, and a rosary, reminding us of the Catholic and spiritist influences on the Santería cult of the dead. Lining the wall are photographs and drawings of the deceased, flanked by fresh flowers. The water in the glasses is fresh and clean, and the attention to the shrine reminds the faithful that the dead continue to be part of the lives of the living.

As with Santería shrines for the dead, the religion's funerary rituals also reflect the merger of Yoruba, Catholic, and Spiritualist influence. Key presumptions in Kongolese cosmology were structurally consistent with these, which together formed the foundation for widespread beliefs in Cuba about *el más allá*, "the other side"; as such, "great numbers of people in Cuba believed the dead were always watching over the living and interfering in their lives, sometimes positively and sometimes negatively" (Sandoval 2006: 36). Death itself is a spirit, furthermore, called "Iku," who "lives in the cemetery, in empty bottles, in piles of trash, and usually comes out at night, searching for victims" (ibid., 109).

Traces of the *engúngún* cult are even less evident in Cuba than in Brazil, a development that Mercedes Sandoval (ibid., 108) attributes in part to "an absence of the patrilineal lineage" in the New World. Also largely absent in Santería is any system of reincarnation, despite strong beliefs in "the other side." Instead, practitioners of Santería generally believe that "the soul of the person, if purified, will go to Ara Onu [Heaven] to enjoy eternal peace." To help out with this purification process and journey to Heaven, the surviving loved ones of the deceased pray novenas and sometimes hold a "spiritualist mass," called *muertería*, for the deceased at the home of a medium, where a *boveda* is erected, "which is a table covered with a white cloth on which glasses filled with water are placed":

> Chairs and sitting arrangements are normally placed to form a circle . . . . After the participants use cologne to rid themselves of evil influences, or currents, passages from Kardec's *Selected Prayers* (1966) are read, and the séance starts. As the spirits possess the mediums . . . they request help and prayers. Meanwhile, the most advanced come to offer advice regarding health and other worldly problems, to warn against possible dangers, and to communicate some message to the participants or their friends. (ibid., 109)

Just as Catholic beliefs about saints held great appeal to the earliest practitioners of Santería in colonial Cuba, so would the methods taught by Kardec for communicating with the dead.

Feting and Joining the Master of Death in Haitian Vodou

There is really no notion of "Heaven" *per se* in Haitian Vodou, but the dead do go somewhere. As in Kongolese religious thought, they cross or go under the water to another land, which, though other and symbolically distant, is spiritually very close to the world of the living. It is widely believed in Vodou that everyone dies to pass a year and one day "at the bottom of a river or a lake" and sometimes then demand that the living ceremoniously extract them from under the water (Métraux, 1972: 258). This belief, along with the thrust of Vodou's funerary traditions and cosmology, are clearly of Central African origin, this river or lake being largely a New World tributary of *nzadi*. That the universe and human fate are so structured (both worlds and life and death being separated and united by a body of water) is, in any case, essential to the Vodouist cosmology.

For its African victims, the brutal oppression of slavery greatly disrupted ancestral spirituality. In West and Central African traditional religion ancestor veneration normally takes place at the burial sites of the dead. As so sadly echoed in Vodouist memory of the Kwala River, mentioned in the initiatory hymn below, African slaves and their descendants in Haiti, unable to offer libations and sacrifices to the dead at African graves, came to perceive of the ancestors as residing collectively in Africa, across or under the water, making both *memorialized* Africa (*Ginen*) and water central to Vodou cosmology:

Dlo kwala manyan, nan peyi sa maman pa konn petit, dlo kwala manyan . . . .
Anba dlo, papa pa konn petit O! . . . .
Men anba tonel la, dlo kwala manyan.
(Water of the Kwala River, in that land a mother does not know her child,
water of the Kwala River . . . . .
Under the water a mother does not know her child, oh! . . . .
Behold under the peristyle roof, the water of the Kwala River.)[8]

The Catholic liturgical calendar offered abundant opportunities for enslaved Africans in Saint-Domingue (the French colony that would become Haiti upon independence in 1804) to perpetuate cultic traditions of the ancestral homeland and thereby overcome some of the deep sadness of the Kwala River. Very early in their exposure to Catholicism (which for many actually began in Central Africa prior to their enslavement), Africans and their descendants conflated African spirits, called *lwa* in Haitian Vodou, with Catholic saints, whose feast days became occasions for Vodouists on which to worship the *lwa*. Similarly, the Catholic feast days of All Saints and All Souls, which occur successively on November 1 and 2, provided a striking opportunity for Africans in the New World to venerate *all* of the dead, those in Africa, *Ginen*, and Haiti, and those who died at sea during the Middle Passage. In Vodou, this would become known as *fet Gede* (Feast of Gede), named for the *lwa* who presides over a whole host of spirits associated with death and dying, like Bawon Samdi (Bawon Lakwa, Bawon Simityè), the ruler of cemeteries.

Being the ruler of *Ginen*, death, and the dead, Gede is one of the few *lwa* with whom all Vodouists must concern themselves, and during *fet Gede* they participate in a range of ancestral venerations, from cleaning graves and feeding the dead, to processing to the cemetery to venerate the ancestors and render homage to Bawon Samdi. And, while much of this ritual activity takes place near the graves of the dead, the various Gede spirits, usually dressed in black and mauve, take to the streets in theatrical performances reminiscent of the *engúngún* festival in Yorubaland, as described here by Laënnec Hurbon (1995: 94–95):

During this period, in the market or in the streets, one might come upon people possessed by the Gédé: for the space of the holiday, these *lwa* take over, and it is imprudent to refuse their attentions. On the day of the dead, however, the appearance of the Gédé also provokes laughter, for they are phallic *lwa* who tell dirty stories, perform lascivious and obscene dances, and spend their time playing jokes on the voodoo faithful, such as stealing their money or personal property.

The phallic symbology of the master of death is similar to that associated with Shiva, the Hindu god of destruction, in the sense that both speak of an eternal return: in Hinduism the universe is destroyed, but in that act is laid the foundation for its recreation; while in Vodou, the dead cross the water to be themselves reborn as members of the family of Gede. Now they serve the living from the land of the dead, just as the living serve the dead from the world in which you have just finished reading this chapter.

Notes

1. Some scholars caution that the term "reincarnation" is inadequate when referring to African cosmologies. MacGaffey (1986: 55) tends to avoid the term, opting instead to explain that "(t)he dead are recycled through this world." Indeed, because it is not the entire soul that transmigrates, and because the same ancestor can be understood to return to life in more than one person, as Idowu opines (1973: 187), "(o)ne can only speak of partial or, more precisely, apparent reincarnation, if the word is to be used at all."

2. Making comparisons with cultures far beyond those in which he did his influential fieldwork among the Ndembu people in Zambia, Victor Turner (1965) went to great lengths to argue that such a white/black/red color triad is universal in human religious consciousness. It is very interesting to note, furthermore, that covering the bodies of corpses in red is one of the oldest funerary practices in human history, suggesting that red is understood to invigorate and aid the departing soul on its journey to the afterlife. Turner, incidentally, characterized the ancestors in Ndembu religion as "moody and punitive."

3. African understandings of souls are highly complex and a discussion of them would require an additional chapter in this book. The *baKongo* generally believes that each of us has two souls, while in Haitian Vodou each person's soul has three parts, which separate at death. Apologetically, I resign myself to glossing over this fascinating dimension of African and African-derived pneumatology in this essay.

4. It is unlikely that the Yoruba conceived of themselves as a single people prior to the transatlantic slave trade, though the Yoruba language served as a *lingua franca* beginning nearly 2,000 years ago for a region of various peoples and kingdoms who were nonetheless participants in a common cultural diffusion. As Matt Childs and Toyin Falola (2004: 5) put it, "a pan-Yoruban identity already existed in Africa but became more pronounced in the Americas."

5. "Egúngún masked performances transform and represent myth through the fragmentation of its narrative structure much in the same way as divination rituals do" (Drewal, 1990: 90). That is to say, just as Yoruba diviners of *Ifá*, which is the most

sophisticated of a variety of divinatory techniques in Yoruba religion, draw upon the religion's corpus of myths to formulated moral prescriptions for its clients, so do *egúngún* for the communities in which they perform. "When reenacted, the precedents documented in myth are carried into the present and are brought to bear on action in much the same way as legal precedents direct court action" (ibid., 91).

6. *Igbas* are "talking drums" used in Yoruba and Candomblé communal ritual.

7. Some practitioners reject the term "Santería" (lit., Way of Saints) because it reflects a Catholic rather than an African idea. Thus, the religion is also referred to as Regla de Ocha and Lucumí.

8. A "peristyle" is the sanctuary of a Vodou temple. Mambo Racine Sans Bout *http://members.aol.com/racine125/vleson2.html* (accessed May 29, 2003). Mambo Racine mistakenly notes West Africa to be where the Kwala River is found. In reality it is located in the "Cuvette Region, on lower reaches of the Likouala-Mossaka, Sangha, and Likouala-aux-Herbes rivers" in the Congo. *www.ethnologue.com/show_country.asp?name=Congo* (accessed May 12, 2003).

Selected Bibliography

Childs, Matt. D., and Toyin Falola. 2004. The Yoruba diaspora in the Atlantic World: Methodology and research. In *The Yoruba Diaspora in the Atlantic World*, Toyin Falola and Matt D. Childs, eds. Bloomington and Indianapolis, IN: Indiana University Press.

Drewal, Margaret Thompson. 1992. *Yoruba ritual: Performers, play, agency*. Bloomington and Indianapolis, IN: Indiana University Press.

Durkheim, Émile. 1995 (1915). *Elementary forms of religious life*. Trans. Karen E. Fields. New York: Free Press.

Echekwube, A. O. 1987. The question of reincarnation in African traditional religion. In *Orita Journal of Religious Studies*, 19(1):10–26.

Evans-Pritchard, E. E. 1956. *Nuer Religion*. New York, NY, and Oxford, UK: Oxford University Press.

Gilliland, William. 1960. Egungun Eshishe. *Man*, 60, 122–123.

Greene, Sandra E. 2002. *Sacred sites and the colonial encounter: A history of meaning and memory in Ghana*. Bloomington, IN: Indiana University Press.

Hurbon, Laënnec. 1995. *Voodoo: Search for the spirit*. New York: Abrams.

Idowu, E. B. 1973. *African traditional religion: A definition*. London: SCM Press.

Kalu, Ogbu U. 2000. Ancestral spirituality and society in Africa. In *African Spirituality: Forms, Meanings, Expressions*, Jacob K. Olupona, ed. New York: Herder and Herder.

MacGaffey, Wyatt. 1994. Dialogues with the Deaf: Europeans on the Atlantic Coast of Africa. In *Implicit Understandings*, S. Schwartz, ed. New York: Cambridge University Press, 249–267.

MacGaffey, Wyatt. 1986. *Religion and society in Central Africa: The BaKongo of Lower Zaire*. Chicago: The University of Chicago Press.

Métraux, Alfred. 1972. *Voodoo in Haiti*. New York: Schocken.

Murphy, Joseph M. 1988. *Santería: African Spirits in America*. Boston: Beacon.

Prandi, Reginaldo. 2008. Axexê Funerary Rites in Brazil's Òrìsà Religion: Constitution, Significance, and Tendencies. In *Òrìsà Devotion as World Religion: The Globalization of Yorùbá Religious Culture*, Jacob K. Olupona and Terry Rey, eds. Madison, WI: The University of Wisconsin Press, 437–447.

Sandoval, Mercedes Cros. 2006. *Worldview, the Orichas, and Santería: Africa to Cuba and Beyond*. Gainesville, FL: University Press of Florida.

Sweet, James H. 2003. *Recreating Africa: Culture, kinship, and religion in the African-Portuguese World, 1441–1770*. Chapel Hill, NC: The University of North Carolina Press.

Turner, Victor. 1965. Color classification in Ndembu ritual: A problem in primitive classification. In *Anthropological Approaches to the Study of Religion*, A.S.A Monograph No. 3. London: Tavistock.

Study Questions

1. Why do practitioners of African and African diasporic religions venerate their ancestors? The author speaks of the "reciprocal relationship of living-dead service" as being central to these religions. What is the place and function of ancestor veneration in this relationship?

2. Describe "reincarnation" as it is traditionally understood in Africa and explain how this understanding is symbolized in Kongolese religion. In doing so, indicate at least two ways in which African systems of reincarnation differ from those found in Hinduism and/or Buddhism.

3. What influences of Kongolese and Yoruba religious thought are reflected in the *tambe* and *axexê* rituals in the Afro-Brazilian religion of Candomblé? What are the chief functions of these rituals and on what occasions are they performed?

4. Compare and contrast the ways in which the living and the dead communicate in Yoruba religion and in Santería. Please include some description of the specific ritual practices in which such communication takes place in each religion.

5. In what ways did African religious practices pertaining to the ancestors change in the New World? In articulating your response, please allude to a substantive example from Haitian Vodou and demonstrate the influence of Catholicism in this particular process of change.